Boston Transit

LEGEND

Transit lines
stops
Terminal station
interchange
other lines

● BLUE LINE
● GREEN LINE

BLUE LINE: Wonderland, Revere Beach, Beachmont, Suffolk Downs, Orient Heights, Wood Island, Airport, Maverick, Aquariu, State

ORANGE LINE: Oak Grove, Malden, Wellington, Sullivan Square, Community College, North Station, Haymarket, State, Downtown Crossi, Chinatown, NE Medical Center, Back Bay, Massachusetts Ave., Ruggles, Roxbury Crossing, Jackson Sq., Stony Brook, Green St., Forest Hills

RED LINE: Alewife, Davis, Porter, Harvard Square, Central Square, Kendall/MIT, Charles/MGH, Park St., Downtown Crossi, South Station, Broadway, Andrew, JFK/UMass, Savin Hill, Fields Corner, Shawmut, Ashmont, Cedar Grove, Butler, Milton, Central Ave., Valley Rd., Capen St., Mattapan, North Quincy, Wollaston, Quincy Adams, Quincy Center, Braintree

GREEN LINE: Lechmere, Science Park, Bowdoin, Gov't Center, Park St., Boylston, Arlington, Copley, Hynes/ICA, Kenmore, BU East, BU Central, BU West, Blandford, Pleasant St., St. Paul St., Boston University, Babcock St., Packards Corner, Harvard Ave., Griggs St., Allston St., Warren St., Washington St., Sutherland Rd., Chiswick Rd., Chestnut Hill Ave., South St., Boston College (B)

Kenmore, Fenway, Longwood, Brookline Village, Brookline Hills, Beaconsfield, Reservoir, Chestnut Hill, Newton Centre, Newton Highlands, Eliot, Waban, Woodland, Riverside (D)

Washington St., Cleveland Circle (C)

Prudential, Symphony, Northeastern, Museum, Brigham Circle, Heath (E)

For Dummies: Bestselling Book Series for Beginners

Boston For Dummies®
2nd Edition

Boston Attractions

Attraction	Transit Stop
Beacon Hill	● Charles/MGH
Boston Common	● ● Park Street
	● Boylston
Boston Public Library	● Copley
Boston Tea Party Ship & Museum	● South Station
Children's Museum	● South Station
The Computer Museum	● South Station
Faneuil Hall	● ● Government Center
	● ● State
Fenway Park	● Kenmore, Fenway
Fogg Art Museum.	● Harvard Square
Franklin Park Zoo	● Forest Hills
	(then bus 16 to main entrance)
Harvard Museum of Natural History	● Harvard Square
Harvard Square/Harvard University	● Harvard Square
Institute of Contemporary Art	● IHynes/ICA
Isabella Stewart Gardner Museum	● Museum
John F. Kennedy Library and Museum	● JFK/UMass *(shuttle bus)*
John F. Kennedy National Historic Site	● Coolidge Corner
John Hancock Observatory	● Copley......... ● Back Bay
Mapparium	● Symphony
	● Massachusetts Ave.
Massachusetts Archives	● JFK/UMass.
Massachusetts Institute of Technology (MIT)	● Central Square or Kendall
Museum of Afro-American History	● Charles/MGH
Museum of Fine Arts	● Museum......... ● Ruggles
Museum of Science	● Science Park
Museum of Transportation	● Reservoir *(then bus no. 51)*
New England Aquarium	● Aquarium
Old North Church	● ● Haymarket
Paul Revere House.	● ● Government Center
Peabody Museum of Archaeology & Ethnology	● Harvard Square
Prudential Center Skywalk	● Copley......... ● Back Bay
Public Garden	● Arlington
Sports Museum of New England	● ● North Station
Symphony Hall	● Symphony

For Dummies: Bestselling Book Series for Beginners

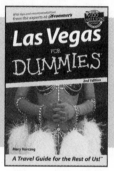

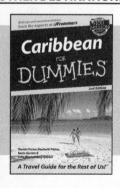
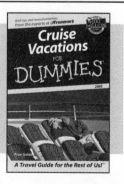

Boston
FOR

DUMMIES®

2ND EDITION

Boston

FOR

DUMMIES®

2ND EDITION

by Marie Morris

WILEY

Wiley Publishing, Inc.

Boston For Dummies®, 2nd Edition

Published by
Wiley Publishing, Inc.
909 Third Avenue
New York, NY 10022
www.wiley.com

For general information on our other products and services or to obtain technical support, please contact our Customer Care Department within the U.S. at 800-762-2974, outside the U.S. at 317-572-3993, or fax 317-572-4002.

Wiley also publishes its books in a variety of electronic formats. Some content that appears in print may not be available in electronic books.

Library of Congress Control Number: 2002114862

ISBN: 0-7645-5491-3

ISSN: 1531-7560

2B/RS/QT/QT/IN

Manufactured in the United States of America

10 9 8 7 6 5 4 3 2 1

About the Author

Marie Morris grew up in New York City, then studied history at Harvard College. She has lived in the Boston area for most of the past two decades. Since 1997, she has written the *Frommer's Boston* travel guide and contributed to *Frommer's New England.* She has also been, among other things, an assistant sports editor at the *Boston Herald* and an editor at *Boston* magazine. She enjoys cooking, entertaining, horse racing, and traveling. Marie lives in the North End, not far from the Freedom Trail, where she often encounters readers — bring along your copy of *Boston For Dummies,* and you might meet her there.

Publisher's Acknowledgments

We're proud of this book; please send us your comments through our Dummies online registration form located at www.dummies.com/register/.

Some of the people who helped bring this book to market include the following:

Editorial

Editors: Lisa Torrance Duffy, Elizabeth Kuball, and Jim Tunstall

Cartographer: Roberta Stockwell

Editorial Supervisor: Michelle Hacker

Editorial Assistant: Elizabeth Rea

Senior Photo Editor: Richard Fox

Front Cover Photo: Boston's Public Garden, © Walter Bibikow/Viesti Collection

Back Cover Photo: Faneuil Hall Marketplace, © Steve Dunwell/ The Image Bank

Cartoons: Rich Tennant, www.the5thwave.com

Production

Project Coordinator: Erin Smith

Layout and Graphics: Seth Conley, Kelly Emkow, Carrie Foster, Stephanie Jumper, Michael Kruzil, Tiffany Muth, Julie Trippetti, Jeremey Unger

Proofreaders: John Bitter, John Tyler Connoley, Dave Faust, Angel Perez, TECHBOOKS Production Services

Indexer: TECHBOOKS Production Services

Publishing and Editorial for Consumer Dummies

Diane Graves Steele, Vice President and Publisher, Consumer Dummies

Joyce Pepple, Acquisitions Director, Consumer Dummies

Kristin A. Cocks, Product Development Director, Consumer Dummies

Michael Spring, Vice President and Publisher, Travel

Brice Gosnell, Publishing Director, Travel

Suzanne Jannetta, Editorial Director, Travel

Publishing for Technology Dummies

Andy Cummings, Vice President and Publisher, Dummies Technology/General User

Composition Services

Gerry Fahey, Vice President of Production Services

Debbie Stailey, Director of Composition Services

Contents at a Glance

Maps at a Glance

Table of Contents

Introduction

Some residents of Boston think of their home as just another large American city. They complain about the traffic, the cost of living, the ceaseless construction, the students who return like locusts every September, and the tourists who flock like lemmings (or students) to the historic sights. Forced to think about why they live here, they admit that Boston has good points, too — "It's near my job," they say.

Sometimes it takes a visit from an out-of-towner to make the locals realize the obvious: Their city must be enjoyable; otherwise, it wouldn't be so popular.

So, in a sense, you're lucky. Even if you've visited Boston before, you can approach the city with a fresh eye and an unjaded attitude. Come for the seafood and stay for the history. Pause as you rush to a meeting and admire the sun-dappled harbor. Seek out some great shopping and stumble upon an impromptu concert. Finally, get into Harvard *and* Fenway Park.

In theory, Boston *is* just another large American city. In practice, it offers a unique blend of elements that make this city a singularly enjoyable destination.

About This Book

Boston For Dummies, 2nd Edition, takes the information you need and breaks it down into manageable pieces. I start with the basics, guiding you from the "I think it may be somewhere in New England" stage all the way through to "I know just what hot spots to hit!"

Treat this book as a reference, not a "travel narrative." Read it cover-to cover or dip into the sections that particularly interest you. If you already know that you'll be staying on your friend's couch, for instance, you can skip the accommodations information without worrying that you're missing something crucial. If you're burning to do some serious shopping . . . well, you probably don't have your nose buried in the Introduction anyway.

In assembling the information, suggestions, and listings in this book, I took a "greatest hits" approach. I present discriminating choices rather than encyclopedic directories. The focus is on what you need to know, not on "in case you were wondering" observations. Throughout, I offer plenty of insider advice to make you feel as comfortable as possible.

In addition, although I can't physically protect you every step of the way, your safety is important to me. I encourage you to stay alert and be aware of your surroundings. Keep a close eye on cameras, purses, backpacks, and wallets — all favorite targets of thieves and pickpockets.

Conventions Used in This Book

Like any reference book, *Boston For Dummies* uses some shorthand phrases and abbreviations. The most obvious are "Boston" and "the Boston area." Throughout eastern Massachusetts, you'll find people born in Newton, raised in Wellesley, educated in Cambridge, and living in Quincy who say they're "from Boston" without thinking twice. Rather than subject you to "Boston, Cambridge, sometimes Brookline, occasionally Somerville, and maybe a few other nearby suburbs," I use the shorter terms. When you need specifics (as in addresses), you get them.

I use the following credit card abbreviations in the text:

AE: American Express

DC: Diners Club

DISC: Discover

MC: MasterCard

V: Visa

The hotel and restaurant reviews in Chapters 8 and 14 employ a system of dollar signs to give you a sense of the price range for each establishment. For a double-occupancy hotel room (not including tax) or dinner for one (not including tax and tip), the ranges are as follows:

Cost	Hotel	Restaurant
$	$125 and less	$20 and less
$$	$126–$225	$21–$30
$$$	$226–$325	$31–$45
$$$$	$326 and up	$46 and up

Please be aware that travel information is subject to change at any time, and that this is *especially* true of prices. I suggest that you write or call ahead for confirmation when making your travel plans.

Also note the "T" that appears in hotel, restaurant, and attraction listings. The T is the name of Boston's rapid transit system, and the listings have the name of the closest T stop.

Foolish Assumptions

This book aims to be as handy for a time-pressed frequent flier as it is for an inexperienced traveler. Which chapters turn out to be most useful depends on you. I assume that you have constraints on your time and your willingness to process boatloads of information, not on your *ability* to do so. (And if those assumptions sound foolish, I can live with that!)

Other assumptions include the following:

✔ Maybe you just don't have time to wade through a conventional guidebook.

✔ Maybe you're an experienced traveler, but you don't have a lot of time to devote to trip planning, or you don't have a lot of time to spend in Boston after you get there. You want expert advice on how to maximize your time and enjoy a hassle-free trip.

✔ Maybe you've visited Boston before, and you suspect (rightly) that there has to be more to this city than crowds from everywhere in the world except New England.

✔ Maybe you've never been on a plane, traveled by train, reserved a room at a B&B, or bought tickets for the symphony — and you want a clear explanation of what to expect.

Whatever you're looking for, I provide as much information as you need.

How This Book Is Organized

This book consists of seven parts that lead you through the process of arriving in and navigating the city, finding a great place to stay, searching out the restaurants that cater to your tastes, discovering the worthwhile attractions and shopping areas, and, well, having a great time.

Part 1: Getting Started

In this part, I describe what you need to know before you go. You get an insider's view of what Boston is really like and the lowdown on the best times to visit. I also help you develop a budget. Here, too, you find information for families, seniors, travelers with disabilities, and gay and lesbian travelers.

Part 11: Ironing Out the Details

Now you move from the theoretical to the specific. How will you get to Boston? Where will you stay? What else do you need to know before you leave home? I answer it all in the chapters in this part.

Part III: Settling Into Boston

You don't truly arrive in Boston until you check into your hotel. In this part, I outline that final leg of your journey, sketch the city's neighbor-hoods, and explain how to get around and between them. I also address the all-important question of where to get cash.

Part IV: Dining in Boston

This part is all about food. From fusion-cuisine hot spots to 175-year-old standbys, Boston is a treat. I tell you where the locals chow down, where foodies dine, and where to go to grab a quick bite.

Part V: Exploring Boston

Here I give you the scoop on the city's sights and attractions — from museums and historic buildings to tours and cruises. If those places sound too highfalutin, check out this part for my tips on sports and shopping. I also recommend some favorite itineraries and day-trips.

Part VI: Living It Up after the Sun Goes Down: Boston Nightlife

Boston makes up for its somewhat anemic nightlife with enough cul-tural offerings to class up a wrestling match — and enough bars and pubs to make up for early closing hours. You can't dance till dawn, but you can have a ball after dark. I set the scene in this section.

Part VII: The Part of Tens

Veteran *For Dummies* readers know about The Part of Tens, and new-comers will recognize the contents of these chapters: interesting stuff that doesn't seem to fit anywhere else. I submit facts, pointers, and observations that complement the rest of this book. Enjoy!

Appendix

Information that could clutter the other chapters migrates here and appears in handy list form. Turn to this Quick Concierge for toll-free numbers and Web sites for airlines and hotels, as well as other sources of information. You're welcome.

Also at the back of the book are yellow planning worksheets. These forms help you set a budget, outline itineraries, and keep track of attractions, hotels, and restaurants that appeal to you. These worksheets make it easy for you to keep all the information you gather in one place.

Icons Used in This Book

In the margins of this book, five icons guide you toward information of your particular interests:

Handy facts, hints, and my insider info. This bull's-eye flags advice about what to do and how to make the best use of your time.

Warnings, tourist traps, rip-offs, travel hazards, and activities that aren't worth the trouble. I steer you away from potential pitfalls with this symbol.

Activities, attractions, and establishments that particularly suit people traveling with children. Boston is an exceptionally family-friendly city; I indicate the standouts with this symbol.

If you want to splurge on one activity, you may need to cut back on another; seek out this icon for pointers on cutting corners (relatively) painlessly, so you can spend your bucks on what you like best.

History flavors nearly everything you see and do in Boston. I use this symbol to single out particularly tasty morsels of information about the city's past.

Where to Go from Here

For most of the past 20 years, I've called Boston home. Friends puzzle over my refusal to relocate — until they hear me talk about my adopted hometown. I still can't get enough of Boston's sights and sounds, its history and geography, its walkability and its proximity to the full range of New England's natural resources. From the salty ocean smell that comes in on the east wind to the United Nations of visitors that come in with the autumn foliage, it's a thrill. And I'm thrilled to be able to share it with you. Here we go!

Part I
Getting Started

The 5th Wave   By Rich Tennant

In this part . . .

Think of planning your trip as a pyramid: The shape begins with a base of nearly infinite possibilities, narrows as you zero in on viable options, and peaks sometime after you scratched "Boston?" on the back of an envelope. Now that you see where your pyramid is pointing, how will you get there?

The four chapters in this part will put you (figuratively and perhaps literally) on the road to Boston. What sights and sensations will you experience? When should you visit? How much will it cost? Where can travelers with special needs turn for information? Here, naturally.

Chapter 1

Discovering the Best of Boston

● ●

In This Chapter

▶ Getting a snapshot of a fun, fascinating destination

▶ Enjoying a taste (just a taste!) of history

▶ Looking at the largest public-works project in the world

● ●

*P*eople from all over the world seem to feel a connection to Boston. Even if you haven't visited the city, you probably know something about Boston. Maybe your best friend went to college here, your next-door neighbor worships the Red Sox, your internist did her residency at Massachusetts General, or your neighborhood *Gilmore Girls* fan shares Rory's obsession with Harvard. You see *Cheers* reruns and the Boston Pops' Fourth of July concert on TV, Fidelity manages your retirement savings, and you remember something about a tea party. You're thinking that Boston sounds like a fun place to visit. You're right.

The city's historic and cultural attractions, entertaining diversions, and manageable size make Boston a popular business, convention, and tourist destination. To help you plan the most enjoyable trip, in this chapter I let you know what to expect.

The Hub of the Solar System

Oliver Wendell Holmes gave Boston perhaps the city's most popular nickname: "The Hub of the Solar System" (which survives partly because headline writers love short words like "Hub"). The solar system may be an exaggeration, but eastern Massachusetts is an important destination for education, high-tech, financial services, and health care.

Don't be too quick to envision legions of pasty-faced techies glowing under fluorescent lights, though. Boston is downright beautiful. Red-brick buildings and cobblestone streets contrast delightfully with modern glass towers (and concrete boxes that seemed like a good idea at the time). Countless millions of dollars went into cleaning up Boston Harbor, and the result is worth every penny. The dot-com meltdown and the post–September 11 economic slump took a toll, but the city remains a vibrant, entertaining destination.

The Athens of America

Boston has a lot of goofy nicknames (I'll get to "Beantown" shortly), but this one is most useful for my purposes. The "Athens of America" description came about because some pointy-headed, 19th-century social critics considered ancient Athens a paragon of education and culture. Lending that city's name to the closest New World equivalent must have seemed perfectly natural, not to mention irresistibly alliterative.

Consider what that comparison means today: Where you find education, you find students. In the Boston area, that means thousands and thousands of college students. With students come noise, crowds, musical innovation, outlandish fashions, cheap diversions, and flat-out fun. Boston and Cambridge positively buzz with youthful energy.

As for culture, Boston is a hot spot. The city is home to some of the world's best and best-loved art, one of the finest symphony orchestras, and countless student efforts in every artistic field. And remember that where you find high culture, you find, well, low culture. Boston is nearly as well known for bar bands, stand-up comedy, and street performance.

Full of Beans

"Beantown" is a nod to colonial Boston, when the Puritans' strict rules about working on the Sabbath meant no cooking on Sunday. A pot of beans could go into the oven in a brick kitchen fireplace on Saturday and cook in the retained heat, emerging for Sunday dinner at noon and giving the world Boston baked beans.

Some traditional restaurants serve beans today, but nobody's coming to Boston for legumes. Folks who come here to dine on fish and shellfish in every imaginable style come to the right place. From cutting-edge cuisine to down-home ethnic fare, nearly every menu includes succulent seafood.

Posterity and Prosperity

If you're like most visitors, you won't get out of Boston without at least a brief, painless history lesson. You can certainly immerse yourself in the past, visit innumerable colonial and Revolutionary landmarks, and stuff your head full of random facts. But you don't need to — merely walking around exposes you to the Boston of a bygone age.

Boston's original landmass was about one-third the size of the modern city. Landfill accounts for the growth, most famously in the Back Bay, the only central area laid out in a grid pattern. Widely circulated myth notwithstanding, the circuitous street patterns in older neighborhoods such as the North End and Beacon Hill don't owe their apparently random designs to cow paths. (These neighborhoods hark back to long-gone property lines and misguided efforts to replicate London's layout.) Every step downtown takes you through centuries' of history, with no exam at the end of the day.

For example, consider Faneuil Hall: Once accessible directly from the harbor, today the area doesn't enjoy a water view. The shops of Faneuil Hall Marketplace stand (on landfill) between the historic building and the shore. A monument to legendary Yankee thrift, the original Filene's Basement, lies a few blocks away. Not far from there, look for the retail fantasyland known as Newbury Street. Between these extremes, Boston offers the full range of retail recreation.

This Is a Hard-Hat Area

Peerless symbol of Bostonian ingenuity or unprecedented pain in the neck? The Central Artery/Third Harbor Tunnel project, better known as the Big Dig, is both.

Interstate 93, the main north-south route through downtown Boston, currently runs on the elevated expressway that separates the waterfront from the rest of downtown. By 2005, when the Big Dig is over, the expressway will be gone. (The demolition began in 2002, while construction was still raging.) Traffic will run through a tunnel and onto a gorgeous bridge over the Charles River. The techniques that are making this happen have construction engineers all over the world salivating — and Boston-area commuters foaming at the mouth.

On a brief visit, you'll probably find the Big Dig inconvenient but fascinating, and perhaps a source of fashion tips. Right around the time many downtown businesses shifted from casual Fridays to casual weekdays, construction workers in the de facto Big Dig uniform (hard hat, orange top, jeans, boots) started turning up all over town. Now that the end is near, suits and ties are regaining ground. Coincidence? It's anyone's guess.

Chapter 2

Deciding When to Go

- -

In This Chapter

▶ Figuring out the best time to visit

▶ Reviewing a month-by-month list of events

- -

*E*very season is a good time to visit Boston. The climate is relatively temperate — with some exceptions, which I'll get to. Citywide events are generally entertaining but not overwhelming — with some exceptions, which I'll get to. The people are typically friendly and welcoming — with some exceptions, which you can (but hopefully won't) discover on your own.

The Secrets of the Seasons

After a kicky New Year's Eve celebration, Boston moves into the slowest travel season of the year. From January through March, many hotels offer great deals, especially on weekends. Conventions, when they happen, tend to be small, short, and local (which means they attract relatively few people who spend the night in town). If you can't take bitter cold and biting winds, plan to concentrate on indoor activities. Snow sometimes overwhelms the city during these months, and some suburban attractions close for the winter.

During the **February** school vacation week (starting with Presidents' Day), kid-oriented places and activities fill up fast. Second honeymooners and other child-free vacationers may want to steer clear.

In **April,** spring comes to the mid-Atlantic states, but in New England snow can linger into the early part of the month. Reluctant outdoors people may want to note this is the height of mud season. (Pack shoes that you don't care about wearing again.) The Boston Marathon, on the third Monday of the month, attracts unbelievable crowds — you'll need a hotel reservation (see Chapter 8) far in advance. The marathon falls on Patriots' Day, a state holiday that marks the start of another school vacation. This week is not a restful time to visit.

A weather report, for better or verse

This poem is the second-best rhyme about Boston to know (after "Paul Revere's Ride"). The description applies to the short column of lights on top of the old John Hancock building in the Back Bay:

Steady blue, clear view;
flashing blue, clouds due;
steady red, rain ahead;
flashing red, snow instead.

(In the summer, flashing red means bad weather has postponed the Red Sox game.)

Between April and November, Boston typically experiences few slow periods. Conventions take place all year, clustering in the spring and fall. The Convention and Visitors Bureau (see the Appendix for contact information) can tip you off to especially large gatherings.

Full-blown spring usually doesn't arrive until early **May,** but that makes the first run of balmy weather all the more enjoyable. This month marks the beginning of college graduation season. Hotels fill in apparently random patterns, and out-of-state drivers flood the city.

Graduation pandemonium lingers into **June,** when pleasant weather and the end of the younger kids' school year translate into a jump in occupancy rates at hotels and crowds all around town.

In **July** and **August,** vacationing families flock to Boston, creating long lines and lots of tantrums. For a week around the Fourth of July, Harborfest draws hordes of people with its extremely fun but crowded activities. Toward the end of August, the flood of returning college students begins.

June, July, and August are about the only months when you may encounter consecutive days of 90-plus temperatures, usually accompanied by debilitating humidity and abysmal air quality. Be ready to concentrate on indoor activities or willing to take it slow outside.

In early **September,** college starts in earnest; watch out for moving vans, especially on September 1. The weather turns cooler, and humidity drops. Foliage season begins in late September and runs to mid-November. Many "leaf-peepers" stay in the Boston area or pass through on their way to northern New England, creating tour-bus gridlock.

September and **October** are the months most likely to include a run of exhilarating weather, with comfortably warm days and cool to chilly nights. The Head of the Charles Regatta, on the third weekend of

October, attracts hundreds of thousands of people; many are students who crash in friends' dorms, but booking a room on short notice may be tough.

November is also when convention business slows. The weather may turn cold and raw, but snow is seldom a problem.

In **December,** the leaves are gone but the meetings linger. You may find a good deal on a weekend, especially at a hotel that offers holiday shopping specials. On New Year's Eve, rooms fill with suburbanites who don't want to deal with driving home after midnight; book far in advance.

Weather Alert

Lots of places claim to be the inspiration for the weather cliché "If you don't like it, wait ten minutes," but a few days in Boston will persuade you that New England's climate inspired the expression. My advice: Think twice before letting the weather determine your plans.

You simply cannot escape New England weather. Steering clear of late winter because you hate the cold, or avoiding midsummer because you can't take humidity, seems to guarantee that you'll miss a spell of especially temperate conditions. (Actually, what trying to avoid bad weather guarantees is that you'll really notice when the meteorologist exclaims over the nice weather in Boston, but that's an issue for the author of *Relativity For Dummies.*) Table 2-1 gives you an idea of the monthly temperatures you can expect.

Table 2-1	Boston's Average Temperatures and Rainfall											
	Jan	Feb	Mar	Apr	May	June	July	Aug	Sept	Oct	Nov	Dec
Temp. (°F)	30	31	38	49	59	68	74	72	65	55	45	34
Temp. (°C)	1.1	–0.5	3.3	9.4	15	20	23.3	22.2	18.3	12.8	7.2	1.1
Rainfall (in.)	4	3.7	4.1	3.7	3.5	2.9	2.7	3.7	3.4	3.4	4.2	4.9

It's a Date: Boston's Calendar of Events

Crowds flood Boston for many of these popular events. Expect full hotels, and booked restaurants. To avoid disappointment, double-check before scheduling a trip to coincide with an event.

Spontaneous travelers and others who haven't planned ahead can pick up suggestions from the event hotline of the **Greater Boston Convention and Visitors Bureau** (☎ 800-SEE-BOSTON or 617-536-4100; Internet: www.bostonusa.com), the "Calendar" section of the Thursday *Boston Globe* (Internet: www.boston.com/globe), and the "Scene" section of the Friday *Boston Herald* (Internet: www.bostonherald.com).

January

Events surrounding **Martin Luther King, Jr., Day** (the third Monday of the month) include gospel celebrations and other musical happenings, lectures, and panel discussions at various venues. Check special listings in the Thursday *Globe* "Calendar" section for specifics.

For **Chinese New Year,** the dragon parade draws a crowd to Chinatown no matter how cold it is, and the **Children's Museum** (☎ 617-426-8855; Internet: www.bostonkids.org) puts on special programs. The date depends on the Chinese lunar calendar: in 2003, February 1; in 2004, January 22. Call the city **Office of Special Events and Tourism** (☎ 617-635-3911) for information.

February

Special museum exhibits and children's programs highlight **Black History Month.** Many institutions schedule concerts, films, and other activities. **National Park Service** rangers (☎ 617-742-5415; Internet: www.nps.gov/boaf) lead tours of the Black Heritage Trail.

During **School Vacation Week,** which starts on Presidents' Day, most elementary and high schools close. Special cultural activities include kid-oriented exhibitions, plays, concerts, and tours. Contact attractions for information on special offerings and extended hours.

March

The **New England Spring Flower Show,** in mid-month, is a perfect antidote to cabin fever. At the end of an especially snowy winter, expect huge crowds. Plan to use public transit. The **Massachusetts Horticultural Society** (☎ 617-536-9280; Internet: www.masshort.org) presents the show at the Bayside Expo Center in Dorchester.

April

The **Big Apple Circus** performs in a heated tent near the South Boston waterfront for about one month every spring (late March through early

May). Proceeds support the Children's Museum. Visit the museum box office or contact **Ticketmaster** (☎ 617-931-ARTS; Internet: www.ticketmaster.com).

On the third Monday of the month, **Patriots' Day** marks the unofficial end of winter. The state holiday commemorates the events of April 18 and 19, 1775, when the Revolutionary War began. Lanterns (as in "two if by sea") hang in the steeple of the **Old North Church** (☎ 617-523-6676; Internet: www.oldnorth.com), and riders dressed as Paul Revere and William Dawes travel from Boston's North End to Lexington and Concord. "Minutemen" and "redcoats" reenact the battles on the town green in Lexington and at the Old North Bridge in Concord. See Chapter 21 for information on visiting Lexington and Concord.

The legendary **Boston Marathon** starts at noon on Patriots' Day. The leaders cross the finish line, on Boylston Street in front of the Boston Public Library, beginning a little after 2 p.m. Good vantage points include Commonwealth Avenue and Kenmore Square. For information, call ☎ 617-236-1652 or visit www.bostonmarathon.org.

May

Usually on the third weekend of the month, **Lilac Sunday** is the only day of the year when the Arnold Arboretum permits picnicking. The gorgeous botanical garden, in Boston's Jamaica Plain neighborhood, boasts sensational spring flowers, including more than 400 varieties of lilacs. Call ☎ 617-524-1717 or visit www.arnold.harvard.edu.

At the end of the month, the **Street Performers Festival** takes over Faneuil Hall Marketplace. Musicians, magicians, jugglers, sword-swallowers, and artists strut their stuff. Call ☎ 617-338-2323 or check www.faneuilhallmarketplace.com for more information.

June

The region's largest gay pride parade is the **Boston Pride March,** on the second Sunday of the month. The procession from the Back Bay to Beacon Hill caps off a week of celebrating diversity in New England. Call ☎ 617-262-9405 or visit www.bostonpride.org.

International headliners and local stars play the **_Boston Globe_ Jazz & Blues Festival,** held the third week of the month. Concerts are indoors and outdoors, at lunch, after work, in the evening, and on the weekend. Some performances require advance tickets; some are free. Call ☎ 617-267-4301 or visit www.boston.com/jazzfestival for more details.

July

The Fourth of July is the high point of the week-long **Boston Harborfest** and a guaranteed blast. Events include fireworks, concerts, guided tours, cruises, the Boston Chowderfest, and the USS *Constitution*'s annual turnaround. Call ☎ **617-227-1528** or visit www.bostonharborfest.com for more information.

The centerpiece of the Fourth of July festivities is the **Boston Pops Concert and Fireworks Display,** at the Hatch Shell amphitheater on the Esplanade. Live music begins in the evening, but this is an all-day affair — fans arrive at dawn to stake out pieces of the lawn in front of the stage. The program includes the "1812 Overture," with actual cannon fire, and amazing fireworks at about 10 p.m. (If you're not keen on roasting in the sun, wait until dark, ride the Red Line to Kendall/MIT, and watch the pyrotechnics from the Cambridge side of the river.) Visit www.july4th.org for more details.

August

The North End is always fun to visit, and during the **Italian-American feasts** on summer weekends, it rocks. The street fairs begin in July, and include food, games, live and recorded music, and dancing in the streets. The Fishermen's Feast (middle of the month) and the Feast of St. Anthony (end of the month) are the biggest. Check their Web sites, www.fishermansfeast.com and www.saintanthonysfeast.com, for highlights.

September

Reports of celebrity sightings jump during the **Boston Film Festival,** at theaters around town in the middle of the month. Stars and directors turn up to promote and discuss their latest independent films; the public is welcome at most screenings. Check the newspapers for schedules; for information, call ☎ **781-925-1373** or visit www.bostonfilmfestival.org.

October

Thousands of rowers plus hundreds of thousands of spectators flood Boston and Cambridge for the **Head of the Charles Regatta,** on the third or fourth weekend of the month. A huge party (without alcohol) rages on the banks of the Charles River and its bridges on Saturday afternoon and all day Sunday. Call ☎ **617-864-8415** or visit www.hocr.org.

In the middle of the month, the **Ringling Brothers and Barnum & Bailey Circus** makes its annual two-week visit to the **FleetCenter** (☎ **617-624-1000;** Internet: www.fleetcenter.com).

Just about all month, the Witch City observes its biggest holiday with **Salem Haunted Happenings.** Special offerings include parades, parties, fortune-telling, cruises, and tours. Visit www.salemhaunted happenings.com for the scoop on the activities.

November

The spirit of the original **Thanksgiving Celebration** endures in Plymouth. The "stroll through the ages" showcases 17th- and 19th-century Thanksgiving preparations in historic homes. **Plimoth Plantation** (☎ **800-262-9356** or 508-746-1622; Internet: www.plimoth. org), which re-creates the colony's first years, offers a reservation-only Victorian Thanksgiving feast (trust me, you're not sorry to miss out on Pilgrim food). Call ☎ **800-USA-1620** or check out www.visit-plymouth.com.

December

Boston Ballet's *Nutcracker,* one of the country's biggest and best, starts its annual run the day after Thanksgiving. The spectacular sets help make the ballet an enticing way to introduce children to theatergoing. Contact **Tele-charge** (☎ **800-447-7400;** Internet: www.telecharge.com) as soon as you plan your trip, ask whether your hotel offers a *Nutcracker* package, or check for returned tickets in person at the Wang Theatre box office at 270 Tremont St.

The year ends with **First Night,** an arts-oriented New Year's Eve blowout all over town from early afternoon to midnight. The parade is in the late afternoon; ice sculptures and art exhibitions dot the city; theatrical performances and other entertainment run all day. The midnight fireworks display explodes over the harbor. For most activities, you need a First Night button, available for about $15 at visitor centers and stores around the city. Call ☎ **617-542-1399** or visit www.firstnight.org.

Chapter 3

Planning Your Budget

● ●

In This Chapter

▶ Finding budgeting strategies for every budget

▶ Unmasking hidden costs

▶ Deciding how to spend: credit cards, traveler's checks, ATMs, and cash

▶ Stretching your money (but not by writing rubber checks)

● ●

Boston has all the elements of an outrageously expensive destina-tion, starting with a shortage of downtown hotels, especially in the non-luxury price ranges. If you're not footing the bill, the limited lodging means your biggest problem at busy times is likely finding someone to take your money. For us regular folks, the hotel shortage means "stay home until you have a workable budget."

You can take a lesson from Boston area's ever-present students. They occupy a parallel universe where food is plentiful and reasonably priced, entertainment is cheap or free, and the whole point of shopping is get-ting the most out of your (and your parents') hard-earned money.

Of course, if you imitate the students too slavishly, you can wind up sleeping in a stranger's bathtub and eating mystery meat. You get the idea, though: Know what's important to you, and try not to overpay for it.

Adding Up the Elements

A well-constructed budget is like a tricky jigsaw puzzle. Making it work can be as satisfying as dropping that 1,000th puzzle piece into place. Think hard (and ask your companions to do the same) about what's important to you.

For instance, corporate travelers rank Boston among the country's most expensive business destinations. If you seal that once-in-a-lifetime deal, though, the high price tag may feel like a bargain. As you determine your budget, flexibility is important, but knowing when you can't be flexible is even more important. Turn to the end of this book for a budget worksheet to help you through this process. Check out Table 3-1 for some other guidelines.

Table 3-1	What Things Cost in Boston
Item	**Cost**
Taxi from airport to downtown or Back Bay	$22–$28
Water shuttle from airport to downtown	$10
Bus from airport to downtown or Back Bay	$6–$8
Subway token	$1
Local bus fare	75¢
Pay phone call	35¢
Double at Omni Parker House	$189–$309
Double at Newbury Guest House	$130–$195
Double at Longwood Inn	$89–$129
Lunch for one at Ye Olde Union Oyster House	$10–$23
Lunch for one at Durgin-Park	$6–$20
Lunch for one at Bartley's Burger Cottage	$4.50–$11
Dinner for one, without wine, at Rialto	$23–$50
Dinner for one, without wine, at Legal Sea Foods	$14–$30
Dinner for one, without wine, at the Elephant Walk	$11–$23
Glass of beer	$2.50–$6
Can of soda	75¢–$1.50
Cup of coffee	$1 and up
Roll of ASA 100 Kodacolor film, 36 exposures	$7–$9
Adult admission to the Museum of Fine Arts	$15
Child (under 18) admission to the Museum of Fine Arts	Free weekdays after 3 p.m. and weekends
Movie ticket	$5–$9
Theater ticket	$30–$90

Lodging

The boom of the late 1990s left its mark on Boston's hotels: Formerly borderline choices upgraded to take advantage of the red-hot market, and construction began on several high-end properties. Although the market was softening even before the terrorist attacks of September 2001, more supply and less demand haven't slashed prices as much as you may hope. Fixed costs are high, and even with a big discount, an outrageous rate drops to merely pricey. The average double-room rate is less than the $180 of the dot-com glory days, but it still flirts with $160.

If you can't book a relatively inexpensive B&B and prefer something nicer than a hostel, expect to spend at least $110 a night. That doesn't include the 12.45% hotel tax. The price of a centrally located chain hotel may seem high (and, except in the dead of winter, probably will be closer to $160 than to $110). Just remember that the lower cost of many suburban establishments doesn't include the time and expense of commuting to downtown attractions and businesses — or the psychic damage Boston-area traffic inflicts.

Transportation

Before discussing anything else, I should point out that many popular destinations are easiest to reach on foot. (If you want to prorate the wear on your walking shoes, be my guest.)

I plan to harp on this until out-of-state drivers are as rare as mastodons: You do not need a car to get around Boston and Cambridge. What you think you get — flexibility and convenience — are exactly the things you sacrifice. Boston in particular is as nightmarish for drivers as New York or San Francisco, and that's before you consider the heavy construction equipment in use on many downtown streets.

 Driving to Boston can appear to be a budget-conscious option, if you resign yourself to parking the car when you arrive and not retrieving it until you leave. But before you shout "road trip," compare the cost of tolls, gas, parking, and incidentals to the best airfare you can find — you may discover that driving isn't such a great deal after all.

Taxis are expensive and can be hard to find, but you'll track one down eventually. The car-rental money you save can pay for several days' worth of cab rides. (See Chapter 11 for information on taxis.)

The Massachusetts Bay Transportation Authority (MBTA), or the T (as it's called by the locals), provides cheap transportation ($1 for a subway token, 75¢ for the local bus) in and around the city. Visitor passes good for unlimited local rides, and sold for one-, three-, and seven-day periods (costing $6, $11, and $22, respectively), can make public transit an even better deal. Note that service shuts down by 1:00 a.m. during the week, 2:30 a.m. on weekends, and doesn't go everywhere — that means more cabs. (For the lowdown on public transit, see Chapter 11.)

Restaurants

Again, thank the students: You can find tasty, inexpensive food all over the place. But don't get carried away. If you've been waiting for years to try fresh lobster, this is not the time to cut corners.

Serious penny-pinchers can enjoy a decent breakfast for $5 or less, lunch for $6 or so, and a more-than-adequate dinner for as little as $15. If your budget, appetite, or both are small, a good strategy is making lunch the big meal of the day. Or start with a bagel and coffee or juice ($2 to $3), lunch on a sandwich or salad ($5), and go wild at dinner.

Attractions

I would be remiss if I didn't tell you that plenty of people visit Boston just to shop, eat, and watch sports (namely the Red Sox, plus the Patriots, Celtics, Bruins, and local colleges). If you can't return home without soaking up a little culture, turn to Part V, make a list, and start adding those admission costs. First, check out potential deals. The Arts/Boston coupon book and Boston CityPass offer good deals on attractions (see Chapter 16 for details), and many institutions, such as the Children's Museum, schedule hours when admission is by donation or free (see "Cutting Costs," later in this chapter).

Shopping

Maybe this activity should fall under "Attractions." (Shopping is an attraction for me!) Budget what you like, not forgetting souvenirs — and not forgetting that a great deal from Filene's Basement makes a better souvenir than a T-shirt or refrigerator magnet ever could. Shopping-wise, Boston is celebrated for high-end arts and crafts, mer-chandise from its dozens of colleges, and deals on clothing. That doesn't mean that prices are especially good (unless, of course, you're at Filene's Basement) — it means the sales tax (5%) doesn't apply to clothing priced below $175. For more information on Boston's shop-ping scene, check out Chapter 19.

Wolves in cheap clothing: Bargains that aren't

Looking back on other trips you've taken, you tend to focus on obvious missteps — the hotel renovation special, the discount tour with a guide your uncle saw on *America's Most Wanted,* and the time you said, "If it were that terrible, would it be a 'featured destination'?" — dumb moves you know not to repeat.

The cost-cutting steps to worry about are the ones that sound so good that you may forget they could be mistakes. Here are two biggies:

✔ **Sacrificing convenience for price.** Sometimes the deal is so good that you can't ignore it. (I've flown out of Providence instead of Boston to save $600, and I'd do it again.) Before you decide to save $50 by leaving at 6 a.m. and returning at 1 a.m. — a mere seven hours before your workday starts — think hard about just how good a deal that is. Are the sacrifices worth the bucks?

✔ **Paying for things you don't need.** The three-day transit pass saves tons of money, but only when you use it enough. If you don't eat breakfast, the room rate that includes a big buffet is subsidizing someone else's meal. The weekend special at a hotel with a great spa is no deal for someone who just wants a lap pool. A bargain is a bargain only if you get something you wanted anyway.

Nightlife

If culture is your main motivation, start with, say, the Boston Symphony Orchestra (known as the BSO), and build the rest of your budget around that. Good seats for the BSO, the Boston Pops, the Boston Ballet, or a Broadway-bound show likely will set you back at least $50 a head. Less expensive but equally enjoyable options include numerous local performing-arts companies and two superb jazz clubs (see Part VI for details).

Even if a splashy night out isn't your thing, consider reserving time, money, and energy for an after-dark excursion. Boston offers lots of relatively inexpensive cultural opportunities, such as half-price theater tickets and cheap or free student performances in every field. Or warm yourself at a congenial pub; a couple of hours and a couple of pints with the locals can often tell you more about the city than an army of tour guides. (For information on the city's nightlife, see Part VI.)

Keeping a Lid on Hidden Expenses

At home, your wallet seems to be made of solid leather (or nylon, or whatever). Your cash is secure inside and doesn't emerge without

careful consideration. Then you leave town, and money starts gush
ing out of your wallet like water from a broken dam. Knowing what to
watch out for can help you stem this spending tide. Let me offer some
advice.

Taxes and fees

These expenses aren't usually paid in cash, so you may not take note of
them as you should. When you arrange any commercial transaction —
hotel rooms, car rentals, sightseeing — be sure to ask for the total cost
as well as the great-sounding price the business quotes you. For
example:

✔ Boston and Cambridge impose 12.45% **lodging** taxes. (Boom! Your
$159 hotel room costs $20 more.)

✔ **Car rentals** that originate in Boston carry a $10 surcharge that
goes toward the construction of a new convention center, and you
agreed to return the gas tank full but didn't leave enough time to
do so. (Cha-ching! That's another $20.)

✔ Most Boston companies that run **guided tours and cruises** are
careful not to mislead potential customers, but some bad apples
may neglect to include taxes when quoting prices. (Shazam! There
goes $5.)

✔ Many **restaurants** add a 15% to 18% gratuity to the bill if your
party is larger than six or eight people; accidentally leave your
own tip and you're out another chunk of change. (Bang! That's an
extra $30 or more.)

Remember to double-check the total and what the bill includes before
you fork over your hard-earned cash.

Gratuities

The average tip for most service providers, such as waiters and cab
drivers, is 15%, rising to 20% for particularly good service. The state
meal tax is 5% — in restaurants, you can triple (or quadruple) the tax
to calculate the tip. A 10% to 15% tip is sufficient if you just drink at a
bar. Bellhops get $1 or $2 a bag, hotel housekeepers should receive at
least $1 per person per day, and valet parking and coat-check atten-
dants expect $1 to $2 for their services.

Incidentals

This low-profile category of expenses is the most insidious. In a day of
spending $1 here and $5 there — on postcards, stamps, water, maps,

snacks, sunscreen, and other random items — you can easily spend $20 or $30 and barely notice it. Budget for these extra expenditures and be a bit more aware of what you're frittering away — you'll save a bundle.

My top tip in this category concerns water. You can bring a bottle from home and fill it at your hotel or from water fountains at attractions and visitor centers. If that seems a bit maniacal, consider picking up a six-pack at a drugstore or supermarket and keeping bottles handy in your room. This suggestion may sound silly, but buying individual bottles (for as much as $3) throughout the day can really add up.

Spending Money: Will That Be Paper or Plastic?

ATMs usually are the easiest way to get cash on vacation. Most cities (including Boston) have plenty of 24-hour machines linked to a national network that probably includes your bank at home. Even if you use traveler's checks, you'll want to keep some cash handy for incidentals.

If you plan to rely on your ATM card, determine which networks accept your bank's cards before leaving home (most cards have this information on the back). **Cirrus** (☎ **800-424-7787** or 800-4CIRRUS) and **Plus** (☎ **800-843-7587**) are the most popular networks; call their toll-free numbers for specific locations of ATMs in their network.

The largest banks in Massachusetts are Fleet and Citizens; smaller institutions and credit unions also operate ATMs. These handy little machines are everywhere, including some subway stations. In busy areas, you'll seldom go more than two blocks without seeing one.

Try not to hit the ATM every time you need 20 bucks, but try not to walk around with a fat roll of bills, either. ATM transactions usually carry service charges, and the fees can add up. Privately operated non-bank ATMs (most commonly found in convenience stores) are especially costly.

Many banks impose a fee every time you use a card from another bank. By law, Massachusetts banks' ATMs must display a message warning you that you're about to be charged and offer you the chance to cancel the transaction. Even if the bank doesn't charge you, *your* bank may tack on its own fee (for using another bank's ATM) of 50¢ to $3.

If your ATM card is also a debit card, consider carrying at least one conventional credit card. When using a debit card, you may forget that you're spending the equivalent of cash and depleting your checking account, instead of running up a credit-card balance. If you don't keep a large balance, be aware that some banks "freeze" part of the money in your account when you use a debit card for a transaction without a set amount (like a car rental or a tank of gas).

All charged up

Credit cards are invaluable when traveling. They're a safe way to carry money and provide a convenient record of your expenses. Most establishments in the Boston area accept major credit cards.

In an emergency, you can get cash advances off your credit cards at any bank. (The fees can be hefty, and interest charges start accruing the moment you receive the cash.) At most banks, you don't need to go to a teller; you can get a cash advance at the ATM if you know your personal identification number (PIN). If you don't know your PIN, call the phone number on the back of your credit card *before you leave home* and ask the bank to send it. You should receive your PIN in five to seven business days. (I offer more details regarding ATMs in Chapter 12.)

Check this out

Traveler's checks are a holdover from the pre-ATM days when out-of-towners couldn't be sure they'd be able to cash personal checks. Because lost or stolen traveler's checks can be replaced, they're still a sound alternative to carrying a lot of cash.

If you feel you need the security of traveler's checks and don't mind the hassle of showing identification every time you want to cash one, you can get checks at almost any bank. **American Express** offers checks in denominations of $10, $20, $50, $100, $500, and $1,000. You pay a service charge ranging from 1% to 4%, although AAA members can obtain checks without a fee at most AAA offices. You can also get American Express traveler's checks over the phone by calling ☎ **800-221-7282;** American Express gold and platinum cardholders who call this number are exempt from the 1% fee.

Citibank offers **Citibank Visa** traveler's checks at Citibank locations across the country and at several other banks. To find the Citibank closest to you, call ☎ **800-541-8882.** The service charge is 1% to 2.5%; checks come in denominations of $20, $50, $100, $500, and $1,000. For information on non-Citibank **Visa** traveler's checks, call ☎ **800-732-1322.** **MasterCard** also offers traveler's checks. Call ☎ **800-223-9920** for a location near you.

Cutting Costs

"Yankee thrift" is not an artifact, it's an art form. Regardless of the economy, saving money is a highly respected pastime. Here are some tips to help you trim your travel costs like a local:

- ✔ **Travel during the off-season.** If you can visit Boston during non-peak times (especially January through March), you'll find hotel prices discounted as much as 50% from their high-season rates.

- ✔ **Fly on off-peak days of the week.** If you can travel on Tuesday, Wednesday, or Thursday, you may lock in a cheaper airfare. When you inquire about airfares, ask if flying on a different day reduces the rate. See Chapter 5 for more tips on getting the best airfare.

- ✔ **Reserve your flight well in advance.** A ticket purchased 14 to 21 days in advance can save you more than $500 on a full fare. See Chapter 5 for details.

- ✔ **Reserve your flight only a couple of days in advance.** Last-minute Internet fares (released Wednesday for the weekend that starts two days later) aren't a sure thing, because you never know what destinations will be included, but they sure are a bargain. Check out Chapter 5 for more information.

- ✔ **Don't fly to Boston.** You'll get to Boston eventually. Flying to Warwick, Rhode Island, or Manchester, New Hampshire, can be *much* cheaper than flying to Boston's Logan International Airport. If you have more time than money, these alternate cities are worth checking out. See Chapter 5 for details.

- ✔ **Weigh that package.** An arrangement that includes airfare, lodging, airport transfers, and perhaps some extras (such as a trolley tour) can save money and time. Turn to Chapter 5 for more details.

- ✔ **Bring only as much luggage as you can carry easily.** A pile of heavy bags weighs you down so much that jumping on the T isn't a reasonable option. So you'll wind up hailing a cab, which costs an awful lot more than that $1 subway token, and possibly tipping skycaps and bellmen. Plan to handle your own lightly packed luggage, and don't forget to leave room for souvenirs you may carry home.

- ✔ **Reserve a hotel room with a kitchen.** It may not feel like as much of a vacation if you do your own cooking and dishes, but eating in restaurants three times a day can be pricey. Even if you only make your own breakfast and take an occasional bag lunch, you'll still save. And you'll never be shocked by a hefty room-service bill.

✔ **Don't be shy about asking for a discount.** All that money you pay to belong to the auto club, AARP, a trade union, or another organization with group bargaining power can pay off — but only if you remember to ask about deals. When you book transportation and accommodations, have your membership cards handy.

✔ **Double up with the kids.** Rates typically are about the same whether you book one bed or two, and many hotels allow children to stay free with their parents or guardian. Plus, an extra bed is much cheaper than an extra room, especially on a long trip.

✔ **Don't rent a car while in Boston.** I'm a tad fixated on this. If you're planning an out-of-town day-trip, go wild. Otherwise, save the expense of renting and parking.

✔ **Buy the MBTA's Boston Visitor Pass.** And use it. The pass can be a great deal if you use it enough (see Chapter 16 for details).

✔ **Buy an ArtsBoston coupon book or a Boston CityPass.** The coupon book's discounts include a wide selection of attractions and activities, such as museums, trolley tours, and sightseeing cruises. The CityPass covers just six attractions (including the Museum of Fine Arts) but represents a 50% discount if you visit all of them. See Chapter 16 for details.

✔ **Take advantage of free or cheap museum admission.** The USS *Constitution* Museum is free; the Children's Museum costs $1 after 5 p.m. on Friday; the Institute of Contemporary Art is free to all after 5 p.m. Wednesday; the Harvard art museums are free before noon Saturday and all day Wednesday; and the Harvard natural history museums are free on Sunday morning year-round and from 3 to 5 p.m. Wednesday during the academic year. The Museum of Fine Arts is pay-what-you-wish — but "suggests" a whopping $14 — after 4 p.m. Wednesday.

✔ **Try expensive restaurants at lunch instead of dinner.** Your lunch tab can be a fraction of the dinner bill at the same establishment, and the menu often includes many of the same specialties.

✔ **Pass on the souvenirs.** Your photographs and your memories should be the best mementos of your trip. If you're worried about money, you can do without the T-shirts and trinkets.

✔ **Let the kids do some planning.** You may be pleasantly surprised to discover that they consider a ride on a swan boat and a session of duck feeding at the Public Garden a full and fulfilling morning. (If your children have champagne taste and you're on a beer budget, forget I said anything.)

Chapter 4

Planning Ahead for Special Travel Needs

● ●

In This Chapter

▶ Setting up a smooth family trip

▶ Traveling senior style

▶ Finding the best places for travelers with disabilities

▶ Getting tips for gay and lesbian travelers

● ●

*O*ne-size-fits-all travel is a myth; all travelers, especially those with particular needs, want their plans custom-tailored. This chapter offers pointers for people in four specific categories: families, senior citizens, travelers with disabilities, and gay and lesbian travelers.

Traveling with the Brood: Advice for Families

Families from around the world flock to Boston, and the ones who prepare wisely return home still on speaking terms. Many, if not most, Boston-area activities appeal to children, and nearly every hotel and restaurant caters to kids. Just getting around Boston becomes a family activity, because you're bound to do a fair amount of hand-in-hand strolling — a positive if walking tires the kids enough to make for a peaceful, early bedtime, but a negative if that walking does the same to you.

The best advice I can offer to family travelers is so simple that it verges on insulting: Give your kids a voice in the planning process. Children have so little control over their daily lives that offering them a bit of power on vacation may go a long way.

Boston on the children's bookshelf

Your kids may know more about these tiny slices of Boston than you do (or more than you remember). Literally hundreds of children's books about Boston are available. Here are three of my favorites:

- ✔ *Make Way for Ducklings,* **by Robert McCloskey.** You may have lost count of how many times you've read this one to your preschoolers. Adorable bronze renderings in their own corner of the Public Garden illustrate the delightful story of the Mallard family.

- ✔ *The Trumpet of the Swan,* **by E. B. White.** He's not as famous as Charlotte the spider, but Louis the trumpeter swan has delightful adventures in Boston. Like the Mallard family, Louis frequents the Public Garden.

- ✔ *Johnny Tremain,* **by Esther Forbes.** This book offers a boy's-eye view (with several strong female characters) of the events that took place in Boston before the Revolutionary War. Johnny's interesting escapades make this a painless introduction to the people and history of the period — and a cracking-good story.

Overall, try to keep your kids' needs in mind when considering the first three stages of your trip: before you leave home, while you're on the road, and when you're in Boston. Look for the Kid Friendly icon throughout this book for family-oriented tips and activities.

Doing your homework

Another borderline-obvious suggestion: Make sure everyone knows what to expect. (This is all too easy to forget even when you're traveling only with adults!) A huge part of Boston's appeal is that this is a working city, not a theme park, but that's no consolation to a child who thinks that *vacation* always means roller coasters and cotton candy.

Children old enough to enjoy traveling can help with planning. (For a lesson in life skills, you may even ask your kids to lend a hand with the vacation budgeting.) Give your children some time with this book and a not-too-overwhelming assortment of other planning materials. After everyone contributes suggestions, all of you will have a better sense of what the other family members have in mind for your Boston vacation.

Spare yourself some angst by including potentially unenthusiastic teenagers early in the planning process. A college tour, time out for mall hopping, or some other inducement may help counteract the totally uncool concept of the family vacation.

Booking a hotel

I want to take the stress out of finding hotel rooms that suit your family and your budget. Here are booking strategies you can follow to simplify the process:

- ✔ **Accommodate the kids' needs first.** If the only thing they care about is a swimming pool (and if they haven't traveled much, they may not know that not every hotel has one), start with confirming that amenity.

- ✔ **Choose a hotel that lets children stay free.** Most do; the cutoff age can be as young as 12 or as old as 19. A room with two double beds typically costs the same as a room with one queen- or king-size bed. Even if a crib or rollaway costs extra, it's cheaper than taking two rooms.

- ✔ **Consider booking a second room or a suite.** Some hotels offer families a deal (usually half-price) on the extra room, which is sometimes an adjoining unit connected by an interior door. Even then, a suite may be less expensive — not to mention more luxurious.

- ✔ **A refrigerator or kitchenette can pay for itself.** Stock up on cereal and juice, make a bag lunch or two, and invest the savings (in money and good behavior) in a fancy dinner.

Don't put off thinking about child care. I *strongly* recommend that you book a sitter in advance — if possible, when you reserve your room. As in other areas of the country, demand for child care is high, and the number of providers is limited. The good news is that most hotels in the Boston area can recommend reliable baby-sitters. If you choose to use a child-care referral service, keep in mind that referral fees are steep. If you're in town on business, ask if your host company has a corporate membership in a child-care referral service. If the company does, you may be able to save some serious money.

The agency **Parents in a Pinch** (☎ **800-688-4697** or 617-739-KIDS; Internet: www.parentsinapinch.com) can line up a carefully screened child-care provider and offer references to parents who request them. The annual registration fee is $150; the per-day referral fee is $40 for evenings and weekends, $60 for weekdays. The sitter gets $10 per hour for one child, $1 an hour for each additional child, reimbursement for transportation (30¢ per mile), and other authorized expenses.

Keeping the peace on the road

Book a nonstop flight. If you can't book a nonstop flight, try to fly early in the day. If you can't fly early in the day, at least try to avoid booking the last flight of the day. A canceled connecting flight may leave you stranded, especially in the winter, when weather delays plague the entire East Coast.

If you fly, remember to pack chewing gum to help with ear-pressure problems.

Flying or not, pack diversionary materials and toys — crayons or markers, a deck of cards, computer game, personal stereo or portable radio with headphones, or a favorite book. Keep a surprise diversion in reserve. These items are handy on the road and can buy weary parents some TV-free downtime in the middle of a busy day in Boston.

Bring more diapers than you think you could possibly need. For a small child, pack a change of clothes where you can reach it easily; for an older child, a clean shirt is always a good idea (let the young-ster carry it).

Exploring the city

Be realistic. You may need to adjust your expectations to accommodate your traveling companions' short legs and shorter attention spans. Here are three important reminders: Don't try to do too much; don't forget to schedule some playtime; and don't assume that more expensive is better.

Remember, children are creatures of habit, and travel is disruptive for everyone. In unfamiliar surroundings, something as simple as a favorite breakfast cereal or flavor of juice may make the difference between wary-but-willing and freaked out.

You probably have a sense of your sightseeing timetable from the groundwork you laid at home. If your schedule isn't set, try this: Ask each child for a short list of top activity picks (no more than three, and no make-or-break choices). Then ask each child to select one activity from someone else's list. This idea may sound a tad crafty, but the plan cuts down on the cries of "this wasn't my idea."

Larger groups may consider splitting up for a while and reuniting to swap notes over a family dinner. This idea works especially well if the children are far apart in age. For example, the teenagers can explore the New England Aquarium while the younger kids check out the Children's Museum. This can help keep the peace and keep everyone satisfied.

Making Age Work for You: Tips for Seniors

Many Boston-area businesses, including hotels, restaurants, museums, and movie theaters, offer discounts to seniors who present valid identification. The cutoff age usually is 65 or (less often) 62. You can find some senior deals through **AARP** (formerly the American Association of Retired Persons); they're available to any member age 50 or older. Membership in AARP, 601 E St. NW, Washington, DC 20049 (☎ **800-424-3410** or 202-434-AARP; Internet: www.aarp.org), costs $12.50 a year and includes discounts on package tours, airfares, car rentals, and hotels — and that's only the travel-related discounts (AARP offers other kinds of discounts as well).

Get in the habit of asking whether a business offers a senior discount. Restaurants and theaters that extend discounts usually do so only during off-peak hours, but museums and other attractions may charge reduced rates at all times. Carry your driver's license or other document that shows your date of birth.

Seniors 65 and over can buy passes that allow them to ride the MBTA (Massachusetts Bay Transportation Authority) subways for 25¢ (75¢ less than the regular fare), and local buses for 15¢ (60¢ less than the regular fare). On zoned and express buses and the commuter rail, the senior fare is half the regular fare. The Senior Pass is available for a nominal fee (currently 50¢) from 8:30 a.m. to 5:00 p.m. weekdays at the Office for Transportation Access, Back Bay Station, 105 Dartmouth St. Or write to the **Office for Transportation Access,** 145 Dartmouth St., Boston, MA 02116 (☎ **617-222-5976** or 617-222-5854 [TTY]; Internet: www.mbta.com). Enclose a 1-x-1-inch photo and a check or money order for 50¢.

A **Golden Age Passport** from the National Park Service is one of the best deals around. For $10, it gives you and immediate family members traveling with you free admission to all recreation areas run by the federal government, including parks and monuments. The passport, which is good for your lifetime, can pay for itself in one visit to the Boston area. For example, it covers the Longfellow House in Cambridge and the Maritime National Historic Site in Salem, among many other destinations. It's available to citizens and permanent residents 62 and older at any Park Service site that charges admission.

At press time, many airlines had discontinued or were cutting back on discount programs for seniors; check around (or ask your travel agent to check around) to be sure you're getting the best available deal.

If you experience mobility difficulties, see the following section for information about getting around Boston.

Accessing Boston: Advice for Travelers with Disabilities

Boston is a generally accessible city, with some exceptions. Widespread construction and uneven walking surfaces can keep you from getting around as quickly as you may like. I recommend that you allow plenty of time to reach your destinations, especially near the Big Dig, which dominates the area between North Station and South Station and can disrupt every mode of transportation in the downtown area (see Chapter 1 for more on the Big Dig).

The narrow streets, cobbled thoroughfares, and brick sidewalks that make older neighborhoods like Beacon Hill and the North End so picturesque can make navigation difficult. However, after you reach the areas, almost all attractions are accessible. Note that the upper levels of some historic buildings — for example, the second floor of the Paul Revere House — can't accommodate wheelchairs. If you have severe mobility issues, contact attractions in advance for accessibility information.

Many North End and Beacon Hill streets don't allow buses and trolleys. Motor tours touch on the edges of these neighborhoods, but the tours don't get up close. If you want to experience these areas, you must disembark from public transit and venture out on your own. (Beware of salespeople who try to tell you otherwise.) For example, the Paul Revere House is four blocks from the closest trolley stop.

VSA Arts Massachusetts (formerly Very Special Arts), 2 Boylston St., Boston, MA 02116 (☎ **617-350-7713;** TTY 617-350-6836; Internet: www. vsamass.org), is an excellent source of information. The comprehensive Web site includes a searchable database of general access information and specifics about more than 200 arts and entertainment facilities in the state.

Finding accommodating accommodations

Most Boston-area lodgings comply with the Americans with Disabilities Act (ADA), but the true level of accessibility can be harder to gauge without asking some pointed questions. Many hotels occupy antique buildings, and the updating process worked better on some than on others. Be explicit about your needs when you make your reservations. If you have a specific concern that a certain hotel can't address, the staff should be able to direct you to a more appropriate establishment.

Some older, smaller hotels and B&Bs comply with federal law only partly or not at all. Large national chain hotels are more likely to offer the full range of ADA-compliant accommodations, including roll-in showers, lower sinks, extra space for maneuvering wheelchairs, and so forth. The **Royal Sonesta Hotel** in Cambridge (☎ **800-SONESTA**) trains its staff in disability awareness; at the **Westin Copley Place Boston** (☎ **800-WESTIN-1**), 48 accessible rooms adjoin standard units.

Getting around

Under the ADA, all forms of public transit must provide special services to patrons with disabilities. Newer stations on the Red, Blue, and Orange lines are wheelchair accessible, and the MBTA is in the process of converting Green Line trolleys. Call ☎ **800-392-6100** (outside Massachusetts) or 617-222-3200 to see if the stations you need are accessible. Make sure you speak to a live person, and make sure the information — especially about functioning elevators — is current.

Don't rely on system maps to tell you which subway stations are accessible; these maps tend to be sorely out-of-date.

All **MBTA buses** are equipped with lifts or kneelers; call ☎ **800-LIFT-BUS** for more information. Some bus routes are wheelchair-accessible at all times, but you may need to make a reservation as much as a day in advance for others. **Boston Cab** (☎ **617-536-5010**) is one taxicab company with wheelchair-accessible vehicles; advance notice is recommended. In addition, the **Airport Accessible Van** (☎ **617-561-1769**) offers wheelchair-accessible service within Logan Airport.

For discounted public-transit fares, persons with disabilities can apply for a $3 **Transportation Access Pass.** The process takes six to eight weeks and may not be worth the trouble for a short visit. Contact the **Office for Transportation Access,** 145 Dartmouth St., Boston, MA 02116 (☎ **617-222-5976** or 617-222-5854 [TTY]; Internet: www. mbta.com).

Gathering general information

Several national organizations provide disabled travelers with the information and tools they need.

The **Society for Accessible Travel and Hospitality** (☎ **212-447-7284;** Internet: www.sath.org) offers a wealth of resources and information for travelers with all types of disabilities. Annual membership costs $45 for adults, $30 for seniors and students.

Access-Able Travel Source (☎ 303-232-2979; Internet: www. access-able.com) is a comprehensive database of travel agents who specialize in travel for people with disabilities; the database also is a clearinghouse for information about accessible destinations around the world.

Many major car-rental companies offer hand-controlled cars for disabled drivers. Avis can provide such a vehicle at any of the company's locations in the United States with 48-hour advance notice; Hertz requires between 24 and 72 hours of advance reservation at most locations. **Wheelchair Getaways** (☎ 800-536-5518 or 606-873-4973; Internet: www.wheelchair-getaways.com) rents specialized vans with wheelchair lifts and other features for the disabled in more than 35 states, including Massachusetts.

Mobility International USA (☎ 541-343-1284 [voice and TTY]; Internet: www.miusa.org) publishes a biannual newsletter; membership costs $35 per year. The organization also publishes *A World of Options,* a 658-page book of resources for travelers with disabilities.

Vision-impaired travelers can get information on traveling with Seeing Eye dogs from the **American Foundation for the Blind,** 11 Penn Plaza, Suite 300, New York, NY 10001 (☎ 800-232-5463).

Stepping Out: Resources for Gay and Lesbian Travelers

Boston is one of the most gay- and lesbian-friendly year-round destinations in New England (Provincetown holds the seasonal title). Boston's South End and Jamaica Plain and Cambridge's Porter Square are home to many gay men and lesbians. A number of nightclubs cater to a gay clientele at least one night a week.

One of the area's best resources, the **Gay and Lesbian Helpline** (☎ 617-267-9001), offers information from 6 to 11 p.m. Monday through Friday, and 5 to 10 p.m. on weekends. The weekly newspaper *Bay Windows* (☎ 617-266-6670; Internet: www.baywindows.com) covers New England and offers extensive cultural listings. The arts-oriented weekly *Boston Phoenix* publishes a monthly supplement, "One in 10," and has a gay-interest Internet area at www.bostonphoenix.com.

The *Pink Pages,* 66 Charles St. #283, Boston, MA 02114 (☎ **800-338-6550**), is a guide to gay- and lesbian-owned and gay-friendly businesses. Check the wide-ranging Web site at www.pinkweb.com/boston.index. html. If you don't have Internet access, you can order a copy of the annual directory for $11, including shipping.

Other information sources include the **Boston Alliance of Gay and Lesbian Youth** (☎ **800-42-BAGLY,** 617-227-4314, or 617-983-9845 [TTY]; Internet: www.bagly.org) and the **Bisexual Resource Center** (☎ **617-424-9595;** Internet: www.biresource.org).

Part II
Ironing Out the Details

The 5th Wave   By Rich Tennant

"The closest hotel room I could get you to Copley Square for that amount of money is in Cleveland."

In this part . . .

*N*ow comes the component of planning that can feel like ditch-digging and pay off like gold-mining. In this part, you discover something about travel agents, package tours, and airfare pricing. You also choose a hotel, weighing lodging options, neighborhoods, and ways of booking a room. Finally, I double-knot the loose ends and send you on your way.

Chapter 5

Getting to Boston

· ·

· ·

*I*f the details of trip planning start to bog you down, you may begin to suspect that the *longest* distance between two points is a straight line. You don't have to feel that way. This chapter outlines your options, from hands-off to hands-on, and explores choices for flying and riding to Boston.

Finding a Good Travel Agent

A good travel agent is like a good mechanic or plumber: hard to find, but invaluable when you find the right one. The best way to find a good travel agent is by word-of-mouth.

To get the most out of your agent, do a little homework. Read up on your destination (you've already made a sound decision by buying this book), and pick some accommodations and attractions that appeal to you. If you have access to the Internet, check prices on the Web (see "Getting the Best Deals on Airfares" later in this chapter) to get ballpark figures. Then, with your guidebook and Web information in hand, ask your agent to make arrangements for you. Because travel agents have access to more resources than even the most complete travel Web site, they generally can get you better prices than you can get yourself. And they can issue your tickets and vouchers right in the agency. In addition, your travel agent can recommend an alternative if the hotel of your choice isn't available.

Travel agents used to work solely on commission. Last year, almost all the major airlines eliminated travel-agent commissions on U.S. flights. Therefore, most agents won't book these services unless you specifically request it. To make up for the loss of revenue on non-commissionable bookings, many agents have started charging customers for services (usually $10 or $20 per ticket).

Buying an All-in-One Package

Say the words *escorted tour* or *package tour* and you may feel as though you're being forced to choose: your money or your lifestyle. Think again, friends. Times — and tours — have changed.

An **escorted tour** does, in fact, involve an escort, but that doesn't mean it has to be dull — or even tame. Escorted tours range from cushy bus trips, where you sit back and let the driver worry about the traffic, to adventures that include walking the Freedom Trail. You do, however, travel with a group, which may be just the thing for you if you're single and want company. In general, your expenses are taken care of after you arrive at your destination, but you still need to cover your airfare.

And this brings me to **package tours.** Unlike escorted tours, these generally "package" costs rather than people. Some tour companies bundle every aspect of your trip, including tours to various sights. However, most tour companies deal just with selected aspects of your trip, allowing you to get good deals by combining airfare and hotel costs, for example. A package tends to leave you a lot of leeway, while saving you a lot of money.

How do you find these deals? Well, I suggest some strategies in the next two sections, but keep in mind that every city is different. The tour operators I mention may not offer deals convenient to your departure city. If that's the case, check with your local travel agent: They generally know the most options close to home and how best to put together things such as escorted tours and airline packages.

Joining an escorted tour

You may love escorted tours. The tour company takes care of all the details and tells you what to expect at each leg of your journey. You know your costs up front, and, in the case of the tamer tours, there aren't many surprises. Escorted tours can take you to the maximum number of sights in the minimum amount of time with the least amount of hassle.

 If you decide to go with an escorted tour, I strongly recommend purchasing travel insurance, especially if the tour operator asks you to pay up front. But don't buy insurance from the tour operator! If the tour operator doesn't provide you with the vacation you paid for, there's no reason to think the operator will fulfill insurance obligations either. Get travel insurance through an independent agency. (I give you more information on the ins and outs of travel insurance in Chapter 9.)

When choosing an escorted tour, along with finding out whether you need to put down a deposit and when final payment is due, ask a few simple questions before you buy:

- ✔ **What is the cancellation policy?** How late can you cancel if you're unable to go? Do you get a refund if you cancel? If they cancel? Does the company keep part of your deposit or refund the whole amount?

- ✔ **How jam-packed is the schedule?** Does the tour try to fit 25 hours into a 24-hour day, or does it give you time to relax or shop? If getting up at 7 a.m. every day and not returning to your hotel until 6 or 7 p.m. at night sounds like a grind, certain escorted tours may not be for you.

- ✔ **How big is the group?** The smaller the group, the less time you spend waiting for people to get on and off the bus. Tour operators may be evasive about this, especially until everybody has made reservations. But the operator should be able to give you a rough estimate.

- ✔ **Does the tour require a minimum group size?** Some tour operators may cancel the tour if the company doesn't get enough bookings. If a quota exists, find out what it is and how close your tour is to reaching the quota. Again, tour operators may be evasive, but the information may help you select a tour that's sure to happen.

- ✔ **What exactly is included?** Don't assume anything. You may be required to get to and from the airport at your own expense. An excursion may include a box lunch, but drinks may be extra.

- ✔ **How much flexibility does the tour offer?** Can you opt out of certain activities, or does the bus leave once a day, with no exceptions? Are all your meals planned in advance? Can you choose your entree at dinner or does everybody get a chicken cutlet?

Picking a peck of package tours

For many destinations, package tours can be a smart way to go. In many cases, packages that include airfare, hotel, and transportation to and from the airport cost less than if you book the individual elements yourself. That's because tour operators buy packages in bulk, then resell to the public. The process is kind of like buying your vacation at a warehouse club — except the tour operator is the one who buys the 1,000-count box of garbage bags (and resells the bags 10 at a time at a cost that undercuts the local supermarket).

A new leaf

Every fall, New England's colorful trees exert a magnetic pull over millions of people. Travelers sign up for bus tours that start and end in Boston and return home with the false impression that they've seen the city. I'm not telling you to skip such tours, but I say this: Foliage season offers no guarantees. "Peak color" may not start or end when you think, and insane traffic and gloomy weather may keep you from making the best of your visit. If you're lucky enough to get a flight to Boston in October, consider making the city your base and scheduling a day-trip or two (after you've seen the forecast) that includes some leaf-peeping.

Ask a lot of questions when you book your trip. Package tour prices vary according to departure city, hotel, and extras such as car rental and side tours. Timing is as important as other options in determining price. Adjusting your travel dates by a week or even a day can yield substantial savings.

Tips for choosing a Boston package

Details of packages to Boston don't vary much, which makes comparison shopping relatively easy. Lodging options aren't extensive simply because of the number of places to stay. The sightseeing component, if there is one, usually is a free or discounted one-day trolley tour rather than a customized offering.

Look into hotel packages that include tickets to a cultural event, such as a major museum show or a Boston Ballet extravaganza (notably *The Nutcracker*). Even if you don't get a discount, landing a hot ticket can be a great time-saver.

Don't automatically add a rental car to your package. If you use the car every day and have access to free parking, it can be a good deal. If the car sits in the hotel garage racking up parking fees, you're wasting money.

On the other hand, an excursion to a suburb can be a worthwhile addition to your vacation. If time is short and you just can't leave town without seeing Plymouth (or Gloucester or another destination), paying someone to handle the logistics of a half- or full-day trip may be worth the money.

Places to find a Boston package

If you decide to investigate these package options further, your next task is to find the package that fits your needs. Check the ads in national magazines like *Arthur Frommer's Budget Travel, Travel + Leisure,* and *Condé*

Nast Traveler. The Travel section of your Sunday newspaper is another place to check, but your best bets are the choices I describe here:

- ✔ **Liberty Travel** (☎ **888-271-1584;** Internet: www.libertytravel.com), one of the biggest packagers in the Northeast, makes up in volume discounts what the company lacks in personalized service.

- ✔ **Yankee Magazine Vacations** (☎ **877-481-5986;** Internet: www.yankeemagazine.com/travel) is a more local option. The add-ons include an impressive variety of excursions to other New England destinations.

- ✔ Airline packages can be a good alternative for some destinations, but Boston (a "spoke" rather than a "hub") isn't always a hot option. At press time, the following offered Boston packages: **American Airlines Vacations** (☎ **800-321-2121;** Internet: www.aavacations.com); **Midwest Express Vacations** (☎ **800-452-2022;** Internet: www.midwestexpressvac.com); **United Vacations** (☎ **888-854-3899;** Internet: www.unitedvacations.com); and **US Airways Vacations** (☎ **800-455-0123;** Internet: www.usairwaysvacations.com). Some deals undercut Amtrak and involve a lot less travel time.

- ✔ If you live close enough to take advantage of **Amtrak Vacations** (☎ **800-654-5748;** Internet: www.amtrak.com), you may find a reasonable option. But don't book a train trip without at least checking your air options. Also, don't assume this is a more reliable choice during bad weather. Snow falls on train tracks, too.

To explore other airline possibilities, see the phone numbers and Web sites listed in the Appendix at the back of this book.

Getting the Best Deals on Airfares

Count the number of passengers in the cabin the next time you fly. You may be counting the number of different fares, too. *Yield management* — making each flight as full and as profitable as possible — can be harsh, but the practice can also work to your advantage.

If you need flexibility, be ready to pay for that luxury. The full fare usually applies to last-minute bookings, sudden itinerary changes, and round-trips that get you home before the weekend. On most flights, even the shortest routes, a full fare can approach $1,000.

You'll pay far less than full fare if you book well in advance, can stay over Saturday night, or can travel on Tuesday, Wednesday, or Thursday. A ticket bought as little as 7 or 14 days in advance will cost only 20% to 30% of the full fare. If you can travel with just a couple days' notice, you may also get a deal (usually on a weekend fare that you book through an airline's Web site — see "Getting tips for weekend warriors," later in this chapter).

Airlines periodically lower prices on the most popular routes. Restrictions abound, but the sales translate into savings. For instance, a cross-country flight may cost as little as $400 (in other words, less than the walk-up shuttle fare for the 218-mile trip from Boston to New York). You may also score a deal when an airline introduces a new route or increases service on an existing one.

Watch newspaper and television ads and airline Web sites (see the Appendix for Web addresses and phone numbers), and when you see a good price, grab the bargain. These sales usually run during slow seasons — for Boston, January through March. Sales rarely coincide with peak travel times such as summer vacation and the winter holidays, when people must fly, regardless of price.

Looking at attractive airport alternatives

If you have lots of time but not lots of money, booking a flight into Warwick, Rhode Island (outside Providence), or Manchester, New Hampshire, can be a great deal. Southwest Airlines broke these markets open, and many other carriers now serve both cities. Getting to Boston can be a hassle, but saving hundreds of dollars to spend on other things makes up for a lot of hassles.

The problem with this approach can be scheduling, because you need extra time to get from these airports to Boston. Plus, if you have to pay a lot for a rental car, there goes your great deal. However, if you have lots of time and you also find a good deal on a rental car, you use public transportation, or you have a friend serve as chauffeur, this could be the way to go.

T. F. Green Airport (☎ **888-268-7222;** Internet: www.pvd-ri.com; Airport code: PVD) is in Warwick, Rhode Island, about 60 miles south of Boston. **Bonanza** (☎ **800-556-3815;** Internet: www.bonanzabus.com) offers bus service ($18 one-way; $32 round-trip) between the airport and Boston's South Station.

Manchester International Airport (☎ **603-624-6556;** Internet: www. flymanchester.com; Airport code: MHT) is about 51 miles north of Boston. **Vermont Transit** (☎ **800-552-8737;** Internet: www. vermonttransit.com) operates bus service to and from South Station and Logan Airport ($11 one-way; $22 round-trip).

Cutting ticket costs by using consolidators

Consolidators, also known as *bucket shops,* are good places to find low fares. Consolidators buy seats in bulk and resell the tickets at prices that undercut the airlines' discounted rates. Be aware that tickets bought this way usually are nonrefundable or carry stiff (as much as 75% of the ticket price) cancellation penalties. *Note:* Before you pay, ask the consolidator for a confirmation number, and then call the airline to confirm your seat. Be prepared to book through a different consolidator if the airline can't confirm your reservation.

Consolidators' small ads usually appear in major newspapers' Sunday Travel sections at the bottom of the page. **STA Travel** (☎ **800-781-4040;** Internet: www.statravel.com) caters to young travelers but offers bargain prices to people of all ages. **The TravelHub** (☎ **800-247-3273;** Internet: www.travelhub.com) represents hundreds of travel agencies, many of which offer consolidator and discount fares. Other reliable consolidators include **1-800-FLY-CHEAP** (☎ **800-359-2432;** Internet: www.1800flycheap.com); **TFI Tours International** (☎ **800-745-8000** or 212-736-1140), which serves as a clearinghouse for unused seats; and *rebaters* such as **Travel Avenue** (☎ **800-333-3335;** Internet: www.travelavenue.com) and the **Smart Traveller** (☎ **800-448-3338** in the U.S. or 305-448-3338), which rebate part of their commissions to you.

Snaring a deal on the Web

Another way to find the cheapest fare is to scour the Internet. Computers can do it best by searching through millions of pieces of data and returning information in rank order. The number of virtual travel agents on the Internet has increased exponentially in recent years.

Checking all the travel booking sites is impossible, but a few of the more respected (and more comprehensive) ones are **Frommer's** (www.frommers.com), **Travelocity** (www.travelocity.com), **Expedia** (www.expedia.com), and **Orbitz** (www.orbitz.com). Each has its own little quirks, but all provide variations of the same service. Just enter the dates you want to fly and the cities you want to visit, and the computer looks for the lowest fares. Several other features have become standard to these sites: the ability to check flights at different times or dates in hopes of finding a cheaper fare, e-mail alerts when fares drop on a route you specified, and a database of last-minute deals that advertises super-cheap vacation packages or airfares for people who can get away at a moment's notice.

Great last-minute deals are also available directly from the airlines themselves through a free e-mail service called E-savers. Each week, the airline sends you a list of discounted flights, usually leaving the upcoming Friday or Saturday, and returning the following Monday or Tuesday. You can sign up for all the major airlines at once by logging on to **Smarter Living** (www.smarterliving.com) or going to each individual airline's Web site. These sites offer schedules, flight booking, and information on late-breaking bargains.

Remember, you don't have to book online; you can ask your flesh-and-blood travel agent to match or beat the best price you find.

Getting tips for weekend warriors

The airlines' Web sites make great last-minute deals available once a week, usually on Wednesday. Flights generally leave on Friday or Saturday (that is, only two or three days later) and return the following Sunday, Monday, or Tuesday. Some carriers offer hotel and car bargains, too.

You can sign up for e-mail alerts through individual Web sites or all at once through **Smarter Living** (www.smarterliving.com). And if you already know what airline you want to fly, consider staying up late on Tuesday and checking the site until the bargains for the coming weekend appear. Book right away and avoid losing out on the limited number of seats.

Finding Other Ways to Reach Boston

Sometimes flying just won't do. Maybe you have mobility issues, you're on a big road-trip vacation, or every flight is booked. Maybe you can't fly, and driving into construction purgatory holds little appeal. Here's the scoop on traveling by car and train.

Driving: A necessary evil

The roads into Boston look perfectly manageable — on paper. If only that map could be three-dimensional. You'd see little construction workers and equipment all over downtown, making the already-dire traffic even worse. I-93, the main north-south highway through town, continues to carry vehicles while its replacement, a tunnel beneath the current road, takes shape. The scheduled completion date for the $14 billion (and counting) Big Dig is 2005. How big is it? It has its own Web site (www.bigdig.com). Highway access *to* the Boston area is good. If you avoid rush hour and venturing all the way into town, your trip probably won't be too awful.

Avoiding cabin fever

Whether you think of flying as an adventure or an ordeal, you're probably not thrilled by the prospect of a bone-dry cabin and a ration of personal space that would make a sardine claustrophobic. (Imagine how I'd sound if I didn't love flying.) Here are some strategies that may make your trip more tolerable:

✔ **Try to get a bulkhead seat, located in the front row of each cabin.** These seats usually offer the most legroom. Don't storm forward just yet. Without a seat in front of you, you must fit your carry-on bag into the overhead bin. The front row may not be the best place to see the in-flight movie, and many airlines save these seats for full-fare frequent fliers.

✔ **Try to get a seat in the emergency-exit row.** Like bulkhead seats, seats in the emergency-exit rows also offer extra legroom. Ask when you check in whether you can be seated in one of these rows; assignment is usually first come, first served. You must be at least 15 years old and able to open the emergency exit door and help direct traffic, if necessary.

✔ **Wear comfortable clothes, and dress in layers.** The supposedly controlled cabin climate can leave you sweltering or shivering. You'll be glad to have a sweater or jacket that can help regulate your body temperature.

✔ **Drink a lot of water.** This won't make you any friends if you're in a window seat, but aisle-huggers won't be sorry. Not only does your body stay hydrated, but walking back and forth to the lavatory helps keep your legs from cramping.

✔ **Bring some toiletries on long flights.** Take a travel-size bottle of moisturizer or lotion to refresh your face and hands at the end of the flight. On an overnight flight (also known as the *red-eye*), always pack a toothbrush. You'll probably also want some petroleum jelly to keep your lips from cracking while you sleep in the dry cabin. If you wear contact lenses, take them out before you board, or at least bring eye drops.

✔ **Order a special meal if you have special dietary needs, or pack your own — a good idea even before cutbacks made the in-flight meal an endangered species.** Most airlines can accommodate dietary restrictions, and nobody has to know that your restriction is that you're a picky eater. The airlines make special meals (vegetarian, kosher, and so forth) to order, unlike the mass-produced chow they feed the other passengers.

✔ **If you're flying with kids, pack chewing gum to help with ear-pressure problems.** Don't forget diapers, toys, and a brand-new distraction (however small) — if a meltdown's looming, you want the element of surprise on your side. See Chapter 4 for other suggestions.

The Massachusetts Turnpike (I-90), or Mass. Pike, is an east-west toll road that runs from the New York border to downtown Boston. The next-to-last exit serves Cambridge. The main north-south route through Boston is I-93, which extends north into New Hampshire. The main north-south route on the East Coast is I-95, which detours around

Boston as a sort of beltway about 11 miles from downtown, where it's better known as State Route 128.

Try not to approach downtown Boston from 7 to 9 a.m. and 3:30 to 6:30 p.m. weekdays. Friday afternoon is especially problematic — make sure the car has plenty of gas and coolant. Here are some basic directions for driving into Boston from other parts of New England:

- ✔ **From New York City, points south, and southwestern Connecticut,** you have several options. My favorite is to take the Hutchinson River Parkway into Connecticut, where it becomes the Merritt/ Wilbur Cross Parkway. Note that you can't use these roads if your car has commercial plates. About 20 miles south of Hartford, follow signs to I-91 north, and take it to I-84 east. At Sturbridge, Massachusetts, pick up the Mass. Pike. (I-95 from New York, a busy truck route, is sometimes a bit faster.)

- ✔ **From Vermont and western New Hampshire,** take I-89 to Concord, New Hampshire, and then I-93 south.

- ✔ **From Maine and southeastern New Hampshire,** take I-95 south to Route 1 or I-93 south.

- ✔ **From Rhode Island and eastern Connecticut,** you're stuck with I-95. Where it intersects with I-93/Massachusetts 128, follow signs to Braintree and Boston.

Arriving by train

Amtrak (☎ **800-USA-RAIL** or 617-482-3660; Internet: www.amtrak.com) runs to Back Bay Station and South Station from the south, and to North Station from the north (Portland, Maine). Use Back Bay Station, on Dartmouth Street across from the Copley Place mall, if you're stay- ing in the Back Bay or the South End. Back Bay is also an Orange Line stop. Go to South Station, on Atlantic Avenue near the waterfront, if you're staying downtown or in Cambridge (South Station is also a Red Line subway stop; you must leave the terminal to reach the T).

Airline-style booking strategies increasingly apply to train travel. Booking far ahead usually will land you a discounted excursion fare. Discounts don't apply during high-volume times such as Friday after- noon, Sunday afternoon, and periods around holidays.

Amtrak also operates **Acela** (www.acela.com) high-speed-rail service on its Northeast Corridor route, between Boston and Washington, D.C. Acela replaced Metroliners between Washington and New York in 2001, cutting the trip time on the Washington-Boston route to just under six hours. Delays and equipment problems have plagued Acela almost since its inception; always call ahead to check the schedule before you run to catch this train. Call Amtrak or check its Web site for more details, schedules, and fares.

Chapter 6

Deciding Where to Stay

*T*aking the time to find the right hotel room is like taking the time to eat breakfast. Skip the most important meal of the day and you probably won't notice until lunchtime, when you're light-headed and crabby. Book the wrong accommodations, and your choice can haunt you hours later, when noise and lumpy beds keep you awake, or weeks later, when you open your credit-card bill and can't *believe* you paid so much.

The Boston area offers travelers many options. Although prices are high, amenities and service are good, and just about every property is in excellent shape. The options that suit your wishes and wallet are out there. This chapter, along with Chapters 7 and 8, helps you find the landing pad that's right for you.

Choosing the Type of Hotel for You

The Boston area offers a full range of accommodations, but not in the same abundant numbers as other destinations. At busy times, "take it or leave it" is more of an affirmation than an idle threat. Here's a look at what to expect.

The Goldilocks factor: What property feels right?

Put some thought into this one, but be ready to compromise, especially if you're traveling during a busy season. Sometimes the best thing about a room is simply that nobody else is in your space.

Giant chain hotels tend to be well appointed, centrally located, and somewhat boring. But don't reflexively dismiss the chains — the benefits of size include a larger supply of rooms and a wider range of prices. The listings in Chapter 8 include some agreeable choices, and the suburbs boast plenty of reliable options as well. (See the Appendix for a list of the major chains' toll-free numbers and Web sites.)

Independent hotels tend to compare favorably with the mega-chains, with less of a cookie-cutter feel and more personal service. These smaller establishments can't compete with chains in every area, though, so know which features are most important to you. (If you *must* swim a mile every morning, even remarkable service won't make a pool materialize.)

Chapter 8 also lists some motels, inns, and guesthouses. These smaller properties tend to be less conveniently located, less luxurious, and less expensive than larger establishments. If all you want is a comfy place to rest your head, this choice can be just right.

The ABCs of B&Bs

Travelers priced out of hotels or tired of generic lodgings are driving a boom in the bed-and-breakfast market. In the Boston area, B&Bs offer everything from simple spare rooms to opulent suites. Most rent only a few units, so unless you have unlimited time to call around until you find a vacancy, your best bet is to use an agency that specializes in B&Bs. Here are some reliable agencies to help with your reservations:

- ✔ **Bed and Breakfast Agency of Boston,** 47 Commercial Wharf, Boston, MA 02110 (☎ **800-248-9262** or 617-720-3540; ☎ 0800-89-5128 from the U.K.; Internet: www.boston-bnbagency.com)

- ✔ **Bed & Breakfast Reservations North Shore/Greater Boston/Cape Cod,** 11A Beach Rd., Gloucester, MA 01930 (☎ **800-832-2632** outside Massachusetts, 617-964-1606, or 978-281-9505; Internet: www.bbreserve.com)

- ✔ **Bed and Breakfast Associates Bay Colony Ltd.,** P.O. Box 57166, Boston, MA 02457 (☎ **800-347-5088** or 781-647-4949; Internet: www.bnbboston.com).

The demand for lodging means you may want to consider the following tips before booking your B&B:

- ✔ **Book as early as possible, especially during busy seasons.** This tip is particularly important if money is tight, because greater demand means higher prices.

- ✔ **Know what you want and what you don't.** Another reason to use an agency: The staff should know enough about each property to keep a guest who starts the day with a muffin over the fax machine away from a host who serves cooing honeymooners eggs Benedict.

✔ **Know your budget.** Expect to pay at least $65 a night, and some-times much more, for a double. Prices soar during high seasons and special events. Most places require a two-night minimum stay, and many offer winter discounts.

Finding the Perfect Location

Considering Boston's well-founded reputation as a city of neighbor-hoods, the question of location is surprisingly easy to answer. The central city is so tiny, and the neighborhoods so small, that the most popular parts of Boston break neatly into two main sections. Spread out a map and find Boston Common. For your purposes, downtown is north and east of this area and Back Bay is west and south. Cambridge and slightly less central areas such as Brookline, which I describe as "in the vicinity," are the other major options. See Chapter 10 for more neighborhood descriptions.

Deciding where to stay downtown

The oldest and newest (that is, still under construction) areas of the city lie between Charles Street and the harbor. Downtown is congested but safe, and notably picturesque. The area encompasses Beacon Hill, the Financial District and Faneuil Hall Marketplace, the North End, Downtown Crossing, Government Center, the gorgeous Waterfront, and the ungorgeous Big Dig. Prices tend to be high, but you're paying for convenience: Most of the Freedom Trail is here, and you can walk everywhere.

Advantages to staying downtown include

✔ Easy access to many popular attractions and business destina-tions.

✔ Convenient public transportation.

✔ The lively atmosphere, especially during the day and around Faneuil Hall Marketplace.

Drawbacks include

✔ The Big Dig. The ever-changing construction site is frantic and noisy. The Big Dig is most problematic if you stay close by, but it influences traffic for miles around.

✔ The distance from the Back Bay and Cambridge. Factor in the time and cost of getting back and forth.

✔ The less-than-lively atmosphere at night, particularly in areas that aren't near Faneuil Hall.

Finding a place to stay in the Back Bay

What I'm calling the Back Bay stretches from Charles Street to the Brookline border. I include in this area the Back Bay proper, the Theater District, and the South End. This area is a safe one, with the exception of the parks and a small part of the Theater District, where you should be cautious at night. Prices tend to be high, but the sheer number of hotel rooms means the spread is broader. One of New England's prime shopping destinations, this area has a posh air but also abounds with budget-conscious students. Here you find the Public Garden, the Prudential Center, Copley Place, the Hynes Convention Center, and Kenmore Square.

The perks of staying in this area include

- ✔ The abundance of hotel rooms.
- ✔ Decent public transportation. The creaky Green Line is no prize, but the Orange Line is reasonably close. The bus to Cambridge runs along Massachusetts Avenue, better known as Mass. Ave.
- ✔ Everything you need to shop till you drop.

Drawbacks include

- ✔ The need to commute to the downtown attractions.
- ✔ The inconvenience of getting to Cambridge (the bus can be slow).
- ✔ Everything you need to shop till you drop.

Determining where to stay in the vicinity

If busier, more centrally located areas aren't for you, consider staying a little farther out. The large town of Brookline begins just past Kenmore Square. Prices are generally lower, life is less rushed, and most of the popular attractions are less convenient. Without a car, you'll essentially be a commuter (it's 15 to 30 minutes to downtown), usually on the ancient Green Line. (One hotel in this area, the Doubletree Guest Suites, isn't on a public-transit line.) Again, check a map — only spoiled Bostonians would seriously think of this area as out of the way, but Brookline can feel inconvenient, especially at night and when you're spending a lot of time in Cambridge.

Good reasons to stay in the vicinity include

〰 Generally lower prices.

〰 A more residential, less frantic atmosphere.

〰 Easy access to the Back Bay and Fenway Park.

Getting out of town: The suburban motel question

When you read the hotel listings in Chapter 8, you'll have an idea of what you can expect to pay for a stay at specific Boston properties. When that cost just won't do, the notion of a moderately priced suburban chain hotel tends to arise. After all, staying outside the city is an excellent option in many other places. Whether this option works for you depends on your answers to the following questions:

〰 **What season is it?** You may not have a choice about this. During the foliage and graduation seasons, just finding a place to stay somewhere in the state of Massachusetts can feel like a triumph.

〰 **Do you mind commuting?** You'll likely drive or take the commuter rail (or both) to downtown Boston. Before you reserve your room, nail down the specifics of the journey, including prices (for train tickets and parking at the station), whether the hotel operates a shuttle to the station, and how late and how often the train runs. If the answer sounds like a hassle, try another place.

〰 **How long will you be in the Boston area?** A few extra days of vacation may mean you don't mind spending some time commuting. In addition, not being stuck downtown can make day-tripping easier.

〰 **Are you behind the wheel?** If you must drive, you may welcome the combination of a chain hotel's free parking (if offered) and driving yourself into the city.

〰 **Are the kids with you?** Their expectations may be entirely different from yours. (A swimming pool, vending machines, and a game room were usually enough to satisfy me and my siblings.) Talk to your kids before booking an expensive hotel with business features youngsters don't care about and easy access to activities that have little appeal to kids.

〰 **How deep are your pockets?** An out-of-the-way location doesn't necessarily mean a deal. Account for hidden costs before you book a room. For example, if you need to drive to Boston or Cambridge, parking fees can easily add $25 a day to your travel expenses. If the "bargain" room rate saves $30 a day, that's no deal.

If you opt for a suburban motel, check with your travel agent, pick one from a guidebook (AAA is my favorite for this sort of thing), or call your favorite chain and ask for a room in the Boston area. (You can find contact information for hotels in the Appendix.) Be sure you understand the definition of *Boston area* before you hang up the phone — Rhode Island and New Hampshire aren't in that area, but you'd never know that to judge from some motels' names.

Drawbacks include

- ✔ The distance from most of the top attractions.
- ✔ The necessity of relying on the Green Line.
- ✔ The inconvenience of getting to Cambridge, unless you rent a car.

Figuring out where to stay in Cambridge

The listings in this section concentrate on Harvard Square, which offers a good mix of transit access, sightseeing, and shopping. This isn't a typical bohemian college town but a generally expensive area that centers on the Harvard T stop. The train station sits beneath the intersection of John F. Kennedy Street, Brattle Street, and Mass. Ave. Moving away from the train station, things grow quieter; the peaceful Charles River is nearby. Downtown Boston is a 15- to 20-minute subway ride away, and the Back Bay is approximately 30 minutes away on the Mass. Ave. bus.

Pluses of staying in Cambridge include

- ✔ The energetic, student-oriented atmosphere.
- ✔ Good public transportation.
- ✔ Excellent shopping and sightseeing options.

Drawbacks include

- ✔ The price of lodging.
- ✔ Crowds of students, shoppers, and sightseers.
- ✔ The commute to Boston attractions.

Choosing a Hotel That's Right on the Money

Each listing in the following section (and in Chapter 8) includes a $ symbol to help you compare prices. The $ symbols correspond to *rack rates* (nondiscounted standard rates), which are what you pay if you walk up to the front desk and ask for a room rate without haggling. Rack rates don't include specials, coupons, or discounts for memberships in travel, retirement, union, or other groups. (Make sure to ask for any of the preceding that apply to you — and make sure never to pay rack rates unless you're coming at peak season and are desperate!) Prices don't include taxes. And remember: Off-season rates and package deals can knock the price down a category or two. (Review the off-season travel periods in Chapter 2.)

Unfortunately, room prices can (and often do) change without notice, so the rates in this book may be different by the time you call the hotel for reservations. Don't be surprised if the rate the hotel offers is lower than the rack rates in this book. Likewise, don't be alarmed if the price is higher.

$ ($125 or less): These hotels offer basic accommodations — essentially, comfortable spots to crash after a day of sightseeing. Don't expect lots of extras, such as room service or a health club, and some may have shared bathrooms. These establishments tend to be small and not all that convenient, but they're clean, safe, and well kept.

$$ ($126–$225): In this category, you find slightly larger rooms with private bathrooms, TVs, and air-conditioning. These establishments generally don't offer room service, but the room rate may include continental breakfast. These places are more centrally located, and some offer access to pools or fitness rooms (ask if an extra charge applies). In a less competitive market, most would be inns and family-run motels. In Boston, many are part of moderately priced chains.

$$$ ($226–$325): Now things get confusing. In this range, the repeat business customer is the gold standard, and these hotels cater to that market. Rooms tend to be decent sized and well appointed, with abundant business amenities. Each hotel offers a range of perks and facilities, but every property defines *essential* differently. For instance, some don't provide minibars or swimming pools, but some do. Ask a lot of questions, and keep asking until you find the place that feels right — or comes closest.

$$$$ ($326 and up): Here you find tycoons, international travelers whose currency is strong against the dollar, and trysting couples. Expect everything you'd get at a $$$ hotel, delivered to your huge room by an employee who can't do enough for you, plus such extras as courtesy cars and personal office equipment. You may reasonably expect your every need to be met.

Remember, downtown Boston has a room shortage. A hotel that doesn't offer every imaginable perk can still get away with charging breathtaking prices. The feature that's most likely to be missing in a less-than-optimal hotel in the $$$ and $$$$ price ranges is an on-premises health club with a pool. If a certain amenity is crucial to you, be sure to ask about it.

Chapter 7

Booking Your Room

• •

In This Chapter

▶ Getting a good deal on your hotel room

▶ Shopping for a hotel on the Internet

▶ Heading to Boston without a reservation

• •

*S*ome people book a room by calling a hotel, asking for a reservation, and agreeing to the price the clerk quotes. These people also pay sticker price for their cars. That won't be you, though, because after reading this chapter, you'll know how to find the best hotel rates.

Uncovering the Truth about Rack Rates

The *rack rate* is the standard amount a hotel charges for a room. If you walked in off the street and asked for a room for the night, you'd pay the rack rate. You sometimes see this rate printed on the emergency-exit diagrams on the back of your hotel room door.

You don't have to pay the rack rate. Hardly anyone does. Perhaps the best way to avoid paying this full rate is surprisingly simple: Ask for a cheaper or discounted rate.

In all but the smallest accommodations, rates depend on many factors, not the least of which is how you make your reservation. A travel agent may be able to negotiate a better deal with certain hotels than you could because hotels sometimes give agents discounts in exchange for repeat business.

Prices also fluctuate with seasons and occupancy rate. If a hotel is nearly full, you're less likely to get a discount. If the hotel is nearly empty, the staff may negotiate. These circumstances can change day to day, so if you're flexible, say so. Business hotels often offer weekend rates and packages. Lodgings in vacation areas may extend midweek discounts, especially during the off-season.

Boston's unpredictable weather makes January through March the only slow season, especially slow if conditions are cold and snowy. (A mild winter can be surprisingly busy.) The hospitality industry aims its "Boston Overnight! Just for the Fun of It" campaign at suburban week-enders, but travelers from farther away can take advantage of discounts, too. Check the Greater Boston Convention & Visitors Bureau Web site (www.bostonusa.com) for information.

Room prices change without notice, so the rates in this book may differ from the rate you receive when you make your reservation.

Throughout this book, you'll see $ symbols for an at-a-glance comparison of the hotels. (See the Introduction for an explanation of the $ rates.) Boston is expensive — the average room rate is around $160 — but packages and other deals may pleasantly surprise you.

Getting the Best Rate for the Best Room

You may have to dig to find the best rate. For example, reserving through the hotel's toll-free number may result in a lower rate than if you call the reservations desk directly. On the other hand, the central reservations number may not know about discounts at specific locations. Local franchises may offer a group rate for a wedding or family reunion but may neglect to tell the central booking line. Your best bet is to call the local number *and* the central number and see which offers a better deal.

Be sure to mention membership in AAA, AARP, and frequent-flier or corporate-rewards programs you belong to when you make your reservation. Your membership may be worth a few dollars off your room rate, especially if you try this: Ask for the price, then mention the status that qualifies you for a discount.

Boston and Cambridge levy a 12.45% room tax. When you make your reservation, be sure to ask whether the quoted rate includes taxes. Package rates generally do. Brookline doesn't charge the 2.75% of the tax that goes for a new convention center, but don't choose a hotel based on that — the savings is negligible and probably won't offset the extra transportation costs.

When you know where you're staying, making a few more requests can help you land the best possible room:

  ✔ **Ask for a corner room.** They're usually larger, quieter, and brighter, but they may cost a bit more.

✔ **Request a room on a high floor.** Upper floors may contain club- or concierge-level rooms; if you don't want to pay for extra features, ask for the highest *standard* floor.

✔ **If the hotel is renovating (ask whether it is), request a room away from the renovation work, and ask again when you check in.**

✔ **Request a room away from restaurants, bars, and meeting facilities, which can be noisy.**

If you aren't happy with your room when you arrive, return to the front desk right away. If another room is available, the staff should be able to accommodate you, within reason.

If you need a room where you can smoke, be sure to request one when you reserve. If you can't bear the lingering smell of smoke, tell everyone who handles your reservation that you need a smoke-free room or floor.

Surfing the Web for Hotel Deals

The Internet is an invaluable resource, allowing you to compare Boston-area properties' features and to see hotels before you book. Reserving online can save time and money — Internet-only deals can represent substantial savings.

Subpar travel arrangements cost time and money. Choosing the wrong hotel can drag down your whole trip. If you aren't satisfied with the information you gather on the Internet, pick up the phone and call the hotel directly. The extra time you spend on a single phone call may help you confirm that the hotel meets your expectations.

You may want to start at a general travel site (see Chapter 5 for more details), at the site of a hotel chain you know and trust (see the Appendix for a list of major chains' toll-free numbers and Web sites), or at a locally oriented site.

The Web sites of the **Greater Boston Convention & Visitors Bureau** (www.bostonusa.com) and the **Massachusetts Office of Travel and Tourism** (www.mass-vacation.com) offer searchable databases and secure online reservations. Don't book through either site until you do enough comparison shopping to know when you find a competitive price.

Reservation bureaus can be a good option if you aren't up for negotiating on your own. These bureaus reserve blocks of rooms, a practice that allows the bureaus to offer rooms in sold-out hotels. Do remember that the deep discounts the bureaus tout generally calculate savings off the rack rate — which you probably wouldn't pay anyway.

Reputable operators include **Citywide Reservation Services** (☎ 800-HOTEL-93; Internet: www.cityres.com), **Hotel Conxions** (☎ 800-522-9991; Internet: www.hotelconxions.com), **Accommodations Express** (☎ 800-906-4685; Internet: www.accommodationsxpress.com), and **Hotel Reservations Network** (☎ 800-715-7666; Internet: www.hoteldiscounts.com). Online, try **Frommer's** (www.frommers.com) or **Expedia** (www.expedia.com).

Use the Web to do some sleuthing. Suppose a hotel description says "overlooking the water" (or a park or some other desirable neighbor), but the site's photos don't show the building in relation to the water. Downloading a map from another source may show an eight-lane highway between the hotel and the beach.

Arriving without a Reservation

You didn't make arrangements in advance? If it's foliage or graduation season, hang your head. Let it droop all the way down to the floor of the airport terminal, because that may be where you spend the night. Or stand up straight and try one or more of the following strategies:

- ✔ **Call the Hotel Hot Line (☎ 800-777-6001), a service of the Greater Boston Convention & Visitors Bureau.** The service can help with reservations even during the busiest times. People, not recordings, handle calls until 8 p.m. weekdays, 4 p.m. weekends.

- ✔ **If you're at the airport, head to the Visitor Service Center in Terminal C.** Staff members with concierge training can lend a hand.

- ✔ **Phone hotels from the airport or train station.** Ask *everyone* you reach who doesn't have a room available to suggest another property.

- ✔ **If you drive from the west, stop at the Massachusetts Turnpike's Natick rest area and try the reservation service at the visitor information center.**

- ✔ **Call a B&B referral agency and ask if any properties have cancellations.** (See Chapter 6 for more details.)

- ✔ **Call a reservation bureau.** These bureaus can save time by checking the availabilities at several lodgings (see "Surfing the Web for Hotel Deals," earlier in this chapter).

- ✔ **Rent a car and head for the suburbs.** Although not being downtown is inconvenient, many lodgings lie within commuting distance. If you have a favorite chain, call the toll-free reservations number for information about Boston-area locations and tips for reaching the properties from the airport. (For the full story, see Chapter 6.)

Chapter 8

Boston's Best Hotels

●●

In This Chapter

▶ Perusing at-a-glance lists arranged by location and price

▶ Looking at Boston's best hotels

▶ Finding more options in case your top picks are full

●●

*A*lthough I complain about Boston's limited lodging choices, keeping this list to a manageable size is difficult. The hotels in this chapter are my favorites, the ones I suggest when friends call to ask for recommendations. Although I list my top picks, these lodgings are by no means the only acceptable choices. Near the end of this chapter, I also include options that can be helpful if you find your favorites booked. I also include indexes that list hotels by neighborhood and price.

Each listing in this chapter includes a $ symbol that indicates the price range of the hotel's rack rates. (***Remember:*** You should never pay the rack rate — always ask about discounts.) Prices are for a standard double room for one night, not including taxes. The $ signs correspond with the following ranges (for more information, see Chapter 6):

> $: $125 and under
>
> $$: $126–$225
>
> $$$: $226–$325
>
> $$$$: more than $326

Also remember that the $ symbols are guidelines. A great off-season rate or package deal can knock a hotel down a category or two, and a huge citywide event can drive up prices even at modest establishments. (See Chapter 7 for pointers on getting the best rates.)

This icon indicates hotels that are especially family-friendly. Most of these accommodations have swimming pools, some offer family packages (usually on weekends), and all supply their all-ages clientele with plenty of patience and good advice. Bear in mind that every hotel in town accommodates children's needs; a listing without this symbol does not mean "kid unfriendly." Most properties allow kids to stay free with their parents, but the cutoff age varies. Always ask when you're booking.

Every hotel in this chapter is clean and safe. As I said, I'd send a friend to any one of these properties — but I wouldn't send every friend to every one. These hotels all offer TVs and air-conditioning; almost all include phones and private bathrooms. With the exception of the Doubletree Guest Suites, every one is within walking distance of the subway, known in Boston as the T. That's where my blanket statements end. For a general discussion of hotel features and amenities, see Chapter 6.

The Lowdown on Boston-Area Hotels

Anthony's Town House
$ In the Vicinity (Brookline)

The Green Line runs past Anthony's Town House, embodying the pluses and minuses of this well-kept, old-fashioned brownstone. The trolley is handy, but the street is busy and can be noisy. The price is great, but you don't get your own bathroom or phone. Each floor holds one bathroom and three good-sized, high-ceilinged rooms with TVs and air-conditioning; units that face the street are larger but less quiet. The agreeable residential neighborhood lies about a mile from Boston's Kenmore Square and 15 to 20 minutes from downtown.

1085 Beacon St. (near Hawes Street). ☎ *617-566-3972. Fax: 617-232-1085. 12 units. T: Hawes Street (Green Line C). Parking: Free. Rack rates: $68–$98. Ask about winter discounts. No credit cards.*

Boston Harbor Hotel
$$$$ Downtown (Waterfront)

This luxurious edifice overlooking the harbor and the Big Dig is the finest hotel downtown. The Boston Harbor offers every perk or appointment you may want or need — from easy access to the airport (the water shuttle docks out back) to top-of-the-line business and fitness facilities, including a 60-foot lap pool. Guest rooms are spacious and plush, with traditional mahogany furniture and great views. The lobby cafe, Intrigue, offers seasonal outdoor dining.

70 Rowes Wharf (entrance on Atlantic Avenue at High Street, off Northern Avenue). ☎ *800-752-7077 or 617-439-7000. Fax: 617-330-9450. Internet:* www.bhh.com. *230 units. T: South Station (Red Line); walk 2½ blocks north. Or Aquarium (Blue Line); walk 2½ blocks south. Parking: Valet $28 per day, self $26 per day; weekend discounts. Rack rates: $365–$555 and up. Ask about weekend packages. AE, DC, DISC, MC, V.*

Chandler Inn Hotel

$$ Back Bay (South End)

You can't beat this location at this price. The rooms and bathrooms are comfortable but small — a real-estate ad might say "cozy," which is accurate in this case. The contemporary-style rooms contain queen-size or double beds or two twin beds, hair dryers, and climate control. Rates include continental breakfast, and the staff is accommodating and friendly. This property is the largest gay-owned hotel in town, and the inn is popular with bargain hunters of all persuasions. Fritz, the bar off the lobby, is a lively neighborhood hangout.

26 Chandler St. (at Berkeley Street). ☎ ***800-842-3450*** *or 617-482-3450. Fax: 617-542-3428. Internet:* www.chandlerinn.com. *56 units. T: Back Bay (Orange Line); cross Columbus Avenue, turn left onto Chandler Street, and walk 2 blocks. Parking: Nearby public garages and lots ($20 and up). Rack rates: $139–$169. Ask about winter discounts. AE, DC, DISC, MC, V.*

The Charles Hotel

$$$$ Cambridge

The most prestigious short-term address in Cambridge, the Charles represents an appealing contrast of sleek, contemporary style and luxurious appointments. In a great location off Harvard Square, the hotel offers large rooms with Shaker-style furnishings and indulgent extras such as a Bose Wave radio in every room and a TV in each bathroom. Room rates include access to the pool and facilities at the adjacent WellBridge Health and Fitness Center. The pool sets aside time each afternoon for children under 16. The hotel complex also includes an excellent day spa, Le Pli. Rialto is the best restaurant in the Boston area (see Chapter 14 for a review). Henrietta's Table serves contemporary American cuisine, and the Regattabar is one of the best jazz clubs in the area.

1 Bennett St. (off Eliot Street, near Mount Auburn Street). ☎ ***800-882-1818*** *outside Massachusetts, or 617-864-1200. Fax: 617-864-5715. Internet:* www.charleshotel.com. *293 units. T: Harvard (Red Line); follow Brattle Street 2 blocks, bear left onto Eliot Street, and go 2 blocks. Parking: Valet or self $18 per day. Rack rates: $349–$429 and up. Ask about weekend, spa, and other packages. AE, DC, MC, V.*

Doubletree Guest Suites

$$–$$$ In the Vicinity (Allston)

The less-than-central location is no bonus, but everything else about this all-suite hotel makes for one of the best deals around. The Doubletree is popular with business travelers and families. Each of the large units contains a living room with a full-size sofa bed, coffeemaker, and refrigerator. Suites on higher floors offer splendid views. The hotel has an indoor

Boston Hotels

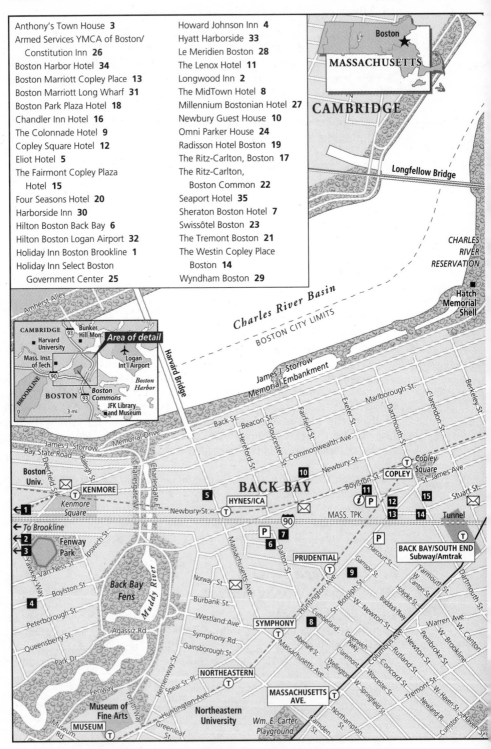

Anthony's Town House **3**
Armed Services YMCA of Boston/
   Constitution Inn **26**
Boston Harbor Hotel **34**
Boston Marriott Copley Place **13**
Boston Marriott Long Wharf **31**
Boston Park Plaza Hotel **18**
Chandler Inn Hotel **16**
The Colonnade Hotel **9**
Copley Square Hotel **12**
Eliot Hotel **5**
The Fairmont Copley Plaza
   Hotel **15**
Four Seasons Hotel **20**
Harborside Inn **30**
Hilton Boston Back Bay **6**
Hilton Boston Logan Airport **32**
Holiday Inn Boston Brookline **1**
Holiday Inn Select Boston
   Government Center **25**

Howard Johnson Inn **4**
Hyatt Harborside **33**
Le Meridien Boston **28**
The Lenox Hotel **11**
Longwood Inn **2**
The MidTown Hotel **8**
Millennium Bostonian Hotel **27**
Newbury Guest House **10**
Omni Parker House **24**
Radisson Hotel Boston **19**
The Ritz-Carlton, Boston **17**
The Ritz-Carlton,
   Boston Common **22**
Seaport Hotel **35**
Sheraton Boston Hotel **7**
Swissôtel Boston **23**
The Tremont Boston **21**
The Westin Copley Place
   Boston **14**
Wyndham Boston **29**

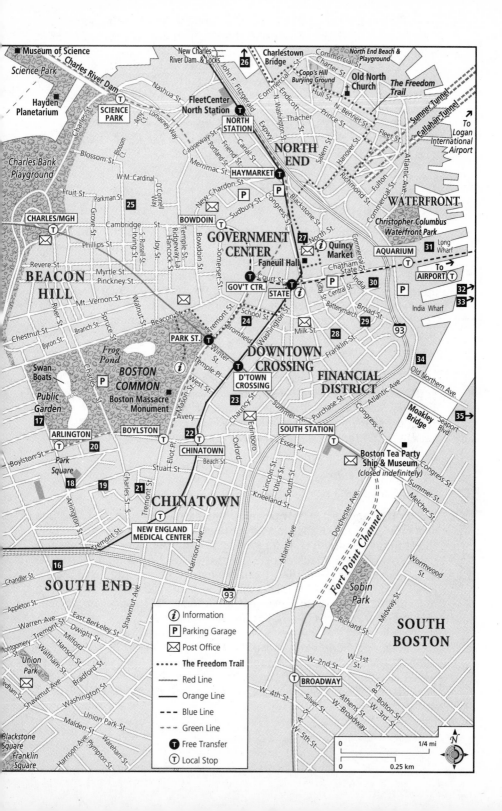

Museum of Science
Science Park
New Charles River Dam & Locks
Charlestown Bridge
Charlestown
North End Beach & Playground
Commercial
Copp's Hill Burying Ground
Charter St.
Old North Church
The Freedom Trail
Charles River Dam
Hayden Planetarium
SCIENCE PARK
Nashua St.
FleetCenter North Station
NORTH STATION
HAYMARKET
N. Washington St.
Endicott
N. Bennet St.
Salem St.
Hull St.
Prince St.
Hanover St.
Fleet St.
Sumner Tunnel
Callahan Tunnel
To Logan International Airport
Charles Bank Playground
Blossom St.
Causeway
Portland St.
Friend St.
Merrimac St.
New Chardon St.
Canal St.
Thacher
Sudbury St.
Blackstone St.
Congress St.
Richmond St.
Fulton
Atlantic Ave.
Commercial
WATERFRONT
Christopher Columbus Waterfront Park
Fruit St.
Parkman St.
W.M. Cardinal
O'Connell Way
25
CHARLES/MGH
Cambridge St.
Temple St.
Ridgeway La.
Hancock St.
Bowdoin St.
BOWDOIN
GOVERNMENT CENTER
27
North St.
Quincy Market
Commercial
AQUARIUM
31
Long Wharf
To AIRPORT
Revere St.
Phillips St.
S. Russell St.
Irving St.
Joy St.
Somerset St.
Faneuil Hall
State St.
Chatham
India
30
32
33
BEACON HILL
Myrtle St.
Pinckney St.
Mt. Vernon St.
Bowdoin St.
GOV'T CTR.
Court St.
STATE
School St.
Kilby St.
Central St.
Batterymarch
Broad St.
India Wharf
Chestnut St.
Byron St.
Branch St.
Spruce St.
Walnut St.
Beacon St.
Tremont St.
Bromfield
Washington St.
Milk St.
Franklin St.
28
29
93
34
Old Northern Ave.
River St.
Frog Pond
PARK ST.
School St.
24
DOWNTOWN CROSSING
FINANCIAL DISTRICT
Swan Boats
BOSTON COMMON
Boston Massacre Monument
Winter
Temple Pl.
West St.
D'TOWN CROSSING
Chauncy St.
Summer St.
Purchase St.
Congress St.
Atlantic Ave.
Moakley Bridge
Seaport Blvd.
35
Public Garden
17
ARLINGTON
BOYLSTON
Avery
Mason
23
Edinboro
SOUTH STATION
Boston Tea Party Ship & Museum (closed indefinitely)
20
Park Square
BOYLSTON
22
CHINATOWN
Beach St.
Essex St.
Lincoln St.
Utica St.
South St.
Summer St.
Melcher St.
Boylston St.
Stuart St.
18
19
21
CHINATOWN
Kneeland St.
Atlantic Ave.
Dorchester Ave.
NEW ENGLAND MEDICAL CENTER
Harrison Ave.
16
SOUTH END
Chandler St.
93
Appleton St.
Warren Ave.
East Berkeley St.
Dwight St.
Milford
Hanson St.
Shawmut Ave.
Union Park
Waltham St.
Bradford St.
Washington St.
Union Park St.
Malden St.
Wareham St.
Plympton St.
Blackstone Square
Franklin Square
Fort Point Channel
Sobin Park
Richard St.
SOUTH BOSTON
Wormwood St.
Midway St.
BROADWAY
W. 1st St.
W. 2nd St.
Silver St.
W. 3rd St.
W. 4th St.
W. 5th St.
W. Broadway
Athens St.
Bolton St.
Congress St.
ⓘ Information
P Parking Garage
✉ Post Office
····· **The Freedom Trail**
Red Line
Orange Line
Blue Line
Green Line
T Free Transfer
Ⓣ Local Stop
0   1/4 mi
0   0.25 km
N

pool, fitness facilities, and a laundry room. The hotel sits across the street from the Charles River and the jogging path that runs along the river's banks. The hotel offers complimentary van service to and from attractions and business areas in Boston and Cambridge. The celebrated Scullers Jazz Club schedules two shows nightly.

400 Soldiers Field Rd. (at Massachusetts Turnpike Allston/Cambridge exit). ☎ *800-222-TREE or 617-783-0090. Fax: 617-783-0897. Internet:* www.doubletree.com. *308 units. Parking: Self $15–$18. Rack rates: $129–$309. Ask about weekend packages and AAA and AARP discounts. AE, DC, DISC, MC, V.*

The Fairmont Copley Plaza Hotel
$$$–$$$$ Back Bay

The Copley Plaza is one of Boston's two stately, old-fashioned luxury hotels (the original Ritz-Carlton is the other); just saying their names evokes an era of grand accommodations, excellent service, and ornate architecture. The Edwardian elegance of this 1912 building belies the up-to-date features of the large guest rooms, which contain every perk you can think of (and then some), including VCRs and oversized towels. The hotel has two restaurants, two bars, a business center, and a fitness center. The Copley Plaza doesn't have an on-premises pool; guests have access to the nearby, coed YWCA.

138 St. James Ave. (at Dartmouth Street, facing Copley Square). ☎ *800-527-4727 or 617-267-5300. Fax: 617-247-6681. Internet:* www.fairmont.com. *379 units. T: Copley (Green Line); cross Copley Square. Or Back Bay (Orange Line); walk 1½ blocks on Dartmouth Street with Copley Place on your left. Parking: Valet $32. Rack rates: $249 and up. Ask about weekend packages. AE, DC, MC, V.*

Four Seasons Hotel
$$$$ Back Bay

This hotel is the best in New England. You may stay here at the same time as a movie star, CEO, rock legend, or head of state, and (here's the key) the staff makes you feel as important as the celebrities. Great service doesn't replace the lack of perks. But that's not a problem here: The accommodations, amenities, business center, health club, and restaurants are all top of the line. The bill is, too. The second-floor restaurant, Aujourd'hui, is one of Boston's best, and the Bristol Lounge serves a celebrated afternoon tea (as well as lunch and dinner).

200 Boylston St. (at Arlington Street). ☎ *800-332-3442 or 617-338-4400. Fax: 617-423-0154. Internet:* www.fourseasons.com. *288 units. T: Arlington (Green Line); walk 1 block on Boylston Street, opposite the Public Garden. Parking: Valet $27. Rack rates: $535–$775 and up. Ask about weekend packages. AE, DC, DISC, MC, V.*

Harborside Inn
$–$$ Downtown (Faneuil Hall Marketplace)

The central location is the main selling point of this renovated 1858 warehouse, which also represents good value for the neighborhood. The Harborside Inn's features can't compete with those of the city's business-oriented pleasure domes — but neither can the price. The location, across the street from Faneuil Hall Marketplace, is an easy stroll from most downtown destinations. Each guest room contains a queen-size bed, hardwood floors, and Oriental rugs. The ceilings are lower in the rooms on the top floor, but the views are better; units that face the atrium are quieter than those that face the street. All local phone calls and voice mail are free, and room service is available until 10 p.m. The inn, under the same ownership as the Newbury Guest House (see later in this section), has a restaurant in the lobby.

185 State St. (between India Street and I-93). ☎ *800-437-7668 or 617-723-7500. Fax: 617-670-2010. Internet:* www.hagopianhotels.com. *54 units. T: Aquarium (Blue Line) or State (Orange Line). Parking: Nearby public garages ($25 and up). Rack rates: $120–$210 and up. Ask about winter discounts. AE, DC, DISC, MC, V.*

Harvard Square Hotel
$$ Cambridge

Comfortable and unpretentious, this well-maintained hotel occupies a great location that makes up for the lack of bells and whistles. In the heart of Harvard Square, the hotel is a good place to retreat after a day of running around (whether sightseeing, visiting a student, or on business). Rooms aren't large, but each has comfortable furnishings, dataports, and voice mail. This hotel is not the place for coddled business travelers, but the low-key atmosphere makes Harvard Square a good alternative to pricier competitors in the area.

110 Mount Auburn St. (at Eliot Street). ☎ *800-458-5886 or 617-864-5200. Fax: 617-864-2409. Internet:* www.doubletree.com. *73 units. T: Harvard (Red Line); follow Brattle Street 2 blocks, bear left onto Eliot Street, and go 1 block. Parking: $20. Rack rates: $129–$209. Ask about corporate, AAA, and AARP discounts. AE, DC, DISC, MC, V.*

Hilton Boston Back Bay
$$–$$$ Back Bay

A business hotel with terrific weekend packages, the Hilton offers a full range of chain amenities in a handy location across the street from the Prudential Center complex. The hotel is near the Back Bay action but not right at the center — which isn't necessarily a bad thing. The large, contemporary rooms are quite plush; units on higher floors offer excellent

Cambridge Hotels

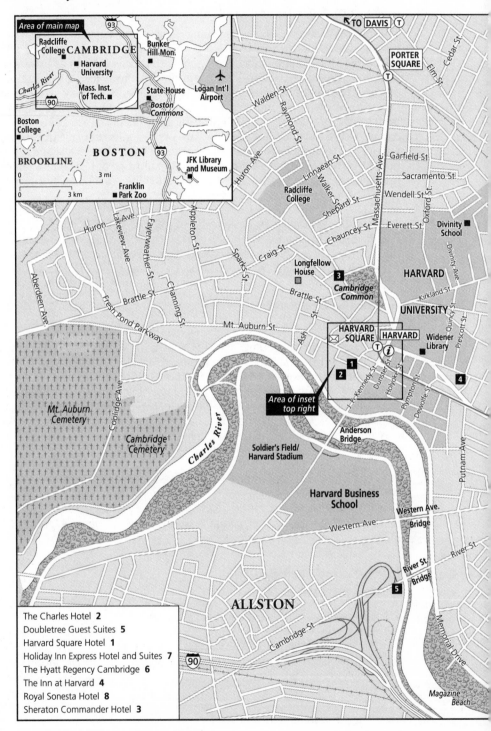

The Charles Hotel **2**
Doubletree Guest Suites **5**
Harvard Square Hotel **1**
Holiday Inn Express Hotel and Suites **7**
The Hyatt Regency Cambridge **6**
The Inn at Harvard **4**
Royal Sonesta Hotel **8**
Sheraton Commander Hotel **3**

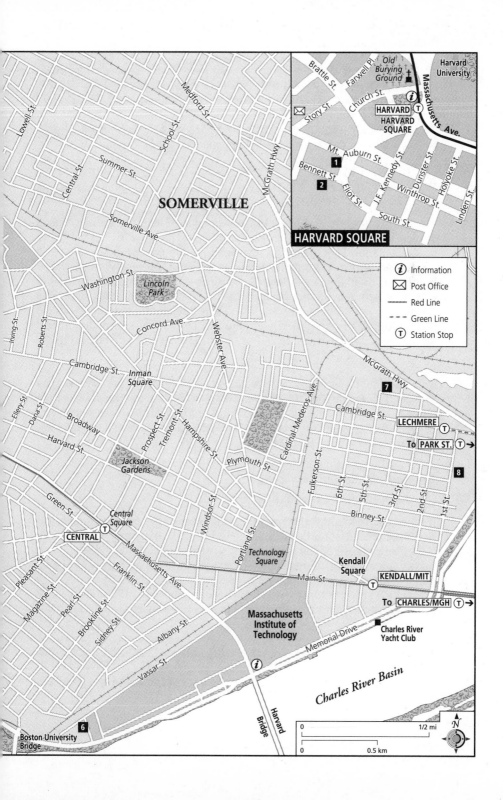

SOMERVILLE

HARVARD SQUARE

Brattle St.
Farwell Pl.
Old Burying Ground
Harvard University
Story St.
Church St.
Massachusetts Ave.
HARVARD
HARVARD SQUARE
Mt. Auburn St.
1
Bennett St.
2
Eliot St.
J.F. Kennedy St.
Winthrop St.
Dunster St.
Holyoke St.
Linden St.
South St.

Information
Post Office
Red Line
Green Line
Station Stop

Medford St.
School St.
McGrath Hwy
Summer St.
Central St.
Lowell St.
Somerville Ave.
Washington St.
Lincoln Park
Concord Ave.
Webster Ave.
Irving St.
Roberts St.
Cambridge St.
Inman Square
Elery St.
Dana St.
Broadway
Harvard St.
Prospect St.
Tremont St.
Hampshire St.
Jackson Gardens
Plymouth St.
Cardinal Medeiros Ave.
McGrath Hwy
7
Cambridge St.
LECHMERE
To PARK ST.
8
Fulkerson St.
6th St.
5th St.
3rd St.
2nd St.
1st St.
Binney St.
Green St.
Central Square
CENTRAL
Massachusetts Ave.
Windsor St.
Portland St.
Pleasant St.
Magazine St.
Pearl St.
Brookline St.
Sidney St.
Franklin St.
Albany St.
Vassar St.
Technology Square
Kendall Square
KENDALL/MIT
Main St.
To CHARLES/MGH
Massachusetts Institute of Technology
Memorial Drive
Charles River Yacht Club
Charles River Basin
Harvard Bridge
6
Boston University Bridge
0   1/2 mi
0   0.5 km
N

views. The hotel has a swimming pool and 24-hour health club, a restaurant, and a bar.

40 Dalton St. (off Boylston Street at Belvidere Street, opposite the Hynes Convention Center). ☎ *800-874-0663, 800-HILTONS, or 617-236-1100. Fax: 617-867-6104. Internet:* www.hilton.com. *385 units. T: Hynes/ICA (Green Line B, C, or D); turn left onto Mass. Ave. and left onto Boylston Street, take the first right onto Dalton Street, and walk 2 blocks. Parking: Valet $24, self $17. Rack rates: $179–$295 and up. Ask about packages and AAA discounts. AE, DC, DISC, MC, V.*

Hilton Boston Logan Airport
$$–$$$ In the Vicinity (Logan Airport)

An airport hotel that courts a business clientele may not seem a logical choice for sightseers. However, the airport Hilton, with proximity to downtown, good access to public transit, and fine weekend packages, is a sensible option for both types of travelers. The newly constructed building (unusual in a market where renovations dominate) opened in 1999. The spacious, quiet guest rooms contain plentiful perks, including wireless Internet access through the TV. A health club with a lap pool is off the lobby; the hotel has a restaurant, a pub that serves lunch and dinner, and a coffee bar. The 24-hour shuttle bus serves all airport destinations, including car-rental offices and the ferry dock.

85 Terminal Rd., Logan International Airport (between Terminal A [a short walk] and Terminal E [a long walk]). ☎ *800-HILTONS or 617-568-6700. Fax: 617-568-6800. Internet:* www.hilton.com. *599 units. T: Airport (Blue Line); take shuttle bus. Parking: Valet $20, self $18. Rack rates: $169–$259 and up. Ask about weekend and other packages. AE, DC, DISC, MC, V.*

Holiday Inn Boston Brookline
$$ In the Vicinity (Brookline)

A pleasant residential setting and good access to downtown make this Holiday Inn a reasonable alternative to hotels that are more convenient but more expensive. The large, well-maintained guest rooms offer no surprises (pleasant or unpleasant) — basically, this is an agreeable chain hotel. The inn has a small indoor pool, whirlpool, and exercise room. The Green Line stops out front; downtown Boston is about 15 minutes away. Coolidge Corner, a non-generic shopping destination, is a ten-minute walk away.

1200 Beacon St. (at St. Paul Street). ☎ *800-HOLIDAY or 617-277-1200. Fax: 617-734-6991. Internet:* www.holiday-inn.com. *225 units. T: St. Paul (Green Line C). Parking: Self $12. Rack rates: $139–$219 and up. Ask about AAA and AARP discounts. AE, DC, DISC, MC, V.*

Holiday Inn Select Boston Government Center
$$ Downtown (Beacon Hill)

This hotel launched Holiday Inn's business brand. The inn lies within easy walking distance of many downtown and Back Bay addresses and the Red Line to Cambridge. The decent-sized rooms include good business features, such as fax machines. Units on higher floors enjoy picture-window views of the city or the State House. The hotel has a business center, an outdoor heated pool, and a small exercise room.

5 Blossom St. (at Cambridge Street). ☎ *800-HOLIDAY or 617-742-7630. Fax: 617-742-4192. Internet:* www.holiday-inn.com. *303 units. T: Charles/MGH (Red Line); walk 3 blocks on Cambridge Street. Parking: Self $25. Rack rates: $200 and up. Ask about weekend and corporate packages and AARP discounts. AE, DC, DISC, MC, V.*

Howard Johnson Inn
$–$$ Back Bay

Proximity to Fenway Park and free parking distinguish this motel, which sits on a busy street in a commercial-residential neighborhood. T access is somewhat inconvenient, but the Back Bay colleges, the Museum of Fine Arts, and the Isabella Stewart Gardner Museum are nearby. Rooms are basic, decent-sized Howard Johnson's accommodations. The outdoor pool is open 9 a.m. to 7 p.m. in the summer.

1271 Boylston St. (at Jersey Street). ☎ *800-654-2000 or 617-267-8300. Fax: 617-267-2763. Internet:* www.hojo.com. *94 units. T: Fenway (Green Line D); follow Brookline Avenue ½ block, turn left (walking around the ballpark) follow Yawkey Way 2 blocks, and turn left. Or Kenmore (Green Line B, C, or D); go left at turnstiles, right at stairs, at first intersection (½ block up), turn left onto Brookline Avenue, cross bridge, pass ballpark, turn left onto Yawkey Way, and take second right onto Boylston Street (whew!). Total walking time: About 10 minutes. Parking: Free. Rack rates: $115–$195. Ask about family packages and senior and AAA discounts. AE, DC, DISC, MC, V.*

Longwood Inn
$ In the Vicinity (Brookline)

This Victorian guesthouse in a quiet residential area projects a homey feel to go with affordable rates. Seventeen units include private bathrooms, and all rooms have air-conditioning and phones. Guests may use the fully equipped kitchen and common dining room, coin laundry, and TV lounge. An apartment, which sleeps four, has a private kitchen and balcony. The tennis courts, running track, and playground at the school next door are open to the public.

123 Longwood Ave. ☎ *617-566-8615. Fax: 617-738-1070. Internet:* go.boston. com/longwoodinn. *22 units. T: Longwood (Green Line D); turn left, walk ½ block to Longwood Avenue, turn right, and walk 2½ blocks. Or Coolidge Corner (Green Line C); walk 1 block south on Harvard Street (past Trader Joe's), turn left, and go 2 blocks on Longwood Avenue. Parking: Free. Rack rates: $89–$109 ($89–$119 for 1-bedroom apartment). Ask about winter discounts. No credit cards.*

The MidTown Hotel
$–$$ Back Bay

This two-story establishment near the Prudential Center is the most centrally located Boston hotel with free parking. The rooms are large and attractively outfitted in contemporary style, but bathrooms are small. Business travelers can request units with two-line phones; families can ask for adjoining rooms with connecting doors. The hotel's popularity with tour groups and convention-goers is a potential drawback, as is the busy street — rooms on the Huntington Avenue side of the low-rise building can be a little noisy. The heated outdoor pool is open from Memorial Day through Labor Day.

220 Huntington Ave. (at Cumberland Street, near Mass. Ave.). ☎ *800-343-1177 or 617-262-1000. Fax: 617-262-8739. Internet:* www.midtownhotel.com. *159 units. T: Symphony (Green Line E); from the corner diagonally across from Symphony Hall, walk 1 block on Huntington Avenue. Or Mass. Ave. (Orange Line); turn left, walk 2 blocks, turn right, and go 1 block on Huntington Avenue. Parking: Free. Rack rates: $139–$269. Ask about winter, AARP, and government-employee discounts. AE, DC, DISC, MC, V.*

Newbury Guest House
$$ Back Bay

The Newbury Guest House was more of a bargain upon its 1991 opening, but considering the location, this is still a deal. In a pair of renovated 19th-century town houses, the Newberry has a comfortable atmosphere and helpful staff. Rooms are modest in size but thoughtfully appointed and mercifully quiet. Rates include a buffet breakfast served in the ground-level dining room, which adjoins a brick patio. This B&B, which has the same owners as the Harborside Inn (see listing earlier in this section), operates near capacity all year; reserve early.

261 Newbury St. (between Fairfield and Gloucester streets). ☎ *617-437-7666. Fax: 617-262-4243. Internet:* www.hagopianhotels.com. *32 units. T: Copley (Green Line); follow Dartmouth Street 1 block away from Copley Square, turn left on Newbury Street, and go 2½ blocks. Or Hynes/ICA (Green Line B, C, or D); exit onto Newbury Street and walk away from Mass. Ave. for 2½ blocks. Parking: Self $15 (reservation required). Rack rates: $140–$195. Minimum 2 nights on weekends. Ask about winter discounts. AE, DC, DISC, MC, V.*

Omni Parker House

$$–$$$ **Downtown (Government Center)**

The Parker House combines historic atmosphere and modern appointments to surprisingly good effect. This establishment is the oldest continuously operating hotel in the country (since 1855). People and rooms were smaller then, but several rounds of renovations since Omni Hotels took over in the early 1990s left the hotel in good shape. Guest rooms aren't large, but well-proportioned furnishings and tons of amenities make most rooms feel cozy, not cramped. The hotel has a business center, exercise facility, restaurant, and two bars. And in case you're wondering, yes, this is the birthplace of Parker House rolls.

60 School St. (at Tremont Street). ☎ *800-THE-OMNI or 617-227-8600. Fax: 617-742-5729. Internet:* www.omnihotels.com. *551 units. T: Government Center (Green or Blue Line); face away from City Hall, turn left, and follow Tremont Street 1 long block. Or Park Street (Red or Green Line); follow Tremont Street away from Boston Common 2 blocks. Parking: Valet $27, self $20. Rack rates: $189–$309 and up. Ask about weekend packages. AE, DC, DISC, MC, V.*

Radisson Hotel Boston

$$–$$$$ **Back Bay (Theater District)**

The central location, business features, and relatively reasonable rates make this Radisson popular with business and leisure travelers. The well-maintained guest rooms are among the largest in the city; each opens onto a private balcony, with terrific views from the higher floors. The hotel has an indoor pool and exercise room. The property also has a restaurant, cafe, and the Stuart Street Playhouse, a professional theater that usually presents one-person and cabaret-style shows.

200 Stuart St. (at Charles Street South). ☎ *800-333-3333 or 617-482-1800. Fax: 617-451-2750. Internet:* www.radisson.com. *356 units. T: Boylston (Green Line); follow Tremont Street away from Boston Common 1 block, turn right onto Stuart Street, and go 2 blocks. Or New England Medical Center (Orange Line); turn left, walk ½ block, turn left, and go 3 blocks. Parking: Self $19. Rack rates: $160–$359. Ask about weekend and theater packages. AE, DC, DISC, MC, V.*

Sheraton Boston Hotel

$$–$$$$ **Back Bay**

Although I'm usually not high on huge hotels, this Sheraton is an exception (the Westin, a little later in this chapter, is another). Direct access to the Prudential Center complex appeals to travelers of all stripes. The Sheraton courts three major markets with scads of meeting space and features for convention-goers, well outfitted rooms for business travelers, and a gigantic indoor/outdoor pool with a retractable dome for vacationers. Rooms are fairly large, with pillow-top beds; bathrooms are medium-sized but (unless you have a magazine named after you) better appointed than your bathroom at home. Units on upper floors afford excellent views. The hotel has a large, well-equipped health club, restaurant, and lounge.

39 Dalton St. (at Belvidere Street, between Huntington Avenue and Boylston Street). ☎ *800-325-3535 or 617-236-2000. Fax: 617-236-1702. Internet:* www.sheraton. com. *1,181 units. T: Prudential (Green Line E); facing tower, bear left onto Belvidere Street and walk 1 block. Or Hynes/ICA (Green Line B, C, or D). Turn left onto Mass. Ave. and left onto Boylston Street, take first right onto Dalton Street, and walk 2 blocks. Parking: Valet $32; self $28. Rack rates: $149–$369 and up. Ask about weekend packages and student, faculty, and senior discounts. AE, DC, DISC, MC, V.*

Sheraton Commander Hotel

$$–$$$$ **Cambridge**

The Sheraton Commander's low-key atmosphere appeals to guests who find the Charles too trendy (and too pricey). The hotel's well-kept guest rooms are moderate in size and traditional in decor. A restaurant, cafe, and small fitness center are on the premises. Harvard Yard is four blocks away.

16 Garden St. (at Waterhouse Street, opposite Cambridge Common). ☎ *800-325-3535 or 617-547-4800. Fax: 617-868-8322. Internet:* www.sheratoncommander. com. *175 units. T: Harvard (Red Line); with Harvard Yard on your right, follow Mass. Ave. north 1 or 2 blocks to Garden Street, turn left, and walk 4 blocks. Parking: Valet $18. Rack rates: $195–$345 and up. Ask about weekend packages and AAA and AARP discounts. AE, DC, DISC, MC, V.*

Swissôtel Boston

$$$–$$$$ **Downtown Crossing**

Weekend travelers, keep reading: This posh hotel, a busy business destination during the week, offers some of the most appealing weekend packages in town. The fanny-pack set creates an interesting contrast with the hotel's European style and lavish business amenities. The spacious guest rooms contain fax machines and everything else you may need to cut a blockbuster deal. The hotel has a restaurant, lounge, 52-foot indoor pool, and fitness center.

1 Avenue de Lafayette (off Washington Street). ☎ *888-73-SWISS or 617-451-2600. Fax: 617-451-0054. Internet:* www.swissotel.com. *501 units. T: Downtown Crossing (Red or Orange Line); walk 1 long block on Washington Street past Macy's and turn left onto Avenue de Lafayette. Or, during daylight hours, Boylston (Green Line); follow Boylston Street away from Boston Common 1 block, turn left onto Washington Street, walk 2 blocks, and turn right onto Avenue de Lafayette. Parking: Valet $30, self $26. Rack rates: $250–$395 and up. Ask about weekend packages. AE, DC, DISC, MC, V.*

The Westin Copley Place Boston
$$$–$$$$ Back Bay

A giant chain hotel that doesn't feel generic is a real find, and this Westin is one (the Sheraton Boston, mentioned earlier in this chapter, is another). This hotel starts with a great location adjoining the Copley Place–Prudential Center complex, adds the full range of business amenities, and throws in an excellent health club with a pool. Guest rooms are large and well appointed, and the views (rooms are all above the seventh floor) are amazing. Two first-class restaurants, the Palm and Turner Fisheries, face the street at ground level; there's a lounge off the second-floor lobby.

10 Huntington Ave. (at Dartmouth Street, accessible through Copley Place). ☎ *800-WESTIN-1 or 617-262-9600. Fax: 617-424-7483. Internet:* www.westin.com. *800 units. T: Copley (Green Line); walk 1 block on Dartmouth Street past the Boston Public Library. Or Back Bay (Orange Line); walk 1½ blocks on Dartmouth Street past Copley Place. Parking: Valet $28. Rack rates: $229–$499 and up. Ask about weekend packages. AE, DC, DISC, MC, V.*

Wyndham Boston
$$–$$$$ Downtown (Financial District)

Three blocks from Faneuil Hall Marketplace and two blocks from the harbor, the Wyndham offers business and leisure travelers a handy location and excellent accommodations. The large, quiet guest rooms abound with amenities, including high-speed Internet access and high ceilings that make them feel even larger. The only potential minuses are the lack of a swimming pool and the (long, by spoiled-Bostonian standards) walk to the T. The hotel has a restaurant off the lobby and a 24-hour fitness center.

89 Broad St. (at Franklin Street). ☎ *800-WYNDHAM or 617-556-0006. Fax: 617-556-0053. Internet:* www.wyndham.com. *362 units. T: State (Blue or Orange Line); follow State Street downhill 2 blocks, turn right, and go 3½ blocks on Broad Street. Parking: Valet $30 weekdays, $16 weekends. Rack rates: $215–$415 and up. Ask about weekend, holiday, and other packages. AE, DC, DISC, MC, V.*

Runner-Up Accommodations

Here are some specific suggestions if your top choices are booked:

Armed Services YMCA of Boston/Constitution Inn
$ Downtown (Charlestown) The Y is not fancy, but the price is right, the location is fairly handy, and guests have access to extensive fitness facilities. ***Note:*** Children under 12 aren't allowed. *150 Second Ave., Charlestown Navy Yard.* ☎ *800-495-9622 or 617-241-8400.*

Boston Marriott Copley Place

$$$ Back Bay   This huge convention hotel has the usual huge-convention-hotel features, including a pool and health club. *110 Huntington Ave., at Harcourt Street (accessible through Copley Place).* ☎ *800-228-9290 or 617-236-5800.*

Boston Marriott Long Wharf

$$$$ Downtown   The great location, within shouting distance of the New England Aquarium and the Financial District, makes up for the generic atmosphere. *296 State St., at Atlantic Avenue.* ☎ *800-228-9290 or 617-227-0800.*

Boston Park Plaza Hotel

$$$ Back Bay   A temple of ornate Old Boston style (the building went up in 1927), the Boston Park has a function and convention clientele that leaves sleek modern competitors in the dust. *64 Arlington St. (1 block from the Public Garden).* ☎ *800-225-2008 or 617-426-2000.*

The Colonnade Hotel

$$$$ Back Bay   The Colonnade is sleek and elegant, with large guest rooms and a seasonal rooftop pool that add to the Euro-chic atmosphere. *120 Huntington Ave., at West Newton Street (opposite the Prudential Center).* ☎ *800-962-3030 or 617-424-7000.*

Copley Square Hotel

$$$ Back Bay   This small hotel puts service and atmosphere ahead of nonstop business perks; you're paying for the location, but what a location this is. *47 Huntington Ave., at Exeter Street.* ☎ *800-225-7062 or 617-536-9000.*

Eliot Hotel

$$$$ Back Bay   A luxurious, romantic all-suite hotel, with superb business amenities; the residential feel and handy location add to the Eliot's considerable appeal. *370 Commonwealth Ave., at Mass. Ave.* ☎ *800-44-ELIOT or 617-267-1607.*

Holiday Inn Express Hotel and Suites

$$ Cambridge (East Cambridge)   The inn is not exactly peaceful or plush, but the convenient location and reasonable prices make this hotel popular with business and leisure travelers. *250 Msgr. O'Brien Hwy. (3 blocks from the Green Line Lechmere stop).* ☎ *888-887-7690 or 617-577-7600.*

Hyatt Harborside

$$$ At the Airport   This hotel's out-of-the-way location isn't great for thrifty sightseers, but the hotel courts business travelers with plenty of amenities and easy access to the Financial District, a seven-minute water-shuttle ride away. *101 Harborside Dr. (at Logan Airport ferry dock, East Boston).* ☎ *800-233-1234 or 617-568-1234.*

The Hyatt Regency Cambridge

$$$ **Cambridge (Central Cambridge)**   Business travelers enjoy tons of perks and proximity to MIT and some high-tech neighbors; fantastic weekend packages help vacationers overlook the scarcity of convenient public transit. *575 Memorial Dr. (near the Boston University Bridge).* ☎ *800-233-1234 or 617-492-1234.*

The Inn at Harvard

$$$ **Cambridge (Harvard Square)**   The inn is elegant and traditional, with good business features and easy access to the university, right across the street. *1201 Massachusetts Ave. (at Quincy Street).* ☎ *800-458-5886 or 617-491-2222.*

Le Meridien Boston

$$$$ **Downtown**   One of the city's best business hotels, Le Meridien offers top-notch weekend packages; the T is a bit of a hike, but downtown and waterfront destinations are nearby. *250 Franklin St. (at Post Office Square).* ☎ *800-543-4300 or 617-451-1900.*

The Lenox Hotel

$$$$ **Back Bay**   This is a boutique hotel in everything but size, with outstanding business amenities in the posh, high-ceilinged guest rooms, a dozen of which have working fireplaces. *710 Boylston St. (at Exeter Street).* ☎ *800-225-7676 or 617-536-5300.*

Millennium Bostonian Hotel

$$$ **Downtown**   Nonstop luxury comes with important extras: The location attracts business travelers and shoppers; romance-minded vacationers revel in the atmosphere of the renovated 19th-century warehouses. *40 North St. (opposite Faneuil Hall Marketplace).* ☎ *800-343-0922 or 617-523-3600.*

The Ritz-Carlton, Boston

$$$$ **Back Bay**   The original Ritz celebrated its 75th birthday in 2002 with a top-to-bottom renovation that updated the accommodations, expanded the dining options, and kept the unfailingly correct service. *15 Arlington St. (at Newbury Street).* ☎ *800-241-3333 or 617-536-5700.*

The Ritz-Carlton, Boston Common

$$$$ **Theater District**   The hot, happening sibling of the city's most traditional hotel, the "new Ritz" offers every amenity you can think of,

including a bath butler and access to the over-the-top Sports Club/LA. *10 Avery St. (between Washington and Tremont streets).* ☎ *800-241-3333 or 617-574-7100.*

Royal Sonesta Hotel

$$$ Cambridge (East Cambridge) Luxurious and contemporary, the Royal Sonesta draws high-tech businesspeople during the week and families (who love the large indoor/outdoor pool) on weekends. *5 Cambridge Pkwy. (around the corner from the Museum of Science).* ☎ *800-SONESTA or 617-806-4200.*

Seaport Hotel

$$$ South Boston Waterfront (Seaport District) Here's a perfect choice if you need to be near the World Trade Center, with great business perks that offset the inconvenient location if you don't. The airport is ten minutes away via the Ted Williams Tunnel. *1 Seaport Lane (off Northern Avenue).* ☎ *877-SEAPORT or 617-385-4000.*

The Tremont Boston

$$$$ Back Bay A Wyndham Grand Heritage hotel, the Tremont is a force in the Theater District's improvement from dicey to decent. The Tremont has a new business center and exercise room. *275 Tremont St., near Stuart Street.* ☎ *800-331-9998 or 617-426-1400.*

Index of Accommodations by Neighborhood

Back Bay

Chandler Inn Hotel ($$)
The Fairmont Copley Plaza Hotel
   ($$$–$$$$)
Four Seasons Hotel ($$$$)
Hilton Boston Back Bay ($$–$$$)
Howard Johnson Inn ($–$$)
The MidTown Hotel ($–$$)
Newbury Guest House ($$)
Radisson Hotel Boston ($$–$$$$)
Sheraton Boston Hotel ($$–$$$$)
The Westin Copley Place Boston
   ($$$–$$$$)

Cambridge

The Charles Hotel ($$$$)
Harvard Square Hotel ($$)
Sheraton Commander Hotel ($$–$$$$)

Downtown

Boston Harbor Hotel ($$$$)
Harborside Inn ($–$$)
Holiday Inn Select Boston Government
   Center ($$)
Omni Parker House ($$–$$$)
Swissôtel Boston ($$$–$$$$)
Wyndham Boston ($$–$$$$)

In the Vicinity

Anthony's Town House ($)
Doubletree Guest Suites ($$–$$$)
Hilton Boston Logan Airport ($$–$$$)
Holiday Inn Boston Brookline ($$)
Longwood Inn ($)

Index of Accommodations by Price

$

Anthony's Town House (In the Vicinity)

Harborside Inn (Downtown)

Howard Johnson Inn (Back Bay)

Longwood Inn (In the Vicinity)

The MidTown Hotel (Back Bay)

$$

Chandler Inn Hotel (Back Bay)

Doubletree Guest Suites (In the Vicinity)

Harborside Inn (Downtown)

Harvard Square Hotel (Cambridge)

Hilton Boston Back Bay (Back Bay)

Hilton Boston Logan Airport (In the Vicinity)

Holiday Inn Boston Brookline (In the Vicinity)

Holiday Inn Select Boston Government Center (Downtown)

Howard Johnson Inn (Back Bay)

The MidTown Hotel (Back Bay)

Newbury Guest House (Back Bay)

Omni Parker House (Downtown)

Radisson Hotel Boston (Back Bay)

Sheraton Boston Hotel (Back Bay)

Sheraton Commander Hotel (Cambridge)

Wyndham Boston (Downtown)

$$$

Doubletree Guest Suites (In the Vicinity)

The Fairmont Copley Plaza Hotel (Back Bay)

Hilton Boston Back Bay (Back Bay)

Hilton Boston Logan Airport (In the Vicinity)

Omni Parker House (Downtown)

Radisson Hotel Boston (Back Bay)

Sheraton Boston Hotel (Back Bay)

Sheraton Commander Hotel (Cambridge)

Swissôtel Boston (Downtown)

The Westin Copley Place Boston (Back Bay)

Wyndham Boston (Downtown)

$$$$

Boston Harbor Hotel (Downtown)

The Charles Hotel (Cambridge)

The Fairmont Copley Plaza Hotel (Back Bay)

Four Seasons Hotel (Back Bay)

Radisson Hotel Boston (Back Bay)

Sheraton Boston Hotel (Back Bay)

Sheraton Commander Hotel (Cambridge)

Swissôtel Boston (Downtown)

The Westin Copley Place Boston (Back Bay)

Wyndham Boston (Downtown)

Chapter 9

Taking Care of the Remaining Details

●●●

In This Chapter

▶ Buying travel and medical insurance

▶ Dealing with illness away from home

▶ Renting a car (and knowing why you don't need to)

▶ Making reservations and getting tickets in advance

▶ Getting tips on packing

●●●

*W*hat's worse than the nagging feeling that you forgot something, but you're not sure what that something is? I'd nominate the sensation of remembering what you forgot just as your plane leaves the ground.

This chapter attempts to relieve that sense of impending doom (or at least inconvenience) with a roundup of topics that can simplify your final trip-planning. Do you need insurance? What if you get sick? What's the story with rental cars? How far ahead can you schedule a fancy dinner and a night at the theater? Perhaps most important, what should you pack?

For more information about money, budgeting, and cost-cutting, turn to Chapter 3. For information on laying your hands on some cash and what to do if someone steals your money, see Chapter 12.

Playing It Safe with Travel and Medical Insurance

Buying insurance is kind of like carrying around an umbrella: If you carry one, the sun will shine. And unlike most umbrellas, insurance can be expensive. So, should you or shouldn't you?

Of the three primary kinds of travel insurance — **trip-cancellation, medical,** and **lost-luggage** — the only one I recommend is trip-cancellation insurance, if you pay a large portion of your vacation expenses up front.

Medical and lost-luggage insurance don't make sense for most travelers. Your existing health insurance should cover you if you get sick while on vacation. (If you belong to an HMO, check to see whether you're fully covered when away from home.) Homeowner's-insurance policies cover stolen luggage if the policy includes off-premises theft. Check your policies before you buy any additional coverage. The airlines are responsible for $2,500 on domestic flights (and $9.07 per pound, up to $640, on international flights) if the airline loses your luggage; if you plan to carry anything more valuable, keep those items in your carry-on bag.

Some credit cards (American Express and certain gold and platinum Visas and MasterCards, for example) offer automatic flight insurance against death or dismemberment in case of an airplane crash. If you feel you need more insurance, contact one of the following companies, but don't pay for more insurance than you need. For example, if you only need trip-cancellation insurance, don't buy coverage for lost or stolen property. Trip-cancellation insurance costs approximately 6% to 8% of the total value of your vacation. The following are among the reputable issuers of all three kinds of travel insurance:

- ✔ **Access America,** P.O. Box 90315, Richmond, VA 23286 (☎ **866-807-3982;** Fax: 800-346-9265; Internet: www.accessamerica.com)

- ✔ **Travelex Insurance Services,** 11717 Burt St., Ste. 202, Omaha, NE 68154 (☎ **800-228-9792;** Internet: www.travelex-insurance.com)

- ✔ **Travel Guard International,** 1145 Clark St., Stevens Point, WI 54481 (☎ **800-826-4919;** Internet: www.travel-guard.com)

- ✔ **Travel Insured International, Inc.,** P.O. Box 280568, 52-S Oakland Ave., East Hartford, CT 06128-0568 (☎ **800-243-3174;** Fax: 860-528-8005; Internet: www.travelinsured.com)

Staying Healthy When You Travel

Medical issues that arise when you're out of town can be tough to resolve. Boston being a health-care mecca, a lot of reliable choices are available if you should (heaven forbid) fall ill. Here are some things to keep in mind:

- ✔ **If you're covered by health insurance, be sure to carry your identification card in your wallet.** Note the emergency number you need to call if your provider requires pretreatment authorization. If you don't think your existing policy is sufficient, consider buying medical travel insurance (see the preceding section for more information).

✔ **Don't forget to pack your medications** (in your carryon, never in checked luggage), as well as a prescription for each one if you think you may run out.

✔ **Pack an extra pair of contact lenses or glasses** in case you lose a pair.

✔ **Remember over-the-counter remedies** for common travelers' ailments such as upset stomach and diarrhea.

✔ **If you suffer from a chronic illness, discuss your trip with your doctor.** For conditions such as epilepsy, diabetes, severe allergies, or heart ailments, wear a MedicAlert identification tag. This tag immediately alerts doctors to your condition and gives access to your medical records through a 24-hour hotline. Membership costs $35, plus a $20 annual fee. Contact the **MedicAlert Foundation,** 2323 Colorado Ave., Turlock, CA 95382 (☎ **888-633-4298;** Internet: www.medicalert.org).

If you need a doctor, ask your hotel's concierge or front desk. Most large hotels can recommend someone at any hour. If the situation is less than dire, try one of the area's many reliable physician-referral services. Options include **Massachusetts General Hospital** (☎ **800-711-4MGH**) and **Brigham and Women's Hospital** (☎ **800-294-9999**).

If you can't get a doctor to help you right away, try a walk-in clinic. You may not get immediate attention, but you won't pay the high price of an emergency-room visit. **MGH Back Bay** (an affiliate of Massachusetts General Hospital), 388 Commonwealth Ave. (☎ **617-267-7171**), honors most insurance plans and accepts credit cards.

If you need a dentist, the **Massachusetts Dental Society** (☎ **800-342-8747** or 508-651-7511; Internet: www.massdental.org) makes recommendations.

See the Appendix for listings of local hospitals.

Detailing the Car Question

You may know someone who claims to have driven all over Boston without a moment's trouble. People handle poisonous snakes every day, too.

Are you sure I don't need to rent a car?

If you visit Boston and Cambridge, you won't have any trouble getting around without a car. Public transportation and your feet are reliable, safe, and cheap. Parking is scarce and expensive — in both categories, among the worst in the country. Traffic is dreadful, worsening the closer you get to downtown, where a traffic jam can spring up at any hour of the day or night. Boston drivers, in particular, are hostile and unpredictable, and the Big Dig isn't helping anyone's disposition.

If you drive to the Boston area, park at the hotel and save the car for day-trips.

Do I need to rent a car for a day-trip?

You can, but you don't need to. Public transportation connects Boston with many popular day-trip destinations (see Chapter 21 for details). If time is short and you don't want to worry about a train or bus schedule, or you want to avoid a tour group, a rental car can be a good investment.

Don't automatically rent a car for the duration of your trip unless you'll use one every day (an easy mistake if you're booking a package). Wait until you know you need a car and save money — not just on the rental, but also on parking. The major agencies operate offices throughout the Boston area. Some companies, including **Enterprise** (☎ **800-736-8222**), offer pickup and drop-off service.

The $10 surcharge on car rentals in Boston goes toward construction of a new convention center. Get around the surcharge by renting in Cambridge, Brookline, or another suburb if you can.

How do I get the best deal?

Car-rental rates vary even more than airline fares. The price depends on the size of the car, the rental period, where and when you pick up and drop off the car, where you drive, and a host of other factors. The following is a list of things to keep in mind to get the best deal:

- ✔ **Weekend rates may be lower than weekday rates.** If you keep the car five or more days, a weekly rate may be cheaper than the daily rate. Ask if the rate is the same for pickup Friday morning as Thursday night, and whether there's a penalty for early drop-off of a weekly rental.

- ✔ **Some companies may assess a drop-off charge.** You may incur this fee if you don't return the car to the pickup location. National is one of the few companies that does not charge this fee.

- ✔ **Find out whether age is an issue.** Many car-rental companies add a fee for drivers under 25 — or don't rent to those drivers at all.

- ✔ **If you see an advertised price in your local newspaper, be sure to ask for that specific rate.** If not, you may be charged the standard (higher) rate. Don't forget to mention membership in AAA, AARP, and trade unions. These memberships usually entitle you to upgrades or to discounts ranging from 5% to 30%.

✔ **Check your frequent-flier accounts.** Not only are your favorite (or at least most-used) airlines likely to send you discount coupons, but most car rentals add at least 500 miles to your account.

✔ **Use the Internet to comparison-shop for a car rental.** All the major booking sites — **Travelocity** (www.travelocity.com), **Microsoft Expedia** (www.expedia.com), **Yahoo! Travel** (www.travel.yahoo.com), and **Cheap Tickets** (www.cheaptickets.com), for example — utilize search engines that can dig up discounted car-rental rates. Just enter the size of the car you want, the pickup and return dates, and the location, and the server returns a price. You can even make the reservation through any of these sites.

What are the additional charges?

In addition to the standard rental prices, other optional charges apply to most car rentals (as do some not-so-optional charges, such as taxes). Many credit-card companies cover the **Collision Damage Waiver (CDW),** which requires you to pay for damage to the car in a collision. Check with your credit-card company before you go so you can avoid paying this hefty fee (as much as $15 a day).

The car-rental companies also offer additional **liability insurance** (if you harm others in an accident), **personal-accident insurance** (if you harm yourself or your passengers), and **personal-effects insurance** (if your luggage is stolen from your car). Your insurance policy on your car at home probably covers most of these unlikely occurrences. However, if your own insurance doesn't cover you for rentals, or if you lack auto insurance, definitely consider the additional coverage (the car-rental companies are liable for certain base amounts, depending on the state). Unless you're toting around the Hope diamond — and you don't want to leave that in your car trunk anyway — you can probably skip the personal-effects insurance. However, driving around without liability or personal-accident coverage is never a good idea; even if you're a good driver, other people may not be, and liability claims can be complicated.

Some companies also offer **refueling packages,** in which you pay for your initial full tank of gas up front and return the car with an empty gas tank. The prices can be competitive with local gas prices, but you don't get credit for any gas remaining in the tank. If you reject this option, you pay only for the gas you use, but you need to return your rental car with a full tank or face charges of $3 to $4 a gallon for any shortfall. In my experience, gas prices in the refueling packages are at the high end. I usually forgo the refueling package and allow plenty of time for refueling en route to the car-rental return. However, if you usually run late and a refueling stop may make you miss your plane, you're a perfect candidate for the fuel-purchase option.

Making Reservations and Getting Tickets Ahead of Time

Boston is one of the best places I know for a fun, spontaneous afternoon or evening. Finding something to do when you get to town is no trouble. But spontaneity will only get you pitying smiles if your impromptu plans include a symphony performance, a high-profile museum exhibition, dinner at a hot restaurant, a Red Sox–Yankees game, or a show on a pre-Broadway run.

Reserving a ticket and getting event information

If you already know what you want to do, you're golden. If you need suggestions, surf ahead and browse around.

✔ Call ahead or visit the Web site of the museum, performing arts company, or sports team that interests you; most sell tickets online or redirect you to an outlet that does.

✔ Check with tourist information offices (see the Appendix for phone numbers and Web site addresses), which often know about big museum and stage shows many months in advance.

✔ If you have a hotel in mind, see whether the property is offering packages that include event or show tickets during the time you're thinking of traveling.

✔ Visit www.boston.com to check out the daily and weekly *Globe* and monthly *Boston* magazine listings.

✔ Check out the weekly *Boston Phoenix,* which not only posts content on www.bostonphoenix.com but also archives back issues. A season preview (the fall preview is the largest) contains listings of selected events for the next several months.

✔ Contact the major ticket agencies, which often make information available even before tickets go on sale. **Next Ticketing** (☎ 617-423-NEXT; Internet: www.nextticketing.com), **Tele-charge** (☎ 800-447-7400; Internet: www.telecharge.com, click on "ACROSS THE USA"), and **Ticketmaster** (☎ 617-931-2000; Internet: www.ticketmaster.com) are the ones that serve Boston.

The concierge or desk staff at your hotel may be your best source for tickets and information about what's going on around town. A good concierge can land you a restaurant reservation, too. And if you loiter in the lobby at a not-too-busy time, ask the bell staff for suggestions.

Reserving a table

If you make your own restaurant reservations, bear in mind that other people also read *Gourmet.* A prominent mention in any national publication, including *The New York Times,* guarantees long waits on the phone and in person. And unless you already have a reservation, don't expect to get near the subject of the weekly *Globe* review, which appears in the Thursday Calendar section, during the next couple of weekends.

 Friday and Saturday are the most popular nights for dining out. Early in the week (especially Sunday or Monday), most restaurants are calmer and less crowded than over the weekend. If you book a table for a slow night at a restaurant with a big-name chef, call a few days ahead to make sure the chef plans to be in the kitchen on the night you'll be there.

Make dinner reservations at every restaurant that takes reservations. Small parties usually don't need lunch reservations. For special-occasion favorites (such as Aujourd'hui, L'Espalier, and Rialto) and the latest hotspots (such as blu, Spire, and Via Matta), book as far ahead as possible. A month is not too far, and sometimes not far enough, especially around the holidays.

As in many other cities, restaurant name-dropping is an excruciatingly popular pastime in Boston. If you can't get a table at the bistro of the moment, don't despair. You may score one at the bistro of ten minutes ago — and just the fact that the eatery is still in business is an indication of the restaurant's worthiness.

Packing It All In

Start by assembling enough clothing and accessories to get you through the trip and making a pile on the bed. Now put half the clothes into your suitcase and return the other half to your dresser and closet.

Pack light, not because you can't take everything you want on the plane — you can, with some limits — but because spraining your back in an attempt to lift your whole summer wardrobe is a poor way to start a vacation. And you certainly can't load up your carry-on without attracting the wrong kind of attention at the airport security checkpoint.

What not to bring

You don't need fancy clothes to visit Boston unless your plans include something fancy, and in certain places "fancy" is one tiny step past "khaki." (In some places, "fancy" *equals* "khaki.") Students and tourists roam the streets in jeans and loose-fitting logo-covered clothing, lowering the fashion bar for everyone. During the day, especially in the summer, just being neat and clean is usually enough.

What to bring

Airlines allow each passenger one piece of carry-on luggage plus a "personal item," such as a purse, briefcase, or laptop. The dimensions vary, so be sure you know what your carrier allows. Be aware that security officers may search your bags at any time — don't pack anything that may embarrass you in front of your fellow passengers. (For more information, see the sidebar "Carry-on luggage do's and don'ts.") In a carry-on bag that you know will get through, pack valuables, prescription drugs, vital documents, return tickets, and other irreplaceable items. Add a book or magazine, anything breakable, and a snack. Leave room for the sweater or light jacket you pull off after a few minutes of hauling bags through the overheated terminal.

Here are some packing specifics:

- ✔ **Start with comfortable, broken-in walking shoes.** This item is perhaps the only one you can't replace on the road, so triple-check this suggestion.

  Note that in downtown Boston, sandals are little magnets for every piece of grit, grime, and gravel the Big Dig generates. Sandals are not a good choice even if you wear socks (which will get you in trouble with the fashion police anyway).

- ✔ **Second most important: Dress in layers.** Indoors or out, the temperature can plummet or soar at a moment's notice, especially in spring and fall. Several thin layers (think T-shirt, fleece pullover, and nylon shell) are more versatile and easier to pack than one thick one (such as a sweatshirt).

- ✔ **Remember your sun hat and sunscreen.** All year. Really.

- ✔ **Winter travelers need a warm jacket or coat, a hat, gloves or mittens, and sturdy boots.** In snowy weather, boots are as acceptable as shoes in nearly every setting. (I've worn mine to some of the city's finest restaurants — the tablecloth hides the boots when you sit down.)

- ✔ **If your plans include an elegant dinner or an evening of theater, classical music, or ballet, you won't feel overdressed in a coat and tie or a dressy outfit.** Pantsuits are okay everywhere.

✔ **Most restaurants don't have dress codes, though a few require jackets for men.** So yes, you probably can get away with just about anything, but have a heart — if you find yourself seated next to a couple celebrating their 50th anniversary, do you really want to be wearing that T-shirt from the most disgusting bar in Key West?

Carry-on luggage do's and don'ts

Airlines restrict each passenger to one carry-on bag and one "personal item" (such as a purse or briefcase). The strictest airlines say carryons must measure no more than 22 x 14 x 9 inches, including wheels and handles, and weigh no more than 40 pounds. These limits are inflexible; don't try to talk your way around them, especially at security-sensitive Logan Airport. Trying to sneak on a bag that's just a smidge over the limit will only make the already-lengthy wait at the security checkpoint that much longer.

You no longer have to leave your eyelash curler at home, but the Transportation Security Administration (TSA), the government agency that now handles all aspects of airport security, continues to bar from airplane cabins sharp items and anything else that may be used as a weapon. That includes utensils with an edge, such as straight razors and scissors, and larger items like golf clubs and ski poles. Visit the agency's Web site (www.tsa.gov) for up-to-date regulations, then double-check with your airline, which may have additional rules.

In addition to going through an x-ray machine, your bags and anything else in your possession may be subject to a hand search by airport security officers. You'll have to turn on your laptop and other electronic devices (to prove that they are what you say they are), and the officer can ask you to take a drink from the coffee cup or water bottle you're carrying. You may have to remove your shoes, too; loafers or slip-ons speed up this process. If the line isn't moving as quickly as you'd like, keep your complaints to yourself. At many airports, including Boston's, these officers are federal employees, and interfering with the officers is serious business. The officers are doing a vital job as quickly as possible; cut them a little slack.

Part III
Settling Into Boston

The 5th Wave   By Rich Tennant

"Where's the North End? Well, that depends. Where's the Big Dig today?"

In this part . . .

*B*oston can be a confusing city to navigate, but it doesn't have to be. (Everyone who lives here has gotten lost at least once.) This section helps clear things up with a look at the airport, the neighborhoods, and the public-transit system. Get these particulars out of the way, and you can move on to the fun part of your trip — spending your money. To that end, I cover the all-important topic of accessing your bucks while in Boston as well.

Chapter 10

Arriving and Getting Oriented

*B*oston's streets appear to have minds of their own. The roads head off in random directions, they change names at the drop of a Red Sox cap, and an awful lot of them aren't wearing signs. How can you find your way around? Ask directions, for one thing. And remember: You can't get *that* lost.

Arriving in Boston

This orientation to Boston begins at your arrival point. I tell you what you need to know if you arrive by plane, train, or car, and how to get to your next destination — your hotel.

By plane

Logan International Airport suffers from insufficient capacity and ongoing construction. Good administration means that neither situation typically causes much trouble, but be ready for air and ground delays all the same.

Logan is one of the most security-conscious airports in the country — both planes that hit the World Trade Center on September 11, 2001, originated in Boston. Expect long check-in lines and don't expect any sympathy if you decide to joke about having a bomb in your luggage. Airport security officers can, literally, make a federal case out of that.

Logan has five terminals, A through E. Terminal A, thanks to construction, was closed at press time (and scheduled to reopen in 2003 at the earliest). Good signage and small terminals make getting lost difficult, except in construction areas, where employees usually can point the way.

In terminals B and C, which serve domestic carriers, gates are on the upper level, and baggage claim and ground transportation are on the first level. Terminals D (domestic and international) and E (international) are one level. Terminal C has children's play spaces. Each terminal has an ATM, Internet kiosks, fax machine, and information booth (near baggage claim). The booth in Terminal C is a Visitor Service Center, where staffers can arrange hotel and restaurant reservations, theater and sports tickets, and tours.

The airport is in East Boston, 3 miles across the harbor from downtown. Signs in the terminals indicate the curbside stops for each mode of transportation (shuttle bus, taxi, and so forth). Nearby tunnels connect "Eastie" to downtown. Sound simple? The Big Dig, like a bad penny, is at the downtown end of the Callahan and Sumner tunnels.

When traffic is heavy — rush hours, Sunday evening, any holiday period — or the weather is bad, public transportation is the fastest way to reach downtown. If you have another destination, crossing the harbor by boat or train and grabbing a cab can still be faster than driving.

The **Massachusetts Port Authority** (☎ **800-23-LOGAN;** Internet: www. massport.com/logan) coordinates airport transportation. The phone line has information about getting to the city and suburbs. The line is open 24 hours a day, with live operators weekdays from 8 a.m. to 7 p.m.

Taking public transportation to your hotel

Free airport shuttle buses run in a loop from 5:30 a.m. to 1:00 a.m. daily. Number 11 runs terminal to terminal; numbers 22, 33, 55, and 66 connect to public transit.

The quickest way to downtown is by water. Take Number 66 to the ferry terminal, buy a $10 ticket if the kiosk is open (if not, buy your ticket on board), and cross the harbor in seven minutes. The **Airport Water Shuttle** (☎ **800-235-6426** or 617-951-0255) runs to Rowes Wharf, off Atlantic Avenue behind the Boston Harbor Hotel. **Harbor Express** (☎ **617-376-8417**) serves Long Wharf, off Atlantic Avenue near the New England Aquarium. (Harbor Express is a good option only from the airport to downtown; on the way back, the express stops first in suburban Quincy.) From April to mid-October, the **Airport Water Taxi** (☎ **617-422-0392**) connects a dozen stops on the harbor, including the ferry dock. The flat fare is $10, and you must call ahead from the dock for service.

The subway is almost as fast and can be more convenient. Shuttle numbers 22 and 33 run to the Blue Line's Airport station. Before 7 a.m. and after 10 p.m., Number 55 covers both. At the station, buy a $1 token or visitor pass (see Chapter 11). The line can be long but moves quickly.

State (for the Orange Line) and Government Center (for the Green Line) are transfer points from the Blue Line. Transfers are free. Trips to Government Center take ten minutes. To reach Cambridge, switch to the Green Line at Government Center, go one stop, and transfer at Park Street to the Red Line.

Taking private transportation to your hotel

Taxis queue up at every terminal. The trip takes 10 to 45 minutes, depending on traffic and time of day. The fare to downtown or the Back Bay should be about $22 to $28.

Boston's cabbies are caught between government entities' attempts to balance budgets, and the cabbies pass along the resulting charges to customers. At press time, these included a $4.50 tunnel fee and a $1.50 airport fee. The meter starts at $1.75, which means you're out $7.75 before you fasten your seatbelt. These surcharges seem to jump every year or so — the staff at the information desk inside the terminal can give you the total. (See Chapter 11 for more information on taxis.)

The Ted Williams Tunnel connects the airport to South Boston. On a map, this looks like a pricey detour. Restrictions on tunnel use and access roads, though, often make this the fastest route to the Back Bay and Cambridge. When traffic is bad, the tunnel is the best way to parts of downtown, too.

Back Bay Coach (☎ **888-BACK-BAY** or 888-222-5229 or 617-746-9909; Internet: www.backbay-coach.com) operates vans from the airport to Boston proper and many suburbs. Prices start at $9 per person. Call or surf ahead for reservations and exact fares.

To arrange limousine service, you must call ahead — drivers can't cruise for fares. Ask if your hotel recommends a company, or try **Carey Limousine Boston** (☎ **800-336-4646** or 617-623-8700) or **Commonwealth Limousine Service** (☎ **800-558-LIMO** outside Massachusetts, or 617-787-5575).

If you don't need a rental car right away, spare yourself the hassle of navigating the airport and pick one up later.

The major rental companies operate shuttles. If you must pick up a car immediately, ask the staff to map a route with the latest traffic patterns and construction sites. Make sure you obtain directions for returning, too, but don't worry if you go astray — the main airport road is a loop.

By train

South Station is a train and commuter rail terminal, bus station, and subway stop at Atlantic Avenue and Summer Street. You must leave the train and bus station to reach the Red Line subway entrance, about five steps from the main exit. Cabs line up on Atlantic Avenue. The area is a major center of Big Dig activity, so be careful (and patient, if you take a cab).

Back Bay Station is on Dartmouth Street between Huntington and Columbus avenues. This is the next-to-last Amtrak stop and serves the Orange Line and commuter rail. Cabs line up on Dartmouth.

North Station is on Causeway Street in the same building as the FleetCenter, near a busy stretch of the Big Dig. Amtrak trains from Portland, Maine, arrive at this station, which also serves the commuter rail. Also here, but not connected to the terminal yet, are the North Station stops on the Green and Orange lines of the T.

By car

If you're staying downtown, call your hotel the day before you plan to arrive. Ask for directions and the latest traffic patterns. For Back Bay hotels, take the Mass. Pike to the Copley exit. For Cambridge hotels, take the Mass. Pike to the Allston/Cambridge exit and follow Storrow Drive to the Harvard Square exit.

Figuring Out the Neighborhoods

These neighborhoods contain the city's main attractions. Most are small and walkable, with loose boundaries and (except in the Back Bay) confusing street patterns. Do yourself a favor and wander a little. (For a map of Boston's neighborhoods, see the inside front cover of this book.)

Downtown

I define *downtown* as the Waterfront, North End, Faneuil Hall Marketplace, Government Center, Beacon Hill, Downtown Crossing, the Financial District, and Charlestown. Here are descriptions of each:

  ✔ **The Waterfront:** Located along Commercial Street and Atlantic Avenue, the Waterfront faces the Inner Harbor. Here you find the New England Aquarium and the wharves that handle tour boats and ferries.

  ✔ **North End:** The Freedom Trail runs through the North End, which lies east of I-93 and north of the Waterfront. The longtime immigrant enclave maintains a reputation as the city's Italian neighborhood (*never* called "Little Italy") through commerce rather than population — newcomers outnumber Italian-American residents. The Paul Revere House and the Old North Church are here.

✔ **Faneuil Hall Marketplace:** Where the North End meets the Waterfront, cross I-93 to find Faneuil Hall Marketplace (also called Quincy Market, the name of the central building). This tourist magnet abounds with shops, restaurants, and bars.

✔ **Government Center:** This cluster of ugly city, state, and federal office buildings is across Congress Street from Faneuil Hall.

✔ **Beacon Hill:** Rest your eyes with a stroll around Beacon Hill, the architectural treasure between Government Center, Boston Common, and the river. If you conjure a picture of Boston, it probably includes Beacon Hill's Federal-style homes and redbrick sidewalks.

✔ **Downtown Crossing:** This shopping and business district is across Boston Common from Beacon Hill. Most of the Freedom Trail is in this area. An area that local PR types have taken to calling the "Ladder District" (between the Common and Washington Street, south of Winter Street) is also here; most locals have yet to go along.

✔ **Financial District:** The Financial District lies east of Downtown Crossing and west of I-93. The area's giant office towers loom over the landmark Custom House and the colorful clock tower.

✔ **Charlestown:** Charlestown is home to the last two stops on the Freedom Trail and lies across the Inner Harbor from the North End.

The Back Bay

For my purposes, "the Back Bay" covers hotels in the centrally located neighborhoods outside downtown, including the Back Bay proper. The other neighborhoods I lump in are (working east to west) Chinatown, the Theater District, the South End, and Kenmore Square. Incidentally, Boston has no "midtown" or "uptown."

The neighborhood Bostonians know as the Back Bay starts at the Public Garden and the river and extends, approximately, to Massachusetts Avenue (or Mass. Ave.) and Huntington Avenue. Boston's finest shopping is along Newbury and Boylston streets. Trinity Church, the Boston Public Library, the Hancock Tower, Copley Place, the Prudential Center, and the Hynes Convention Center also are in this area.

Remember "two if by sea"? Incredibly, the Back Bay was the "sea." (In the Longfellow poem, Paul Revere watched the steeple of the Old North Church for a signal telling him whether to alert the minutemen to watch for British troops approaching over land — one lantern — or by water.)

This neighborhood was a marshy body of water until 1835, when development began pushing west from downtown. The Back Bay attained its current contours by 1882. In 1775, when British troops set out for Lexington and Concord, present-day Charles Street (between Boston Common and the Public Garden) was the shoreline.

Chinatown is a congested area where you'll find an enormous assortment of Asian restaurants and shops. This neighborhood lies south of Downtown Crossing and west of I-93. The **Theater District,** a small area around the intersection of Tremont and Stuart streets, holds the largest professional Boston theaters.

Victorian brownstones distinguish the **South End,** which lies south of the Back Bay proper. The landmark district underwent extensive gentrification beginning in the 1970s. The South End has a large gay community and some of the best restaurants in the city.

At Beacon Street and Commonwealth Avenue, **Kenmore Square** spreads out below an enormous white-and-red Citgo sign, one of the city skyline's most famous features. Fenway Park lies three blocks away.

Cambridge

The Red Line of the subway cuts through the city known as "Boston's Left Bank." **Harvard Square,** where you'll find upscale shops, historic landmarks, and, oh yeah, a big university, is the most popular destination. The city's other world-famous institution is Massachusetts Institute of Technology (MIT), in and around Kendall Square. **Central Square,** a rapidly gentrifying area that abounds with ethnic restaurants and clubs, lies between the two. **Porter Square,** where you'll find quirky shops like those that once characterized Harvard Square, is one stop past Harvard.

Knowing Where to Get Information in Person

Make your first stop the concierge or front-desk staff at your hotel. Many hotels have racks full of brochures and other information.

The **Boston National Historic Park Visitor Center,** 15 State St. (☎ 617-242-5642), across the street from the Old State House and the State Street T station, is another good resource. The center is open 9 a.m. to 5 p.m. daily except January 1, Thanksgiving Day, and December 25.

The Freedom Trail begins at the **Boston Common Information Center,** 146 Tremont St., on the Common (open 8:30 a.m. to 5:00 p.m. Monday through Saturday, 9 a.m. to 5 p.m. Sunday). The **Prudential Information**

Center, on the main level of the Prudential Center, is open 9 a.m. to 8 p.m. Monday through Saturday, 11 a.m. to 6 p.m. Sunday. The **Greater Boston Convention & Visitors Bureau** (☎ 888-SEE-BOSTON or 617-536-4100) operates both.

A small booth is at **Faneuil Hall Marketplace,** between Quincy Market and the South Market Building. The booth is staffed in spring, summer, and fall from 10 a.m. to 6 p.m. Monday through Saturday, noon to 6 p.m. Sunday.

In Cambridge, a kiosk (☎ 617-497-1630) in the heart of **Harvard Square,** near the T entrance at Mass. Ave. and John F. Kennedy Street, is open 9 a.m. to 5 p.m. Monday through Saturday, 1 to 5 p.m. Sunday.

Chapter 11

Getting Around Boston

. . . .

In This Chapter

▶ Exploring on foot

▶ Navigating the T (subway, bus, and boat)

▶ Getting around on wheels (taxi or car)

. . . .

Some people consider an African safari an adventure. Others say whitewater rafting in the Rockies is a daring experience. Still others, perhaps overdramatic but no less serious, may call navigating Boston's downtown streets a courageous undertaking.

Congestion, construction, unmarked streets — Boston has it all. My goal is to scare you into walking everywhere. (How'm I doing so far?) But sometimes you can't — destinations are too far or you're too late or tired. This chapter contains pointers for getting from place to place by foot and, because you may need to take another means of transportation, by subway, bus, boat, taxi, and car — all without steering you into adventure territory.

Should you find yourself in a sightseeing mood in the early morning or late afternoon, no matter what your mode of transportation, remember you're essentially a commuter. If you're on the move between 7 and 9 a.m. or 4 and 7 p.m., be patient while in transit. And don't stop in the middle of a busy sidewalk or intersection to check your map.

Hitting the Bricks: Foot Traffic

You packed your good walking shoes, right? The compact size and baffling layout of the central city make this a pedestrian's pleasure. Everywhere you turn, something picturesque catches your attention, and not being in a speeding vehicle means you can check out sights for as long as you like.

Here are some trekking tips to keep in mind:

> ✔ The only steep areas are Beacon Hill and Copp's Hill, in the North End behind the Old North Church.

> ✔ All over town, brick and cobblestone sidewalks ripple gently, just waiting to trip you and mess up the heels of your good shoes. Step carefully.

> ✔ The Back Bay is the only neighborhood laid out in a grid. The cross streets begin at the Public Garden with Arlington Street and proceed alphabetically (until Mass. Ave. jumps in after Hereford).

> ✔ At many downtown intersections, the timing mechanism that controls the traffic light allows pedestrians just 7 seconds to walk (sprint, really) across. Ignore the locals and stay put until the light changes.

> ✔ Always look both ways before crossing — careless drivers, bikers, and skaters don't worry about one-way signs.

Hot T: Public Transit

The full name of the T is the **Massachusetts Bay Transportation Authority,** or MBTA (☎ **800-392-6100** outside Massachusetts, or 617-222-3200; Internet: www.mbta.com). The system operates subway lines, surface transit, and trains to the suburbs. Call the main information number for round-the-clock automated information, and assistance from live operators from 6:30 a.m. to 8:00 p.m. Monday through Friday, 7:30 a.m. to 6:00 p.m. weekends. Visit the Web site to view maps and schedules and to buy passes online (subject to a service charge).

You'll hear subway stops called "T stops," "T stations," and just "T," as in "I'll meet you near the Government Center T." If someone gives you directions that include a subway ride, be sure you know which exit to use (most stations have more than one).

On subways and buses, kids under age 5 accompanied by an adult ride free, and kids ages 5 to 11 get a 50% discount. The commuter rail family fare (equal to twice the adult fare) also applies to one adult traveling with as many as four kids under 18.

The **MBTA visitor pass** (☎ **877-927-7277** or 617-222-5218; Internet: www.mbta.com) covers the subway, local buses, commuter rail zones 1A and 1B, and two ferries. Passes are available over the phone or on the Web (a shipping charge applies), and in person at the Airport, Government Center, and Harvard T stops, South Station, Back Bay Station, and North Station. The Boston Common, Prudential Center, and Faneuil Hall Marketplace information centers and some hotels sell passes, too. The price is $6, $11, or $22, respectively, for one day, three consecutive days, or seven consecutive days.

Boston Transit

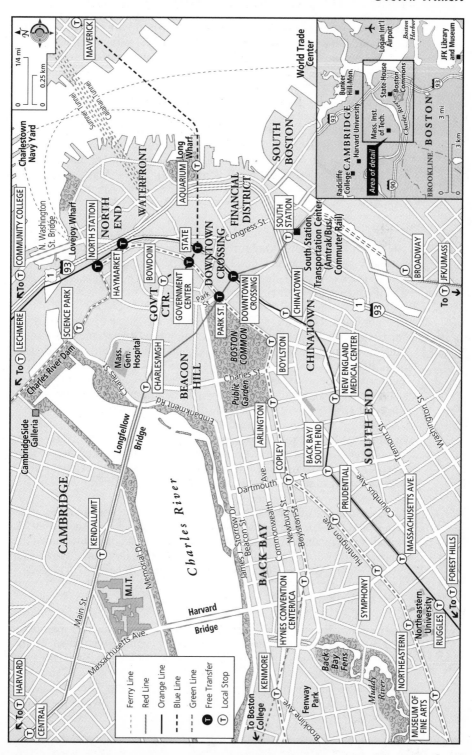

The subway and trolley systems

Red, Orange, and Blue line subways and **Green Line trolleys,** which cover most areas you're likely to want to visit, are the quickest non-pedestrian way to get around. The T is generally dependable and safe, with a couple of caveats: The Green Line is sometimes unreliable, and you should take the precautions (such as watching out for pickpockets) that you would on any big-city transit system.

The local fare is $1, and transfers are free. You need a token or visitor pass to enter subway stations; if you're boarding a Green Line trolley above ground (as you leave the Museum of Fine Arts, for instance), pay at the front of the first car. Tokens are for sale at booths in every station and machines at many stops. Buy an extra token for your return trip.

The T operates from about 5:15 a.m. until at least 12:30 a.m., but no later than 1:00 a.m., Sunday through Thursday. For information about bus service until 2:30 a.m. on Friday and Saturday, see the "Late-night weekend bus service" sidebar. On New Year's Eve, service is free after 8 p.m. and shuts down at 2 a.m.

The antiquated Green Line, which serves many areas of interest to visitors, is the most complicated. When riding the Green Line, make sure you know which branch (B, C, D, or E) you need. Each starts and ends at a different station; all four serve every stop between Government Center and Copley. If you take the wrong westbound train, you may need to backtrack and switch lines; ask the conductor to leave you at the right stop.

System maps, available on request from most token-booth clerks, display the subway lines (in the designated colors) and commuter rail (in purple). The maps in this book also show subway stops. To get route and fare information before your visit, check the Web site.

Renovations are under way to make the Green Line wheelchair-accessible. Updated system maps show accessible stations on other lines, but not all stations display up-to-date maps (check the date, if you can find one). To find out more, call the main information number (☎ **800-392-6100**) or contact the **Office for Transportation Access (☎ 617-222-5976** or 617-222-5854 [TTY]; Internet: www.mbta.com). Also see Chapter 4 for more information.

Check a map that shows T stations superimposed on a street map before automatically hopping on the subway to get around downtown. South Station to Aquarium, for example, is a three-train trip but an easy ten-minute walk.

Late-night weekend bus service

The MBTA operates Night Owl bus service Friday and Saturday until 2:30 a.m. (In Boston, that's late.) Several popular routes continue after regular closing time, and additional bus routes parallel the subway lines above ground. Introduced on a trial basis in 2001, the Night Owl was under evaluation at press time but appeared likely to continue. The fare is one token or $1 in coins. For information and to make sure the service is still operating, check with the T (☎ **800-392-6100** outside Massachusetts or 617-222-3200; Internet: www.mbta.com).

The bus system

T buses and *trackless trolleys* (electricity-powered buses) serve Boston, Cambridge, and other nearby suburbs. The local fare is 75¢. Fare boxes accept tokens but don't make change. Express bus fares start at $1.50. Buses with wheelchair lifts cover many routes; call ☎ **800-LIFT-BUS** for information.

Here are local routes you may find useful:

- ✔ **Number 1,** along Mass. Ave. from Dudley Station in Roxbury through the Back Bay and Cambridge to Harvard Square. During off-peak hours, this route is usually faster than the subway.

- ✔ **Numbers 92 and 93,** between Haymarket and Charlestown. Freedom Trail walkers may be too tired for anything except the bus, but the ferry (see the following section, "The ferry system") is more fun.

- ✔ **Number 77,** along Mass. Ave. north of Harvard Square to Porter Square, North Cambridge, and Arlington.

The ferry system

Water-transportation options change periodically, according to demand and other factors. Two popular routes cross the Inner Harbor. The first connects Long Wharf, on State Street near Atlantic Avenue, with the Charlestown Navy Yard; this is a good break from the Freedom Trail. The second runs from Lovejoy Wharf, near North Station and the FleetCenter, off Causeway Street, to the World Trade Center, on Northern Avenue. The fare is $1.25; you can use your visitor pass on both routes. Call ☎ **617-227-4321** for more information.

Cab Session: Taxis

Taxis are pricey and can be tough to hail. At busy times such as rush hours and early morning (when bars and clubs are closing), you shouldn't have much trouble — the drivers go where the business is. Otherwise, find a cab stand or call a dispatcher.

Cabs line up near hotels and at designated stands. You'll find cabs queuing at Faneuil Hall Marketplace (on North Street), South Station, Back Bay Station, and at two stretches of Mass. Ave. in Harvard Square, near Brattle Street and near Dunster Street.

If the hour is late and you're desperate, look in front of a 24-hour business such as Dunkin' Donuts.

To call ahead for a cab, try the **Independent Taxi Operators Association** (☎ 617-426-8700), **Boston Cab** (☎ 617-536-5010), **Town Taxi** (☎ 617-536-5000), or **Metro Cab** (☎ 617-242-8000.** In Cambridge, call **Ambassador Brattle** (☎ 617-492-1100) or **Yellow Cab** (☎ 617-547-3000). Boston Cab can dispatch a wheelchair-accessible vehicle; advance notice of an hour or so is recommended.

The *drop rate* (the rate for the first ¼ mile) is $1.75. After that, the fare adds up at 30¢ per ⅛ mile. *Wait time* (the time the driver waits for you) is extra, and the passenger pays all tolls, as well as $6 in fees (which include the tunnel toll) on trips leaving Logan Airport. The law forbids charging a flat rate within Boston. If you need a cab to a suburb, the driver will charge you the price on the Police Department's list of flat rates (and show the list to you if you ask).

Cabs licensed in Boston are painted mostly white. Strenuously enforced regulations call for acceptable maintenance of vehicle and driver.

Although the practice is technically illegal, out-of-town cabs sometimes pick up fares in Boston; you won't be the one stuck with the fine, but you may be stuck with a driver who doesn't know the city.

Always, always ask for a receipt, which should state the name of the company. If you lose something or want to report a problem, call the **Police Department** (☎ 617-536-8294).

Engine Block: Driving in Boston

Driving is not a good idea, but sometimes you have no choice. Start by buckling up, even if you never do at home. No kidding.

When you reach Boston or Cambridge, park the car, then walk or use public transportation. Do all you can to stay off the roads during rush hours and weekend afternoons. Make sure you have a map and, if possible, a cool-headed navigator. Most streets are one-way, and your out-of-state plates make you more of a moving target than an object of sympathy.

Be alert — no snacks or phone calls. (Those bumper stickers that say HANG UP AND DRIVE come from Cambridge.) Watch out for cars that change lanes or leave the curb without signaling. Look both ways at intersections, even on one-way streets. Also keep an eye out for wrong-way bicyclists.

Enough! Where can I leave the car?

Not on the street, unless you're very lucky. Meters regulate most spaces, where nonresidents may park for no more than two hours (sometimes much less), and only between 8 a.m. and 6 p.m. The penalty is a $25 ticket, and parking-enforcement officers work long hours every day except Sunday. Most Boston and Cambridge meters take quarters only. In busy areas, that quarter only buys you 15 minutes — start hoarding now.

To see if your "missing" car is in the city tow lot, call ☎ 617-635-3900. Make sure you have your wallet — the fines and fees can easily top $100. Then take a taxi to 200 Frontage Rd., South Boston, or ride the Red Line to Andrew and flag a cab.

A parking lot or garage is easier but still no prize. The daily rate downtown, reputedly tops in the country, can be as much as $35; hourly rates (as much as $15) are outrageous, too. Weekends and evenings usually are cheaper. Many establishments discount weekday rates if you enter and exit before certain times. Some restaurants have deals with nearby garages; ask when you make your reservation.

Prices are slightly lower than public lots at the city-operated garage under Boston Common (☎ 617-954-2096). The entrance is on Charles Street between Boylston and Beacon streets. The Prudential Center garage (☎ 617-267-1002) offers a discount if you make a purchase at the Shops at Prudential Center and have your ticket validated. Enter from Boylston Street, Huntington Avenue, Exeter Street, or Dalton Street (at the Sheraton Boston Hotel). The Copley Place garage (☎ 617-375-4488) extends a discount to shoppers, too. The garage is off Huntington Avenue near Exeter Street. Many Faneuil Hall Marketplace shops and restaurants validate parking at the 75 State St. Garage (☎ 617-742-7275).

Other good-sized garages can be found at Government Center off Congress Street (☎ 617-227-0385), Sudbury Street off Congress Street (☎ 617-973-6954), the New England Aquarium (☎ 617-723-1731), Zero Post Office Square (☎ 617-423-1430), and near the Hynes Convention Center on Dalton Street (☎ 617-247-8006).

Harvard Square is even less hospitable to motorists than downtown Boston. The area is congested with a few costly garages and parking lots, and many tow-away zones disguised as tempting university spaces. Be patient and have a backup plan and budget in case you don't find a metered space (maximum stay, 30 minutes to 2 hours).

Parking is free on North Harvard Street and Western Avenue, on the Boston side of the Charles River near Harvard Business School. Harvard Square is some distance away (use the bridge at Memorial Drive and John F. Kennedy Street), but this is not a bad walk, and the price is right.

Rules of the road

You may turn right at a red light after stopping when traffic permits, unless a sign says otherwise. Seat belts are mandatory for adults and children, children under 12 must ride in the back seat, and infants and children under 5 must be strapped into car seats.

Under state law, pedestrians in the crosswalk have the right of way, and vehicles already in a *rotary* (traffic circle or roundabout) have the right of way. Most suburbs post and enforce the crosswalk law; signs state the right-of-way law in every rotary, with little discernible effect.

Chapter 12

Managing Your Money

● ●

In This Chapter

▶ Getting cash on the road

▶ Coping with stolen money

▶ Dealing with taxing matters

● ●

*Y*ou may hear that Boston is a great bargain because the city is a college town. Well, a typical college kid isn't buying meals, snacks, subway tokens, and souvenirs for a family of four. This chapter discusses where to get money and where to turn for help if someone else makes off with yours. Check out Chapter 3 for more money-management strategies.

Where to Get Cash in Boston

The largest banks in Massachusetts are **Fleet** (☎ 800-841-4000) and **Citizens** (☎ 800-852-5577); their ATMs accept most networks' cards, and impose fees for these services. State law says banks must warn you before imposing a fee for using a "foreign" bank card and offer you the chance to cancel the transaction.

You'll find ATMs at grocery and convenience stores, most department stores, and some subway stations. Most are in safe, well-lit areas. If you don't feel secure, keep walking; you'll pass another machine soon.

When using the ATM, use the same caution you would at home. Protect your password and don't be complacent.

The largest networks are **Cirrus** (☎ 800-424-7787) and **Plus** (☎ 800-843-7587). Also, the **NYCE** network (Internet: www.nycenet.com) operates in the eastern U.S. Check before leaving home (the logo should be on the back of your ATM card) to see which network accepts your bank's cards.

The **SUM** network (Internet: www.sum-atm.com) gives customers of smaller banks and credit unions free access to other members' ATMs. Check to see whether your bank belongs to the SUM network or has another arrangement that can help you avoid fees.

Even if the Massachusetts bank doesn't charge you, your home bank may. Weigh the cumulative cost against the risk of carrying a wad of cash and adjust your withdrawal patterns accordingly.

Knowing What to Do if Your Money Gets Stolen

Most credit-card companies operate toll-free numbers to call if your credit card is stolen. Your card issuer may be able to wire you a cash advance and provide an emergency replacement card in a day or two.

Check the back of your card for the issuing bank's number before you leave home. Keep the number separate from your wallet. You also can call toll-free directory assistance (☎ **800-555-1212**) to find your bank's number.

Visa and MasterCard have global service numbers: for **Visa,** ☎ **800-847-2911**; for **MasterCard,** ☎ **800-307-7309.** (Both suggest you contact your card issuer directly.) **American Express** cardholders and traveler's check holders should call ☎ **800-221-7282.**

If you carry traveler's checks, keep a record of the serial numbers so you can handle such an emergency. Keeping a record of your credit card numbers and the companies' emergency numbers also is a good idea.

Always notify the police if your wallet is stolen. You probably won't get the wallet back, but you may need a copy of the police report for your insurance or credit-card company.

Taxing Matters

The 5% Massachusetts sales tax does not apply to food, prescription drugs, newspapers, or clothing that costs less than $175. The 5% meal tax applies to restaurant food and takeout orders. In Boston and Cambridge, the total lodging tax is 12.45%.

Part IV
Dining in Boston

The 5th Wave   By Rich Tennant

"How you doin', sir? Why don't you let me show you an old New England way of getting meat out of a lobster?"

In this part . . .

One of the liveliest restaurant markets in the country, Boston offers choices to suit every budget, taste, and style. Volatility coexists with stability — you can enjoy back-to-back meals at a place that opened 18 days ago and a place that opened in the 1800s. This part explores your options, describes my favorite restaurants, and sets you on the path to dining well.

Your table is ready.

Chapter 13

The Scoop on the Boston Dining Scene

● ●

In This Chapter

▶ Enjoying hot spots and local favorites

▶ Paying the check without getting heartburn

▶ Figuring out reservations, dress codes, and other considerations

● ●

*O*ut-of-towners ask the same question everywhere: Where do people who live in Boston (or Paris or Seattle or Harrisburg) go to eat? This chapter offers an overview of the local dining scene, plus pointers about the mechanics of getting strangers to bring you food. Turn to Chapter 14 for specifics about my favorites and to Chapter 15 if you're just grabbing a quick bite. For the locations of restaurants mentioned in this chapter, see the "Boston Dining" and "Cambridge Dining" maps in Chapter 14.

Finding Out What's Hot Now

New England cuisine abounds with seafood and local produce, but there's no particular "Boston style." Thanks to constant turnover, though, every chef in town seems to have supervised or worked for nearly every other chef. Many kitchens show signs of similar influences, particularly in the mingling of ethnic elements and ingredients, a practice that has become increasingly apparent on menus across the country.

Boston has shaken a reputation for stodgy food and stodgier restaurants, even among hard-core snobs and wanna-be New Yorkers. Pockets of Gotham-esque see-and-be-seen action have sprung up in some improbable neighborhoods. The hottest places as I write (they could be different as you read) are **blu,** in the Ritz-Carlton, Boston Common, 4 Avery St., Downtown Crossing (☎ **617-375-8550**); **Mantra,** 52 Temple Place, Downtown Crossing (☎ **617-546-8111**); and **Via Matta,** 79 Park Plaza, Back Bay (☎ **617-422-0008**).

Locating Where the Locals Eat

First, let me assure you that you're not going to get scurvy from eating *only* New England clam chowder, Boston baked beans, and Boston cream pie. The menus here offer a lot more than stereotypical New England food; in fact, the renowned chowder, beans, and pie went out with disco and platform shoes — the first time around. The locals eat tons of seafood, appreciate chefs' increasing interest in local and organic produce, and demonstrate a willingness to try just about anything once.

Remember, many locals are students, who come from all over the world with lots of ambition and tuition, and often not much else. When going out to eat, collegians are willing to experiment but not overpay. Seek out a busy place near a college campus when you're looking for generous portions and reasonable prices.

As in any city of neighborhoods, the local standby occupies an honored place. Depending on the neighborhood, this dependable eating establishment may be a pocket-sized bistro, an ethnic counter, a diner, or just about anything else. I'll suggest a few in Chapter 14, but never dismiss a restaurant just because you can't find the name in a guidebook. Your friends who can't shut up about the great place around the corner may be ahead of the curve.

Tasting Boston's Ethnic Eats

Head to the North End — which would be Boston's Little Italy if anyone ever used that term — for good Italian food in every price range. Hanover and Salem streets are the main drags, with some good spots on the streets nearby. In Chinatown, you'll find excellent and affordable Chinese, Japanese, Korean, Vietnamese, and Malaysian food. Start at Beach Street and wander the streets that intersect Beach.

Ethnic restaurants thrive all over Cambridge. Along Mass. Ave. in Central Square, you'll find a particularly appealing, eclectic mix.

Dressing to Dine

Boston is a college town with a down-to-earth attitude. A few lonely restaurants still ask that men wear jackets at dinner, but most have no formal dress code. At casual restaurants near campuses and in tourist areas, just about anything goes, particularly at lunch. That includes shorts in the summer and jeans and sneakers all year.

Hot on the trail of celebrity chefs

So you've seen a certain Boston-area chef on TV, in a national magazine, or at a culinary expo. The thrill of dropping a big name may not compare with being the first to "discover" an emerging talent, but the big name usually is a reliable indicator of excellent dining. In cooking, unlike a lot of other reputation-driven fields, fame generally does correlate with talent.

Important note: Celebrity is time-consuming; if you're planning a special trip to bask in the glow, call ahead to make sure the chef whose name you want to drop plans to be behind the stove — or, is still in the kitchen.

Here's a selection of Boston's noted chefs and the restaurants the chefs own or run (most do both):

✔ Todd English: **Olives,** 10 City Sq., Charlestown (☎ 617-242-1999); **Bonfire,** in the Boston Park Plaza Hotel, 50 Park Plaza (☎ 617-262-3473); and **KingFish Hall,** 1 Faneuil Hall Marketplace (☎ 617-523-8862), reservations only for six or more.

✔ Gordon Hamersley: **Hamersley's Bistro,** 553 Tremont St., South End (☎ 617-423-2700).

✔ Ken Oringer: **Clio,** in the Eliot Hotel, 370 Commonwealth Ave., Back Bay (☎ 617-536-7200).

✔ Lydia Shire: **Locke-Ober,** 3–4 Winter Place (☎ 617-542-1340). Jackets are suggested for men; no shorts or sneakers allowed.

✔ Jasper White: **Summer Shack,** 149 Alewife Brook Parkway, Cambridge (☎ 617-520-9500). Reservations are not accepted.

The key phrase in the previous paragraph was *at casual restaurants.* At the more upscale places, if you take the time to look presentable, you should fit in better, and the staff may even take you more seriously. Save your breath — I've heard all the arguments. In theory, yes, you should get the same treatment whether you're in footie pajamas or a tux. Get over that attitude.

Unmoved? I'll appeal to your conscience. Even if you're not paying, consider the people who chose that expensive restaurant for the eatery's "wow" factor, and try not to look as if you're about to come in off the bench.

Trimming the Fat from Your Budget

Boston dining is terrific, but this city isn't New Orleans or San Francisco — you're not here just to eat. You'll probably want some cash left over for other activities.

The best cost-cutting move is to eat your big meal at lunch. Many restaurants serve dinner only, but the ones that open at midday (or even for breakfast) offer great values at lunch.

Other strategies include the following:

✔ Split an appetizer or dessert.

✔ Skip the alcohol or enjoy a before- or after-dinner drink from your private (and cheaper) stash in your room.

✔ If possible, skip beverages altogether — those $2 Diet Cokes can really add up.

✔ Order the fixed-price or *prix-fixe* menu (not available everywhere but always a good deal).

✔ Plan a picnic for lunch (see Chapter 15 for suggestions) and run up the bill at dinner.

A server who rattles off daily specials without prices may be busy or forgetful — or may be counting on your reluctance to look cheap in front of your friends or family. Always ask, and no $23 plate of noodles (true story) will ever sneak up on you.

A final thought: A fancy dinner every night is no vacation for anyone but a hard-core foodie. Give yourself a break, dip into the less-expensive categories, and chow down. You just may like the experience.

Tackling Tipping, Taxes, and Trimmings

The Massachusetts meal tax (which also applies to take-out food) is 5%. Tip three or four times the tax, and you're set. Don't leave less than 15% unless the service was awful, and round up, not down — that extra dollar means more to your server than to you.

If you're with a large group (six, eight, or more, depending on the restaurant), the check may include a service charge. Examine the total before accidentally tipping twice.

Also, valet parking can cost up to $18 at restaurants, so ask before making your reservation.

Making Reservations

 Reserve a table for Friday or Saturday night at any restaurant that takes reservations. If you already know where you want to eat, try to call before you leave home. If the night you want is booked, call when you reach Boston and ask if there have been any cancellations. At lunch, a party of two usually shouldn't have trouble landing a table, but a reservation is a good idea for larger groups.

Boston is an early city, even on weekends. Don't count on dropping in and getting a table at what seems to you to be an off-peak hour. "Early" is 5:30 or 6:00 p.m., and "too late" can be as early as 9:30 p.m.

 Some places let you eat at the bar without a reservation. The location is not ideal — the menu may have different choices from the menu in the dining room, and you'll probably be breathing secondhand smoke — but this option works if you're desperate to check out a particular restaurant. Make sure the host or hostess knows you're willing to move if there's a last-minute cancellation.

Lighting Up — or Not!

You'll find smoked food at a ton of establishments, but smoking people are less welcome. The law is tough: *Most restaurants ban smoking in dining areas,* and smaller places don't allow diners to light up at all. If you must have a smoke, say so when you make your reservation, and expect to wind up in or near the bar.

Look, up in the sky — it's a restaurant!

Boston has not one but two high-altitude restaurants that attract tourists and people celebrating special occasions. The food at The Bay Tower and Top of the Hub is quite good, but what you're paying for is the view. Ask for a table by the window when you make your reservation (The Bay Tower has more front-row seats than Top of the Hub). If the person you talk to can't guarantee a seat with a view, just enjoy a drink in the lounge, and eat somewhere else.

The Bay Tower (☎ **617-723-1666;** Internet: www.baytower.com) is on the 33rd floor of 60 State St., overlooking Faneuil Hall Marketplace, downtown, and the airport. This restaurant serves dinner Monday through Saturday. **Top of the Hub** (☎ **617-536-1775**) is on the 52nd floor of the Prudential Tower, 800 Boylston St., Back Bay. The Top serves lunch Monday through Saturday, Sunday brunch, and dinner daily.

Chapter 14

Boston's Best Restaurants

● ●

In This Chapter

▶ Eating in my favorite places

▶ Stalking the neighborhoods

▶ Categorizing by price, location, and cuisine

● ●

*B*y now you're probably pretty hungry, so I'll jump right in. This
chapter lists and reviews my favorite restaurants. I also give you
suggestions on neighborhoods to wander when you're hungry but not
set on where you want to eat.

The Kid Friendly icon indicates restaurants your family will like, and
that will like your family. Most have children's menus; all offer friendly
service and not-too-challenging fare that can make any homesick young-
ster feel a little more settled. (Adventurous palates will find reasonable
options, too.) As with hotels, the absence of the icon doesn't mean kids
are unwelcome — but think twice if your heirs tend to get rambunctious.
If you're unsure, ask someone at the restaurant before you make a
reservation.

Keep in mind that when reservations are recommended, that means for
dinner, and for large parties at lunch.

The $ symbols that accompany each review give an idea of the price of
dinner for one. That covers an appetizer, main course, dessert, and one
nonalcoholic drink, not including tax and tip. The listings also include
a price range (see Table 14-1) for main courses. The price ranges are
estimates — adjust accordingly if you order truffles, lobster, and wine
from Château d'Expensive, or if you split an appetizer, drink water,
stick to pasta, and skip dessert.

Table 14-1	Key to Restaurant Dollar Signs
Dollar Signs	*Price Range*
$	$20 and less
$$	$21–$30
$$$	$31–$45
$$$$	$46 and up

For restaurant locations, see the "Boston Dining" or "Cambridge Dining" maps in this chapter. (Eateries described in Chapters 13 and 15 also appear on these maps.)

My Favorite Boston-Area Restaurants

Aujourd'hui
$$$$ Back Bay CONTEMPORARY AMERICAN

The restaurant that puts the "special" in "special occasion" and the "expense" in "expense account" occupies a striking space on the second floor of the luxurious Four Seasons Hotel. The excellent cuisine incorporates seasonal ingredients and inventive preparations, but this *is* a hotel dining room, so don't expect anything too wild. Seafood is a marvelous choice (there's always a lobster dish), and the desserts are amazing. The element that makes the experience unforgettable is service so good that *superlative* doesn't go far enough.

In the Four Seasons Hotel, 200 Boylston St. (opposite the Public Garden). ☎ 617-351-2071. Reservations suggested (required on holidays). T: Arlington (Green Line); walk one block on Boylston Street opposite the Public Garden. Parking: Valet. Main courses: $35–$45. AE, DC, DISC, MC, V. Open: Mon–Fri 6:30–11:00 a.m., Sat–Sun 7–11 a.m. (breakfast); Sun–Fri 11:30 a.m.–2:30 p.m. (lunch; brunch Sun); Mon–Sat 5:30–10:30 p.m., Sun 6:00–10:30 p.m (dinner).

The Blue Room
$$$$ Cambridge/Kendall Square ECLECTIC

The trek to the Blue Room is more like a pilgrimage for diners who seek unusual cuisine in unusual locations. Tech-heavy East Cambridge is not a fine-dining mecca, but the Blue Room is a revelation: Steve Johnson grills, roasts, and braises up a storm, creating gutsy, flavorful food in a sleek but comfortable setting. You'll find the best roast chicken in town among the inventive main courses, which always include admirable vegetarian options. In warm weather, seating on the brick patio is available.

1 Kendall Sq. (off Hampshire Street). ☎ *617-494-9034. Reservations recommended. T: Kendall (Red Line); cross through the Marriott lobby, turn left, follow Broadway two long blocks (across the train tracks), bear right onto Hampshire Street, and walk ½ block. Main courses: $18–$24. AE, DC, DISC, MC, V. Open: Sun–Thurs 5:30–10:00 p.m., Fri–Sat 5:30–11:00 p.m. (dinner); Sun 11:00 a.m.–2:30 p.m. (brunch).*

Bob the Chef's Jazz Cafe

$$ South End   AMERICAN

Southern food and jazz are a match made in heaven, so I guess that makes Bob the Chef's heavenly. Here you'll find "glorifried" chicken, meat loaf, pan-fried catfish, barbecued ribs, and more, served with your choice of two side dishes. I like the mac and cheese and the collard greens; your friendly server can help you decide. The sophisticated setting brings to mind a jazz club, and that's the soundtrack here — live Thursday though Saturday nights and at Sunday brunch.

604 Columbus Ave. (at Northampton Street). ☎ *617-536-6204. Reservations not required. T: Massachusetts Avenue (Orange Line); turn right, follow Mass. Ave. to Columbus Avenue, turn right, and walk one block. Main courses: $9–$15. AE, DISC, MC, V. Open: Tues–Wed 11:30 a.m.–10:00 p.m., Thurs–Sat 11:30 a.m. to midnight; Sun 11 a.m.–9 p.m. (brunch until 3 p.m.).*

Border Café

$$ Cambridge/Harvard Square   SOUTHWESTERN

Huge crowds don't necessarily mean high quality, unless the crowds have been huge since the mid-'80s. The nonstop party at the Border Café runs on heaping portions of Tex-Mex, Cajun, and occasionally Caribbean food — and, of course, beer and margaritas. The cheerful but frantic staff keeps the peace with plenty of chips and salsa. Except at off-hours, there are no quick meals (the wait for a table can stretch out), so be in the mood to linger and join the party.

32 Church St. (at Palmer Street). ☎ *617-864-6100. Reservations not accepted. T: Harvard (Red Line); use Church Street exit (at front of Alewife-bound train), go right at turnstiles, and walk one block. Main courses: $7–$15. AE, MC, V. Open: Mon–Thurs 11 a.m.–1 a.m.; Fri–Sat 11 a.m.–2 a.m.; Sun noon to 11 p.m.*

Buddha's Delight

$ Chinatown   VEGETARIAN VIETNAMESE

Things are not always what they seem: A dingy staircase leads to a comfortable second-floor dining room, the sleek decor belies the friendly service, and the delicious food is actually good for you. Buddha's Delight doesn't serve meat, poultry, fish, or dairy (some beverages are made with condensed milk). Instead, the chefs transform tofu and gluten into

Boston Dining

Au Bon Pain (Prudential Center) **8**
Au Bon Pain (State St.) **42**
Aujourd'hui **24**
The Bay Tower **41**
Ben & Jerry's **13**
Bertucci's (Back Bay) **16**
Bertucci's (Faneuil Hall) **40**
blu **48**
Bob the Chef's Jazz Café **9**
The Bristol Lounge **24**
Buddha's Delight **53**
Café Jaffa **7**
Caffè dello Sport **31**
Caffè Graffiti **36**
Caffè Paradiso **38**
Caffè Vittoria **29**
Casa Romero **4**
Chau Chow City **51**
China Pearl **52**
Clio **2**
Daily Catch **35**
Durgin–Park **40**

The Elephant Walk **1**
Emack & Bolio's **6**
Empire Garden Restaurant **54**
Giacomo's **34**
Grill 23 & Bar **17**
Grillfish **18**
Hamersley's Bistro **20**
Hard Rock Café **15**
Herrell's **12**
Icarus **19**
Il Panino Express **28**
JP Licks **3**
KingFish Hall **40**
La Summa **32**
Legal Sea Foods
  (Copley) **14**
Legal Sea Foods
  (Park Square) **23**
Legal Sea Foods
  (Prudential) **10**
Legal Sea Foods
  (Waterfront) **45**

Le Gamin Café **21**
L'Espalier **5**
Les Zygomates **50**
Locke-Ober **46**
Mamma Maria **33**
Mantra **47**
Mike's Pastry **30**
Olives **27**
Piccola Venezia **37**
Pizzeria Regina **27**
Ritz Lounge **25**
Savenor's
  Supermarket **26**
Sel de la Terre **44**
Souper Salad
  (Center Plaza) **39**
Souper Salad
  (State St.) **43**
Souper Salad
  (Summer St.) **49**
Top of the Hub **11**
Via Matta **22**

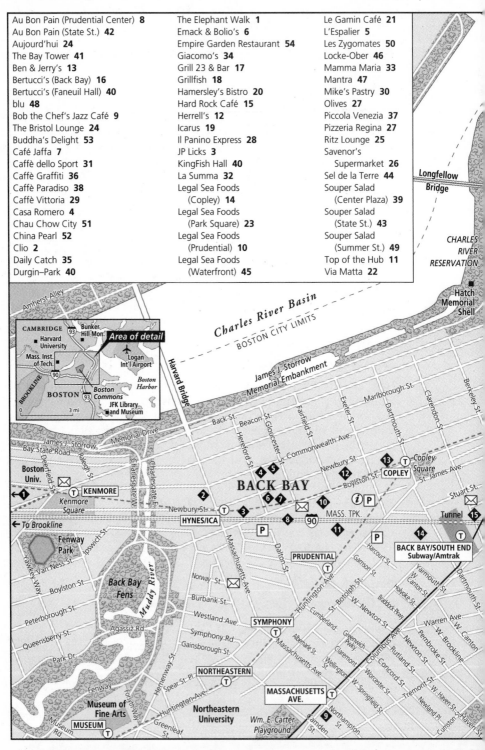

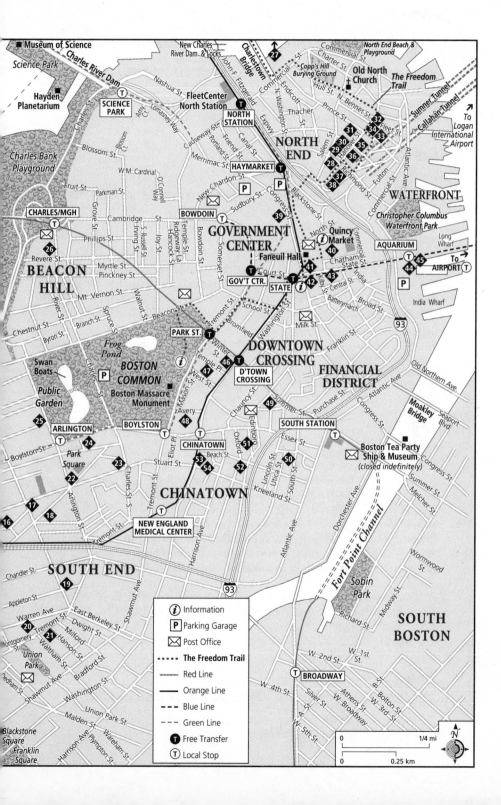

chicken, pork, beef, shrimp, and even lobster taste-alikes. This restaurant produces bounteous portions of unusual but delicious food. Try the delightful fresh spring roll appetizer; then start experimenting.

5 Beach St. (at Washington Street), 2nd Floor. ☎ *617-451-2395. Reservations not required. T: Chinatown (Orange Line); follow Washington Street (past the China Trade Center) one block. Main courses: $6–$12. MC, V. Open: Sun–Thurs 11:00 a.m.–9:30 p.m.; Fri–Sat 11:00 a.m.–10:30 p.m.*

Café Jaffa
$ Back Bay   MIDDLE EASTERN

Newbury and Boylston streets are consumer central, and the last thing you want in the middle of a shopping spree is a meal that weighs you down — physically or financially. Café Jaffa is a favorite with shoppers and students, who come here for low prices, high quality, and good-sized portions. Traditional Middle Eastern dishes such as falafel, baba ghanoush, and hummus make a not-too-filling break from bargain hunting; lamb, beef, and chicken kabobs, burgers, and steak tips are heartier and equally tasty. The exposed-brick, glass-fronted room makes a good setting for mid-afternoon coffee, too.

48 Gloucester St. (between Boylston and Newbury streets). ☎ *617-536-0230. Reservations not required. T: Hynes/ICA (Green Line B, C, or D); use Newbury Street exit, turn right, walk two blocks, and turn right. Main courses: $5–$13. AE, DC, DISC, MC, V. Open: Mon–Thurs 11:00 a.m.–10:30 p.m.; Fri–Sat 11 a.m.–11 p.m.; Sun 1–10 p.m.*

Casa Romero
$$$ Back Bay   CLASSIC MEXICAN

Hidden in an alley, Casa Romero is a romantic destination a stone's throw from busy Newbury Street. The peaceful atmosphere and dimly lit rooms almost make the food secondary, but this food demands attention. The authentic cuisine is nothing like what you find at Tex-Mex drive-throughs — the food is fresh, savory, and not too heavy. Unusual ingredients (cactus salad is an unexpectedly good starter) and flavor-layered sauces make meat, poultry, and seafood shine. The enclosed garden is pleasant in warm weather, but seating is on plastic furniture.

30 Gloucester St. (off Newbury Street; entrance in alley). ☎ *617-536-4341. Reservations recommended. T: Hynes/ICA (Green Line B, C, or D); turn right onto Mass. Ave. and right onto Newbury Street, walk two blocks, and turn left. Main courses: $14–$27. DISC, MC, V. Open: Sun–Thurs 5–10 p.m.; Fri–Sat 5–11 p.m.*

Daily Catch
$$ Downtown/North End   SEAFOOD AND SOUTHERN ITALIAN

For a true North End experience, try this tiny storefront under an awning that reads "Calamari Café." The open kitchen cranks out hearty, garlicky food that often revolves around squid, right down to the garlic-and-oil pasta sauce (which includes chopped calamari) and the black pasta (which includes squid ink). The casual atmosphere — some dishes land on the table still in the cooking skillet — is part of the fun.

323 Hanover St. (between Richmond and Prince streets). ☎ *617-523-8567. Reservations not accepted. T: Haymarket (Green or Orange Line); cross under Expressway, turn right, follow Cross Street to Hanover Street, turn left, and go 1½ blocks. Main courses: $12–$19. No credit cards. Open: Sun–Thurs noon to 10:30 p.m.; Fri–Sat noon to 11 p.m.*

Dalí

$$ Cambridge/Somerville   SPANISH

Appetizers with no main course make a good dinner-party menu at home — and they can be even better at a restaurant. The main attraction at this boisterous place is delectable *tapas*. The appetizer-like plates of hot or cold meat, seafood, vegetables, and cheese are so tasty that you won't miss the big platter of one boring thing. Instead, you'll want to ask for another order or two of sausages, cold potato salad, salmon croquettes, or whatever catches your fancy. The wait at the bar can be long, but the atmosphere is festive and the payoff huge — unlike the bill. (A conventional meal of Spanish classics will push the tab into $$$ territory.)

415 Washington St., Somerville. ☎ *617-661-3254. Internet:* www.Dali Restaurant.com. *Reservations not accepted. T: Harvard (Red Line); cross through Harvard Yard and follow Kirkland Street from the back of Memorial Hall to the intersection of Washington and Beacon streets. It's a $5 cab ride. Tapas: $4–$8. Main courses: $17–$21. AE, DC, MC, V. Open: Daily 6–11 p.m. in summer; 5:30–11:00 p.m. in winter.*

Durgin-Park

$$ Downtown/Faneuil Hall Marketplace   NEW ENGLAND

If you prefer hearty food and sassy service to fancy ingredients and unpronounceable dishes, Durgin-Park is the classic New England experience. Bostonians and out-of-towners come to the long, multiple-party tables (smaller ones are available) for generous helpings of delicious, down-to-earth fare. The cornbread and baked beans are famous, the prime rib and fresh seafood are delicious, and the strawberry shortcake is as fresh as some of the waitresses. That's right — like a 19th-century theme restaurant, Durgin-Park (founded in 1827) has a shtick: borderline-belligerent service. Far from being cranky, many waitresses are actually pleasant, but a trip into the orbit of someone who takes the job seriously can be an eye-opening experience.

340 Faneuil Hall Marketplace (in the North Market building). ☎ *617-227-2038. Reservations accepted for parties of 15 or more. T: Government Center (Green or*

Cambridge Dining

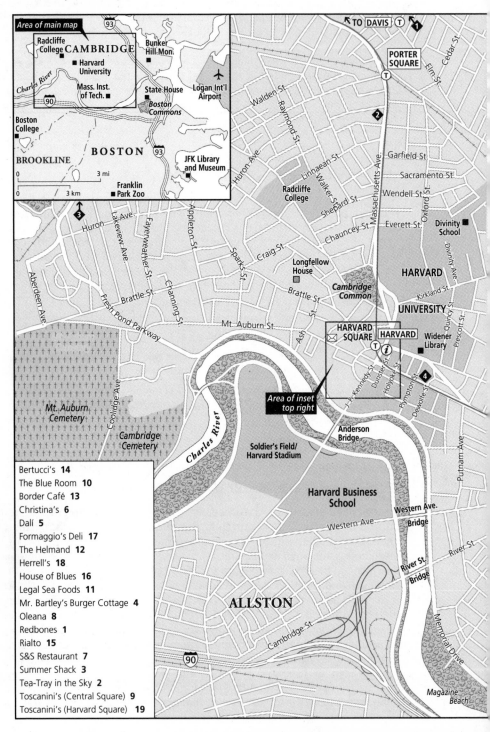

Area of main map

93

Radcliffe College CAMBRIDGE

Bunker Hill Mon.

Harvard University

Charles River

90

Mass. Inst. of Tech.

State House

Boston Commons

Logan Int'l Airport

Boston College

BROOKLINE

BOSTON

93

JFK Library and Museum

0   3 mi
0   3 km

Franklin Park Zoo

TO DAVIS

PORTER SQUARE

Cedar St.

Elm St.

Walden St.

Raymond St.

Garfield St.

Sacramento St.

Huron Ave.

Linnaean St.

Walker St.

Shepard St.

Massachusetts Ave.

Wendell St.

Oxford St.

Everett St.

Divinity School

Huron Ave.

Lakeview Ave.

Fayerweather St.

Appleton St.

Sparks St.

Craig St.

Chauncey St.

Radcliffe College

Longfellow House

Divinity Ave.

HARVARD

Aberdeen Ave.

Brattle St.

Channing St.

Fresh Pond Parkway

Mt. Auburn St.

Brattle St.

Ash St.

Cambridge Common

Kirkland St.

UNIVERSITY

Quincy St.

Prescott St.

HARVARD SQUARE

HARVARD

Widener Library

Coolidge Ave.

Mt. Auburn Cemetery

Cambridge Cemetery

J. F. Kennedy St.

Dunster St.

Holyoke St.

Plympton St.

DeWolfe St.

Area of inset top right

Charles River

Anderson Bridge

Soldier's Field/ Harvard Stadium

Putnam Ave.

Harvard Business School

Western Ave.

Western Ave.

Bridge

ALLSTON

River St.

Bridge

River St.

Memorial Drive

90

Cambridge St.

Magazine Beach

Bertucci's **14**
The Blue Room **10**
Border Café **13**
Christina's **6**
Dalí **5**
Formaggio's Deli **17**
The Helmand **12**
Herrell's **18**
House of Blues **16**
Legal Sea Foods **11**
Mr. Bartley's Burger Cottage **4**
Oleana **8**
Redbones **1**
Rialto **15**
S&S Restaurant **7**
Summer Shack **3**
Tea-Tray in the Sky **2**
Toscanini's (Central Square) **9**
Toscanini's (Harvard Square) **19**

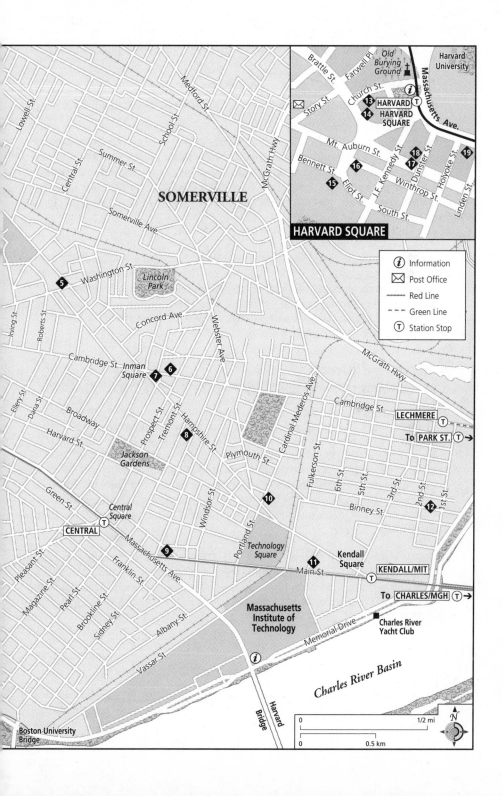

HARVARD SQUARE

i Information

✉ Post Office

—— Red Line

--- Green Line

Ⓣ Station Stop

Blue Line) or Haymarket (Orange Line); follow the crowds. Main courses: $5–$25; specials $19–$40. AE, DC, DISC, MC, V. Open: Mon–Thurs 11:30 a.m.–10:00 p.m., Fri–Sat 11:30 a.m.–10:30 p.m., Sun 11:30 a.m.–9:00 p.m. (lunch menu until 2:30 p.m.).

The Elephant Walk

$$$ Back Bay/Kenmore Square   FRENCH AND CAMBODIAN

This restaurant is the worst-kept "secret" on the Boston culinary scene, but the Elephant Walk does feel like a great find. The unique combination of French and Cambodian isn't the mishmash that plagues fusion cuisine; rather, each side of the menu stands alone and complements the other. On the French side, you may find pan-seared filet mignon. On the Cambodian side, *curry de crevettes* (yup, that's French) is a perfect shrimp dish. The accommodating staff offers excellent advice, and tofu can replace animal protein in many dishes.

900 Beacon St. (at St. Mary's Street; four blocks past Kenmore Square). ☎ *617-247-1500. Internet:* www.elephantwalk.com. *Reservations suggested at dinner Sun–Thurs, not accepted Fri–Sat. T: St. Mary's (Green Line C). Parking: Valet at dinner only. Main courses: $10–$24. AE, DISC, MC, V. Open: Mon–Sat 11:30 a.m.–2:30 p.m.; Mon–Thurs 5–10 p.m.; Fri 5–11 p.m.; Sat 4:30–11:00 p.m.; Sun 4:30–10:00 p.m.*

Giacomo's Ristorante

$$ Downtown/North End   SEAFOOD AND SOUTHERN ITALIAN

For pure inconvenience — long lines, no credit cards, improbably cramped space — you'll have a hard time beating Giacomo's. So why the crowds? You also can't beat the food. Go early, before the queue gets too long. Check the board for outstanding daily specials, take the chef's advice, or create your own dish from the list of ingredients and sauces. Salmon with sun-dried tomatoes over fettuccine is my favorite, but I've never had anything short of fabulous. Portions are large, and even dainty eaters who declare themselves stuffed can't help trying just one more mouthful.

355 Hanover St. (near Fleet Street). ☎ *617-523-9026. Reservations not accepted. T: Haymarket (Green or Orange Line); cross under Expressway, turn right, follow Cross Street to Hanover Street, turn left, and walk three full blocks. Main courses: $14–$20. No credit cards. Open: Mon–Thurs 5–10 p.m.; Fri–Sat 5:00–10:30 p.m.; Sun 4–10 p.m.*

Grill 23 & Bar

$$$$ Back Bay   AMERICAN

The best steakhouse in Boston earns that title with an irresistible mix of macho atmosphere and splendid food. Grill 23 is a favorite business destination with a raucous crowd that seems to have sealed a deal minutes before. If they're smart, the young (and old) turks give a moment's thought to their plates. The steak and chops are magnificent, and the more inventive options — for instance, top-notch meatloaf — are equally satisfying but not as *Flintstones*-like. As at any self-respecting steakhouse, the side dishes (à la carte) and desserts are diet-busting delights.

161 Berkeley St. (at Stuart Street). ☎ *617-542-2255. Internet:* www.grill23.com. *Reservations recommended. T: Arlington (Green Line); follow Boylston Street one block away from the Public Garden, turn left, and walk two full blocks. Parking: Valet. Main courses: $21–$40. AE, DC, DISC, MC, V. Open: Mon–Thurs 5:30–10:30 p.m.; Fri–Sat 5:30–11:00 p.m.; Sun 5:30–10:00 p.m.*

Grillfish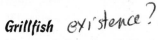

$$ Back Bay/South End   SEAFOOD

The specialty at this cavernous, clamorous restaurant is grilled seafood, a somewhat neglected option in Boston. Prepared over an open fire, menu standards and daily specials pick up a hint of smoke; each comes with sweet onion or garlic-tomato sauce. Marsala or piccata sauce accompanies sautéed dishes, and pasta comes with several kinds of grilled shellfish (including shrimp scampi with tomatoes). The jovial crowd can get noisy, so ask for a table near the windows or on the small seasonal patio if you're in the mood for conversation. Grillfish is part of a small chain with roots in the Miami area and some locations around Washington, D.C.

162 Columbus Ave. (between Arlington and Berkeley streets). ☎ *617-357-1620. Internet:* www.grillfish.com. *Reservations accepted for parties of six or more. T: Arlington (Green Line); follow Arlington Street away from the Public Garden, cross Columbus Avenue, turn right (at the Park Plaza Castle), and walk ½ block. Main courses: $10–$22. AE, DISC, MC, V. Sun–Mon 5:30–10:00 p.m.; Tues–Thurs 5:30–11:00 p.m.; Fri–Sat 5:30 p.m. to midnight.*

The Helmand

$$ Cambridge/Kendall Square   AFGHAN

In Cambridge's United Nations of dining, the Helmand stands out. This restaurant offers the tasty food, friendly service, and reasonable prices of an ethnic restaurant in an elegant setting that may make you wonder what the catch is. (The Helmand is *too* popular, would be my grumpy answer — as was the case even before the world turned its attention to Afghanistan.) Afghan cuisine is Middle Eastern with Indian and Pakistani influences, filling but not heavy, redolent of spices. Vegetarians will be happy; meat accents many dishes instead of dominating, and many meatless choices are available. My pick is baked pumpkin with meat sauce, but that's a tough decision — everything is flat-out delicious.

143 First St. (at Bent Street). ☎ *617-492-4646. Reservations recommended. T: Lechmere (Green Line); walk past rear of trolley, pass through tunnel on right, and go 6½ short blocks on First Street, passing CambridgeSide Galleria mall. Main courses: $10–$18. AE, MC, V. Open: Sun–Thurs 5–10 p.m.; Fri–Sat 5–11 p.m.*

Icarus

$$$$ South End ECLECTIC

This subterranean hideaway is the most romantic restaurant in town (an insanely competitive category), a grand space that abounds with personal touches. The regularly changing menu is equally quirky and equally enjoyable. Chef-owner Christopher Douglass simply transforms his fresh local ingredients. The no-nonsense descriptions (lemony grilled chicken with garlic and herbs, polenta with braised exotic mushrooms) can't do justice to the imaginative interplay of flavors and textures. Save room for an unbelievable dessert; even chocolate fiends love the fruit sorbets.

3 Appleton St. (off Tremont Street). ☎ *617-426-1790. Reservations recommended. T: Arlington (Green Line); follow Arlington Street away from the Public Garden, across the Mass. Pike. (about six blocks), bear right onto Tremont Street, and go one long block. Or Back Bay (Orange Line); use Clarendon Street exit (at back of Forest Hills–bound train), turn right, walk four blocks, turn left onto Appleton Street, and go two blocks. Parking: Valet. Main courses: $21–$33. AE, DC, DISC, MC, V. Open: Mon–Thurs 6–10 p.m.; Fri 6:00–10:30 p.m.; Sat 5:30–10:30 p.m.; Sun 5:30–10:00 p.m. Closed Sun July–Aug.*

La Summa

$$ Downtown/North End SOUTHERN ITALIAN

As newcomers push the North End up the *nouveau* scale, neighborhood favorites such as La Summa tick along, offering homey food in a welcoming atmosphere. House-made pasta and desserts attract locals and savvy passersby to a restaurant that also serves terrific seafood and meat dishes. Check the specials board on the way in, and if lobster ravioli is on there, don't hesitate. Just be sure to save room for sweets.

30 Fleet St. ☎ *617-523-9503. Reservations recommended. T: Haymarket (Green or Orange Line); cross under Expressway, turn right, and follow Cross Street to Hanover Street. Follow Hanover Street to Fleet Street, turn right, and go 1½ blocks. Main courses: $11–$24. AE, DC, DISC, MC, V. Open: Daily 4:30–10:30 p.m.*

Legal Sea Foods

$$$ Back Bay, Downtown/Waterfront, other locations SEAFOOD

Out-of-towners arrive in Boston, unpack, and demand seafood. The ones who wind up here are in for a treat: the freshest seafood around. From roots as a counter in a fish store, "Legal's" has grown into a sprawling chain that incorporates no-frills filets and inventive preparations. This is the place for perennial favorites (lobsters the size of a laptop, every species of fish that's available fresh on the day you eat here) and seasonal specials (shad roe, soft-shell crabs). Legal Sea Foods is the place for do-believe-the-hype clam and fish chowder, sublime raw-bar offerings, and even scrumptious desserts. This eatery is never quiet, and service is pleasant but somewhat slapdash — that's part of the experience.

Until recently, the long wait for a table was also part of the experience. The Prudential Center branch takes reservations at lunch only, so go there if you can't abide waiting. Another good strategy: Go for a late lunch or early dinner. Or put your name on the list and see what *not* being an out-of-towner feels like.

Also at 255 State St. (☎ **617-227-3115**; T: Aquarium [Blue Line]), one block from the New England Aquarium, Waterfront; 36 Park Sq., between Columbus Avenue and Stuart Street, Back Bay (☎ **617-426-4444**; T: Arlington [Green Line]); Copley Place, second level, Back Bay (☎ **617-266-7775**); and 5 Cambridge Center, Kendall Square, Cambridge (☎ **617-864-3400**; T: Kendall/MIT [Red Line]).

800 Boylston St., in the Prudential Center. ☎ 617-266-6800. Internet: www.legalseafoods.com. *Reservations recommended and only accepted at lunch. T: Prudential (Green Line E) or Copley (Green Line); follow Boylston Street three blocks, past the Boston Public Library. Main courses: Dinner $14–$29; lobster is market price (at least $15 a pound). AE, DC, DISC, MC, V. Open: Mon–Thurs 11:30 a.m.–10:30 p.m.; Fri–Sat 11:00 a.m.–11:30 p.m.; Sun noon to 10 p.m.*

Le Gamin Cafe
$ South End FRENCH

Everything old really is new again: Here's a classic cafe in the trendy South End. The top-notch food and reasonable prices make Le Gamin a neighborhood favorite. Everything from ultra-rich hot chocolate to crackling-fresh salad is just what you'd expect; sandwiches with fillings you choose are just what you want. The loiterer-friendly atmosphere makes Le Gamin a good choice for coffee or a glass of wine with a friend. This location is the first outoftown branch of a small New York chain.

550 Tremont St. (at Waltham Street). ☎ 617-654-8969. Internet: www.legamin.com. *Reservations not required. T: Back Bay (Orange Line); use Clarendon Street exit (at back of Forest Hills–bound train), turn right, and walk five blocks. Main courses: $5–$12. MC, V. Open: Mon–Fri 10 a.m. to midnight; Sat–Sun 8 a.m. to midnight.*

L'Espalier
$$$$ Back Bay NEW ENGLAND AND FRENCH

Diners disappear into this elegant townhouse off Newbury Street like guests arriving at a dinner party, and in a way, that's just what guests are (well, except for the pesky matter of money). The gorgeous 19th-century dining rooms contrast pleasingly with chef and co-owner Frank McClelland's innovative, deliriously good food. French techniques and fresh local ingredients — seafood, game, unusual produce, artisan cheeses — collide to produce unusual dishes that never cross the line into brain-teaser territory. The dessert cart is worth a look, and this is one of the only places in town where the after-dinner cheese tray gets deserved attention.

30 Gloucester St. (off Newbury Street). ☎ *617-262-3023. Internet:* www. lespalier.com. *Reservations required. T: Hynes/ICA (Green Line B, C, or D); turn right onto Mass. Ave. and right onto Newbury Street, walk two blocks, and turn left. Parking: Valet. Prix fixe: $68 (three courses). Degustation menu (seven courses; tables for two or more): $85. AE, DISC, MC, V. Open: Mon–Sat 6–10 p.m.*

Les Zygomates
$$$ Downtown FRENCH BISTRO

A Parisian accent in the middle of the Big Dig, Les Zygomates (lay *zee-go-mat*) is a loose, lively antidote to the pandemonium outside. Primarily a wine bar, this bistro serves an excellent selection by the bottle, glass, and 2-ounce taste. Classic but original, the food is an artful mix of local ingredients and bistro favorites, such as braised lamb shank with garlic puree. The quirky neighborhood (technically the Leather District) attracts business lunchers and a stylish dinner crowd that lingers for live jazz.

129 South St. (between Tufts and Beach streets; two blocks from South Station). ☎ *617-542-5108. Internet:* www.winebar.com. *Reservations recommended. T: South Station (Red Line); cross Atlantic Avenue, turn left, walk one block to East Street, turn right, and walk one block to South Street. Or ask a construction worker. Parking: Valet at dinner only. Main courses: $15–$25; prix-fixe lunch: $15; prix-fixe dinner (Mon–Thurs only): $21. AE, DC, DISC, MC, V. Open: Mon–Fri 11 a.m.–1 a.m. (lunch menu until 2 p.m.); Sat 6 p.m.–1 a.m.*

Mamma Maria
$$$$ Downtown/North End NORTHERN ITALIAN

A fine-dining destination in a pasta-and-pizza neighborhood, Mamma Maria is the best restaurant in the North End. Plenty of competitors serve excellent food in no-frills settings, but this elegant townhouse a stone's throw from the Paul Revere House is the champ. The romantic atmosphere makes Mamma's a popular place for marriage proposals and anniversary dinners. The exquisite cuisine, which changes seasonally, always includes fabulous seafood dishes, daily pasta specials, and fork-tender osso buco. You won't even miss the pizza.

3 North Sq. (at Prince Street). ☎ *617-523-0077. Internet:* www.mammamaria.com. *Reservations recommended. T: Haymarket (Green or Orange Line); cross under*

Expressway, turn right, follow Cross Street to Hanover Street, and turn left. Walk two full blocks, go right onto Prince Street, and walk one block. Parking: Valet. Main courses: $19–$35. AE, DC, DISC, MC, V. Open: Sun–Thurs 5:00–9:30 p.m.; Fri–Sat 5:00–10:30 p.m.

Mr. Bartley's Burger Cottage

$ **Cambridge/Harvard Square   AMERICAN**

Down-to-earth burger joints are scarce in Harvard Square, which is more retail haven than college campus. But even Harvard students need ground beef (and turkey), and this is a great place for both. The college-town atmosphere is authentic, from the vintage posters to the chummy wait staff. Although meat is the main event, vegetarians can eat surprisingly well. Sublime onion rings round out a perfect burger-joint meal.

1246 Massachusetts Ave. (between Plympton and Bow streets). ☎ 617-354-6559. Reservations not required. T: Harvard (Red Line); with the Harvard Coop at your back, follow Mass. Ave. 3½ blocks. Main courses: $9 or less. No credit cards. Open: Mon–Wed, Sat 11 a.m.–9 p.m.; Thurs–Fri 11 a.m.–10 p.m.

Oleana

$$$ **Cambridge/Inman Square   MEDITERRANEAN**

Oleana is a sunny destination on even the dreariest night. The menu of seasonal offerings and timeless classics has something for everyone — adventurous or timid, vegetarian or meat-lover. Flavors are bold but not overwhelming, and the kitchen pays just as much attention to the little things (delectable deviled eggs) as to the more complicated creations. In the summer, ask for a table on the peaceful patio.

134 Hampshire St. (at Columbia Street). ☎ 617-661-0505. Reservations recommended. T: Central (Red Line); turn right on Prospect Street (at Starbucks), go four blocks, turn right onto Inman Street and go five blocks (a ten-minute walk). Main courses: $17–$24. AE, MC, V. Open: Sun–Thurs 5:30–10:00 p.m.; Fri–Sat 5:30–11:00 p.m.

Piccola Venezia

$$ **Downtown/North End   SOUTHERN ITALIAN**

Piccola Venezia probably loses some business because of location: the first block of the North End's main drag. Banish "maybe we'll find something better" from your mind — you won't be sorry. The menu combines home-style specialties with less red-sauce-intensive options, all in generous quantities. To give you some idea of the scope, tripe is a house specialty, polenta with mushrooms is a great starter, and a recent daily special of seafood lasagna made a delectable dinner *and* a filling lunch the next day. It's a cliché, but spaghetti and meatballs is a good choice, too.

263 Hanover St. ☎ 617-523-3888. Reservations suggested at dinner. T: Haymarket (Green or Orange Line); cross under Expressway, turn right, follow Cross Street to Hanover Street, turn left, and walk ½ block. Main courses: $10–$20; lunch special-ties: $5–$8. AE, DISC, MC, V. Open: Daily 11 a.m.–10 p.m. (lunch menu weekdays until 4 p.m.).

Pizzeria Regina
$ North End   ITALIAN

Regina's is the only Boston pizza place that competes with New York in quality and ambience. True, this restaurant is hard to find and the line can be long (though quickly moving). The too-good-to-be-true atmos-phere is the real thing, though, right down to waitresses who call you "honey" while warning you not to burn your mouth on the bubbling-hot pie that just arrived. The pizza, fresh from the brick oven, is that hot. And that good.

11½ Thacher St. (at North Margin Street). ☎ 617-227-0765. Reservations not accepted. T: Haymarket (Green or Orange Line); cross under Expressway, go straight onto Salem Street for three blocks, turn left onto Cooper Street, take next right onto North Margin Street, and go two blocks to Thacher Street. Pizza: $9–$16. No credit cards. Open: Mon–Thurs 11:00 a.m.–11:30 p.m.; Fri–Sat 11 a.m. to mid-night; Sun noon to 11 p.m.

Redbones
$$ Cambridge/Somerville   BARBECUE

"New England barbecue" doesn't exactly roll off the tongue. But you'll want these treats rolling right into your mouth after just one whiff of this place. The festive crowd and whimsical decor make an appealing first impression, and the down-home food backs things up. Expatriate Southerners, ravenous college students, and celebratory families relish the lively atmosphere and authentic fare. Barbecue in all incarnations shares the menu with Southern specialties such as catfish and pecan pie — all in abundant portions. Try to get a table at street level, not in the barlike space downstairs. Suck down a beer, make a dent in a pile of pulled pork or baby-back ribs, and you'll understand why there's a stack of paper napkins on every table.

55 Chester St. (off Elm Street), Somerville. ☎ 617-628-2200. Internet: www.red bonesbbq.com. *Reservations accepted for parties of 11 or more, Sun–Thurs. T: Davis (Red Line); right at turnstiles, right at exit, walk three blocks on Elm Street, and turn right onto Chester Street. Main courses: $7–$19. No credit cards. Open: Sun–Thurs noon to 10:30 p.m., Fri–Sat noon to 11:30 p.m. (lunch menu until 4 p.m.).*

Rialto

$$$$ **Cambridge/Harvard Square** **MEDITERRANEAN**

Rialto is my favorite Boston-area restaurant. This eatery has the sleek-chic vibe you'd expect at the Charles Hotel but never to the point of feeling snooty. Rialto assembles the elements that make a memorable dining experience unforgettable: a glamorous but comfortable space, attentive service, and, most important, Jody Adams's amazing food. She makes good use of seasonal local products, creating an overall effect of a sun-drenched field overlooking the Mediterranean. Try any seafood dish, any vegetarian option — anything, really. Now you're *so* cutting edge.

1 Bennett St. (in the Charles Hotel). ☎ *617-661-5050. Reservations suggested. T: Harvard (Red Line); follow Brattle Street two blocks, bear left onto Eliot Street, and go two blocks. Parking: Valet and validated. Main courses: $20–$36. AE, DC, MC, V. Open: Sun–Thurs 5:30–10:00 p.m.; Fri–Sat 5:30–11:00 p.m.*

S&S Restaurant

$ **Cambridge/Inman Square** **AMERICAN**

The best brunch in the area draws huge crowds to this Inman Square standby, which is also a fine place for a tasty meal during the week. Never mind the long walk from the T — on the way back, you'll be working off calories from the huge omelets, inventive pancakes and waffles, and excellent baked goods. On weekends, arrive early or schedule your day to allow for waiting time (and people watching). During non-brunch hours, the traditional deli menu includes breakfast anytime.

1334 Cambridge St. (at Hampshire Street). ☎ *617-354-0777. Reservations not accepted. T: Central (Red Line); turn right on Prospect Street (at Starbucks), go five blocks to Cambridge Street, and turn left. Or Harvard (Red Line); use Church Street exit (at front of Alewife-bound train), and turn left at turnstiles; then take Number 69 (Harvard-Lechmere) bus to Inman Square or walk ⁷/₁₀ mile up Cambridge Street It's a $5 cab ride. Main courses: $4–$12. No credit cards. Open: Mon–Sat 7 a.m. to midnight, Sun 8 a.m. to midnight (brunch weekends until 4 p.m.).*

Sel de la Terre

$$$ **Downtown/Waterfront** **MEDITERRANEAN**

The atmosphere at this upscale-but-not-too-upscale cousin of L'Espalier may be the neatest trick in town: Sel de la Terre is smack in the middle of the Big Dig, and inside you'd never know. Not that you'll imagine you're in Provence, but that's clearly where executive chef Geoff Gardner's heart is. Gardner transforms fresh local ingredients (especially seafood) into luscious food that's flavor-packed but never overwhelming. The crowd is businesslike at lunch, chic at dinner. And you don't even need to ruin your appetite by filling up on the delicious breads — which are for sale at the *boulangerie* near the entrance.

255 State St. (at Atlantic Avenue; one block from the New England Aquarium). ☎ *617-720-1300. Internet:* www.seldelaterre.com. *Reservations suggested. T: State (Blue or Orange Line) or Aquarium (Blue Line), if open; walk four blocks toward the harbor on State Street. Main courses: All $23. AE, DISC, MC, V. Open: Daily 11:30 a.m.–2:30 p.m. and 5:30–10:00 p.m.*

Hunting grounds: Restaurant-rich neighborhoods

Boston and Cambridge boast a number of areas where hungry people can scout around and emerge well fed. You don't want to be the first one through the door in these neighborhoods (trust me, the empty places are empty for a reason), but don't let a less-than-full room stop you, especially on a weeknight. Here's a list of Boston's neighborhoods and what to expect in each area's eateries:

✔ Head to the **North End** (Haymarket stop on the Green or Orange Line) for Italian food of every description in every price range. Ordinarily, I can't abide waiting, but in this area, lines are good. You'll see some locals in restaurants on high-traffic Hanover and Salem streets, but the neighborhood places are on the side streets.

✔ **Chinatown** (which has an Orange Line stop) is another promising neighborhood, and not just for Chinese food. Reasonably priced Asian cuisine abounds on Beach Street and the narrow streets that branch off between Washington Street (where the T stop is) and the Surface Artery (where the landmark Chinatown Arch is).

✔ Generally more expensive and more upscale, the **South End** (Back Bay stop on the Orange Line) is home to some big names and big budgets. Still, this is a neighborhood like any other, and people who live here need to eat, too — check out the area around Tremont and Clarendon streets, or stroll over to Washington Street.

✔ In Cambridge, **Harvard Square** (Red Line to Harvard) offers a good mix of places where students go with other students and places where visiting parents give their kids a break from the dining hall.

✔ **Central Square** is a social and culinary melting pot, with food from almost every corner of the globe. Follow Mass. Ave. in either direction from the T stop (Red Line to Central) and you'll probably find something that gets your nose's attention.

✔ Take the Red Line to Central and walk up Prospect Street (turn the corner at Starbucks) to **Inman Square,** where you'll find everything from Brazilian barbecue to Korean food within about five blocks.

Tea-Tray in the Sky
$ Cambridge   AMERICAN

Just walking into this little tearoom gives me a buzz, and I'm never sure if that's the caffeine or the trippy, *Alice's Adventures in Wonderland* decor. The mind-blowing selection of tea includes the pedestrian and the unusual, and complements scrumptious food and baked goods (made in-house). The pastries can substitute for "real" food but don't have to — unlike the dreary fare at some beverage-oriented places, the soups, salads, and focaccia sandwiches are outstanding. If you're shopping in Harvard and Porter squares, a stop here is a must.

1796 Mass. Ave. (at Lancaster Street). ☎ *617-492-8327. Reservations not accepted. T: Porter (Red Line); walk four blocks south on Mass. Ave. Main courses: $5–$12. AE, DISC, MC, V. Open: Tues–Thurs noon to 8:30 p.m.; Fri–Sat noon to 10 p.m.; Sun noon to 7 p. m. (closed Sun in summer).*

Index of Restaurants by Neighborhood

Back Bay
Aujourd'hui (Contemporary American, $$$$)
Café Jaffa (Middle Eastern, $)
Casa Romero (Classic Mexican, $$$)
The Elephant Walk (French and Cambodian, $$$)
Grill 23 & Bar (American, $$$$)
Legal Sea Foods (Seafood $$$)
L'Espalier (New England and French, $$$$)

Cambridge
The Blue Room (Eclectic, $$$)
Border Café (Southwestern, $$)
Dalí (Spanish, $$)
The Helmand (Afghan, $$)
Legal Sea Foods (Seafood, $$$)
Mr. Bartley's Burger Cottage (American, $)
Oleana (Mediterranean, $$$)
Redbones (Barbecue, $$)
Rialto (Mediterranean, $$$$)
S&S Restaurant (American, $)
Tea-Tray in the Sky (American, $)

Chinatown
Buddha's Delight (Vegetarian Vietnamese, $)

Downtown
Durgin-Park (New England, $$)
Legal Sea Foods (Seafood, $$$)
Les Zygomates (French Bistro, $$$)
Sel de la Terre (Mediterranean, $$$)

North End
Daily Catch (Seafood and Southern Italian, $$)
Giacomo's Ristorante (Seafood and Southern Italian, $$)
La Summa (Southern Italian, $$)
Mamma Maria (Northern Italian, $$$$)
Piccola Venezia (Southern Italian, $$)
Pizzeria Regina (Italian, $)

South End
Bob the Chef's Jazz Cafe (American, $$)
Grillfish (Seafood, $$)
Icarus (Eclectic, $$$$)
Le Gamin Café (French, $)

Index of Restaurants by Cuisine

American
Aujourd'hui (Back Bay, $$$$)
Bob the Chef's Jazz Cafe (South End, $$)
Durgin-Park (Downtown, $$)
Grill 23 & Bar (Back Bay, $$$$)
L'Espalier (Back Bay, $$$$)
Mr. Bartley's Burger Cottage (Cambridge/Harvard Square, $)
Redbones (Cambridge/Somerville, $$)
S&S Restaurant (Cambridge/Inman Square, $)
Tea-Tray in the Sky (Cambridge, $)

Asian
Buddha's Delight (Chinatown, $)
The Elephant Walk (Back Bay/Kenmore Square, $$$)

Eclectic
The Blue Room (Cambridge/Kendall Square, $$$)
Icarus (South End, $$$$)

French
The Elephant Walk (Back Bay/Kenmore Square, $$$)
Le Gamin Café (South End, $)
L'Espalier (Back Bay, $$$$)
Les Zygomates (Downtown, $$$)

Italian
Daily Catch (North End, $$)
Giacomo's Ristorante (North End, $$)
La Summa (North End, $$)
Mamma Maria (North End, $$$$)
Piccola Venezia (North End, $$)
Pizzeria Regina (North End, $)

Mediterranean
Dalí (Cambridge/Somerville, $$)
Oleana (Cambridge, $$$)
Rialto (Cambridge/Harvard Square, $$$$)
Sel de la Terre (Downtown, $$$)

Seafood
Daily Catch (North End, $$)
Giacomo's Ristorante (North End, $$)
Grillfish (South End, $$)
Legal Sea Foods (Back Bay and other locations, $$$)

South of the Border
Border Café (Cambridge/Harvard Square, $$)
Casa Romero (Back Bay, $$$)

Other Ethnic
Café Jaffa (Middle Eastern, Back Bay, $)
The Helmand (Afghan, Cambridge/Kendall Square, $$)

Index of Restaurants by Price

$$$$
Aujourd'hui (Contemporary American, Back Bay)
Grill 23 & Bar (American, Back Bay)
Icarus (Eclectic, South End)
L'Espalier (New England and French, Back Bay)
Mamma Maria (Northern Italian, North End)
Rialto (Mediterranean, Cambridge/Harvard Square)

$$$
The Blue Room (Eclectic, Cambridge/Kendall Square)
Casa Romero (Classic Mexican, Back Bay)
The Elephant Walk (French and Cambodian, Back Bay/Kenmore Square)
Legal Sea Foods (Seafood, Back Bay and other locations)

Les Zygomates (French Bistro, Downtown)

Oleana (Mediterranean, Cambridge/Inman Square)

Sel de la Terre (Mediterranean, Downtown/Waterfront)

$$

Bob the Chef's Jazz Cafe (American, South End)

Border Café (Southwestern, Cambridge/Harvard Square)

Daily Catch (Seafood and Southern Italian, North End)

Dalí (Spanish, Cambridge/Somerville)

Durgin-Park (New England, Downtown)

Giacomo's Ristorante (Seafood and Southern Italian, North End)

Grillfish (Seafood, South End)

The Helmand (Afghan, Cambridge/Kendall Square)

La Summa (Southern Italian, North End)

Piccola Venezia (Southern Italian, North End)

Redbones (Barbecue, Cambridge/Somerville)

$

Buddha's Delight (Vegetarian Vietnamese, Chinatown)

Café Jaffa (Middle Eastern, Back Bay)

Le Gamin Café (French, South End)

Mr. Bartley's Burger Cottage (American, Cambridge/Harvard Square)

Pizzeria Regina (Italian, North End)

S&S Restaurant (American, Cambridge/Inman Square)

Tea-Tray in the Sky (American, Cambridge)

Chapter 15

Snacks and Meals on the Go

● ●

In This Chapter

▶ Getting out: picnic food (and where to eat it)

▶ Linking with the chains

▶ *Tea*ing off

▶ Experiencing dim sum

▶ Finding the best coffee and ice cream

● ●

*M*ultiple courses, starched tablecloths, and courtly service have a time and place; that's usually *not* in the middle of a busy day of sightseeing. Here you'll get the scoop on grabbing a bite (outdoors and indoors), plus pointers on afternoon tea, dim sum, coffee, and ice cream.

For the locations of places mentioned in this chapter, see the "Boston Dining" and "Cambridge Dining" maps in Chapter 14.

Picking the Picnic Option

With the harbor here and the river there, Boston and Cambridge offer acres of waterfront space perfect for picnicking, and plenty of places to outfit your metaphorical picnic basket. Here are some airy options:

✔ Gathering food for your outdoor feast is a picnic (ouch!) at the **Colonnade food court** at Faneuil Hall Marketplace (T: Government Center [Green or Blue Line] or Haymarket [Orange Line]), which has plenty of variety, including enough to satisfy a large group. When you're set, cross Atlantic Avenue (under the Expressway) and discover the plaza at the end of **Long Wharf** or the benches and lawns of **Christopher Columbus Park.**

✔ In the North End, **Il Panino Express,** 266 Hanover St. (T: Haymarket [Green or Orange Line]; ☎ 617-720-5720), cranks out superb sandwiches, pasta, and pizza. Cross Hanover Street to Richmond Street and follow it four blocks downhill to **Christopher Columbus Park.**

✔ At the foot of Beacon Hill (near the Esplanade, a destination for concerts and movies all summer), **Savenor's Supermarket,** 160 Charles St. (T: Charles/MGH [Red Line]; ☎ **617-723-6328**) lets you load up on gourmet provisions before heading across the footbridge to the **Charles River Basin.**

✔ Harvard Square also affords easy access to the Charles. **Formaggio's Deli,** 81 Mount Auburn St., in the Garage mall (T: Harvard [Red Line]; ☎ **617-547-4795**), is more gourmet-sandwich mecca than traditional deli, with sandwiches that are stuffed yet sophisticated. Stake out a bench on the riverbank or a comfy spot at **John F. Kennedy Park,** at Kennedy Street and Memorial Drive.

Bound for Chains

National chains abound, but really, can't you do that at home? Two exceptions are especially useful if you're traveling with teenagers:

✔ The **Hard Rock Cafe,** 131 Clarendon St. (off Stuart Street), in the Back Bay (T: Back Bay [Orange Line]; ☎ **617-424-ROCK**), is the usual. If you don't know what to expect, ask the kids.

✔ The original **House of Blues** is at 96 Winthrop St. (off John F. Kennedy Street), Harvard Square, Cambridge (T: Harvard [Red Line]; ☎ **617-491-BLUE**). The drawing card is live music by talented locals and name visitors; the eclectic menu includes pizza and inventive pasta dishes, with Southern specialties at the Sunday gospel brunch. (See the listing in Chapter 23 for a more complete review.)

Local chains offer a less generic experience. Check out my favorite picks:

✔ The upscale pizzerias of **Bertucci's** appeal to adults and kids. The little ones can concentrate on the wood-burning brick ovens, and their caddies can exclaim over the plain and fancy pizzas and pastas. Handy branches are at Faneuil Hall Marketplace (behind Abercrombie & Fitch; ☎ **617-227-7889**); 43 Stanhope St. (around the corner from the Hard Rock Cafe); Back Bay (T: Back Bay [Orange Line]; ☎ **617-247-6161**); and 21 Brattle St., Harvard Square, Cambridge (T: Harvard [Red Line]; ☎ **617-864-4748**).

✔ The fresh, tasty sandwiches and baked goods at **Au Bon Pain** are never particularly unusual or disappointing. Locations are all over town, including the Prudential Center, 800 Boylston St., Back Bay (T: Prudential [Green Line E] or Hynes/ICA [Green Line B, C, or D]; ☎ **617-421-9593**); and 53 State St. (T: State [Blue or Orange Line];

☎ **617-723-8483**). The patio at the Harvard Square location, in Holyoke Center, 1350 Mass. Ave., Cambridge (T: Harvard [Red Line]; ☎ **617-497-9797**) is one of the best people-watching perches in New England.

✔ Time-sensitive sightseers and downtown workers benefit equally from the lickety-split self-service salad bars at **Souper Salad,** where you can eat in or take out. Branches near the Freedom Trail are at 3 Center Plaza (T: Governement Center [Green or Blue Line]; ☎ **617-367-6067**); 82 Summer St. (T: Downtown Crossing [Red or Orange Line]; ☎ **617-426-6834**); and 103 State St. (T: State [Blue or Orange Line]; ☎ **617-227-9151**).

Taking Tea Time

The original Boston Tea Party, a colonial rebellion, couldn't be farther from the experience of proper afternoon tea in a posh hotel. Finger sandwiches, pastries, scones, clotted cream, and other niceties make this the most polite way I know to make a pig of yourself. These hotels are within walking distance of the Arlington T stop (Green Line). You'll need a reservation, especially on weekends. Put on your daintiest attitude and "tea" off at:

✔ The Four Seasons Hotel, 200 Boylston St. **The Bristol Lounge** (☎ **617-351-2053**) serves tea daily from 3:00 to 4:30 p.m. Expect to pay $24 per person, more if you spring for the signature kir royale (a champagne cocktail).

✔ The Ritz-Carlton, Boston, 15 Arlington St. (☎ **617-536-5700**). The legendary **Ritz Lounge,** newly renovated and expanded, serves tea between 3:00 and 5:30 p.m. for about $23 a person.

Bao, Wow: Dim Sum

Dim sum, a Chinese midday meal, is a perfect way to sample a variety of small dishes. To get the most, go on a weekend with at least one other person. Waitresses make the rounds, pushing carts loaded with *bao* (steamed buns), steamed and fried dumplings, spring rolls, sweets, and more. Point at what you want (unless you speak Chinese), and the waitress stamps your check with the symbol of the dish; most cost $1 to $3. For around $10 per person, this is a thoroughly satisfying experience.

If you don't care for fried food, pork, or shrimp, dim sum may leave you feeling more deprived than satisfied.

The top dim-sum destinations, all near the Chinatown T stop (Orange Line), include the following:

- ✔ **Empire Garden Restaurant,** 690–698 Washington St., 2nd floor (☎ 617-482-8898)

- ✔ **China Pearl,** 9 Tyler St., 2nd floor (☎ 617-426-4338)

- ✔ **Chau Chow City,** 81 Essex St. (☎ 617-338-8158)

Espresso Express

Boston and Cambridge overflow with congenial coffee outlets (college and stimulants seem to go together), but the classic caffeine-related experience is a spell in a North End *caffè*. Check out the pastries, order an espresso or cappuccino (decaf, if you insist), sit back, and watch the world go by. The following keep long hours; all but Mike's (which is a pastry shop, not a *caffè*) permit smoking. To get to the North End, take the T to Haymarket (Green or Orange Line) and cross under the Expressway.

My favorite destinations include **Caffè dello Sport,** 308 Hanover St. (☎ 617-523-5063), and **Caffè Vittoria,** 296 Hanover St. (☎ 617-227-7606). **Caffè Paradiso,** 255 Hanover St. (☎ 617-742-1768), is *the* place to watch big European soccer matches. **Mike's Pastry,** 300 Hanover St. (☎ 617-742-3050), is a popular bakeshop with table service. Find what you want in the case; then sit down and order.

1 Scream, You Scream

The New Yorker in me can't believe the year-round popularity of ice cream in the Boston area. (That's not a complaint!) After encyclopedic research and great personal sacrifice, I can attest to the quality of the following.

In the Back Bay:

- ✔ **Emack & Bolio's,** 290 Newbury St. (T: Hynes/ICA [Green Line B, C, or D]; ☎ 617-247-8772)

- ✔ **Herrell's,** 224 Newbury St. (T: Hynes/ICA [Green Line B, C, or D]; ☎ 617-236-0857)

- ✔ **JP Licks,** 352 Newbury St. (T: Hynes/ICA [Green Line B, C, or D]; ☎ 617-236-1666)

- ✔ **Ben & Jerry's,** 174 Newbury St. (T: Copley [Green Line]; ☎ 617-536-5456)

In Cambridge:

✔ **Herrell's,** 15 Dunster St., Harvard Square (T: Harvard [Red Line]; ☎ **617-497-2179**)

✔ **Toscanini's,** 899 Main St., Central Square (T: Central [Red Line]; ☎ **617-491-5877**), and 1310 Mass. Ave., Harvard Square (T: Harvard [Red Line]; ☎ **617-354-9350**)

✔ **Christina's,** 1255 Cambridge St., Inman Square (T: Central [Red Line], turn right onto Prospect Street (at Starbucks) and go five blocks; ☎ **617-492-7021**)

Part V
Exploring Boston

"We've seen the *Cheers* bar, the *St. Elsewhere* hospital, and the courthouse from *The Practice.* I'm not sure why, but I feel like just going back to the hotel and watching TV."

In this part . . .

Now we reach the heart of the matter, the singular experiences and activities that led you to choose Boston over every other potential destination. (And if the meeting planners or the bride and groom or your parents chose for you, think of this as the "maybe it won't be so bad" section.)

You can approach Boston as a history lesson, an art gallery, a seafood buffet, or even a giant shopping center. You can concentrate on a specific interest or skip around. You can spend a day, a weekend, or a month, and only scratch the surface. Weigh the innumerable options, don't try to do too much, and soon you'll be on your way to a good time. Here's the information that will help you mix and match a trip that's just right for you.

Chapter 16

Boston's Top Sights

*B*oston stimulates all your senses: You see great paintings and sculpture, hear classical and popular music, taste ocean-fresh seafood, smell the perfume of Public Garden flowerbeds, and feel the breeze off the harbor in your hair. The preceding chapters address getting to Boston and finding shelter and food. Now, how will you spend your time? This chapter describes the most popular attractions and contains a separate section on the world-famous Freedom Trail. (Turn to Chapter 17 for descriptions of more-specialized experiences.) I also include indexes that organize the city's top sights by neighborhood and type.

The best thing you can do at this stage is to forget that you know the words *should* and *ought*. Yes, you can immerse yourself in history, art, science, or any number of other topics. But if a certain subject feels more obligatory than fun, that's probably not a great option.

Listen to yourself (and me, of course), not to the friends who say you *must* see or do something that sounds, to you, as dull as watching paint dry. You may want to practice smiling and saying, "That sounded great, but there wasn't time." (Your well-meaning neighbor doesn't need to know that you're thinking, "and there won't be, even if I live to be 100.")

Many Boston-area attractions are government (federal, state, and city) property, with the same concern for security Americans have come to expect at other government institutions. You may have to pass through a checkpoint, have your bag inspected, or stay a certain distance from some buildings or public spaces.

Time- and money-saving suggestions

Here are two good options for visitors spending more than a day or two:

✔ The **Boston CityPass** includes tickets to the John F. Kennedy Library, Harvard Museum of Natural History, Museum of Fine Arts, Museum of Science, New England Aquarium, and Prudential Center Skywalk. The price is subject to change as museum fees skyrocket. At press time, adults paid $30.25; children 3 to 17, $18.50. For adults, that's a 50% savings if you visit all six attractions (and you don't need to wait in line!). The passes, good for nine days from the date of purchase, are sold at participating attractions as well as at the Boston Common and Prudential Center visitor information centers, through the Greater Boston Convention and Visitors Bureau (☎ 800-SEE-BOSTON), at some hotel concierge desks, and from www.citypass.net.

✔ The **Arts/Boston coupon book** (☎ 617-482-2849; Internet: www.boston.com/ artsboston) includes discounts to museums and attractions such as the Museum of Fine Arts, New England Aquarium, Kennedy Library, Massachusetts Bay Lines cruises, and Beantown and Old Town trolley tours. The coupon book isn't worth the money (currently $9) for single travelers because many of the coupons are two-for-one deals. Arts/Boston coupon books are on sale at BosTix booths at Faneuil Hall Marketplace (on the south side of Faneuil Hall) and in Copley Square (at the corner of Boylston and Dartmouth streets).

For locations of the various attractions described here, see the "Boston Attractions" and "Cambridge Attractions" maps in this chapter, unless otherwise noted. (These maps also include attractions from Chapter 17.)

The Top Attractions

Dreams of Freedom
Downtown

A multimedia experience illustrating Boston's immigrant history, Dreams of Freedom covers everyone from the Puritans to the folks alighting from planes today. The artifacts, photographs, backdrops, and re-creations of other elements of immigration (such as a ship's hold) make the center entertaining and informative. Set aside at least 90 minutes to make your way through the exhibits with virtual host Benjamin Franklin.

Pause as you enter or leave to check out the second-floor facade, which honors your tour guide with the proclamation, BIRTHPLACE OF FRANKLIN.

1 Milk St. (off Washington Street). ☎ *617-338-6022. Internet:* www.dreamsof freedom.org. *T: Downtown Crossing (Red or Orange Line); follow Washington Street past Filene's for two blocks and turn right. Admission: $7.50 adults, $3.50 children 6–18, free for children under 6. Open: Daily 10 a.m.–6 p.m.*

Faneuil Hall Marketplace
Downtown

The city's most popular attraction is an agreeable amalgam of recreation, retail, and restaurants. Brick plazas and plenty of outdoor seating surround the five-building "festival-market" complex, which buzzes with activity from just past dawn 'til well past dark in pleasant weather year-round. Dozens of stores, shops, boutiques, and pushcarts share space with restaurants, bars, and food counters.

The marketplace is busiest in summer and fall; these seasons are peak travel times when street performers and musicians make the rounds. The shopping ranges from generic to quirky, the dining from fast to fancy. The central building, **Quincy Market,** contains a food court that runs the length of the building. You don't need to spend a penny to enjoy the fun, though: Between buskers and visitors from all over the world, the marketplace also offers great people-watching. True, this is touristy, especially in warm weather — but sometimes you just need to relax and let your inner tourist look around.

See "The Freedom Trail" section in this chapter for information about **Faneuil Hall.**

Between North, Congress, and State streets and I-93. ☎ *617-338-2323. T: Government Center (Green or Blue Line); cross the plaza, walk down the stairs, and cross Congress Street. Or Haymarket (Orange Line); follow Congress Street (with I-93 on your left) for two to three blocks. Open: Marketplace Mon–Sat 10 a.m.–9 p.m.; Sun noon to 6 p.m. Food court opens earlier; restaurant hours vary.*

Harvard University
Cambridge

Harvard has educated many notable people. The mystique of the country's oldest (established in 1636) and best-known college draws visitors to a school that is the alma mater of five American presidents. The heart of the campus, two hopelessly picturesque quadrangles known as **Harvard Yard** (or just "the Yard"), sits behind the brick walls that run along Mass. Ave. and Quincy and Cambridge streets.

The Yard is the oldest part of the campus and contains Harvard's oldest building, **Massachusetts Hall** (1720), home to the university president's office. Also in the Yard, in front of University Hall, you'll find the **John Harvard Statue** (1884), a magnet for photographers from all over the world. Campus legend gives the nickname "the Statue of Three Lies" to the sculpture, whose inscription reads "John Harvard — Founder — 1638." The truth: The college dates to 1636; Harvard bestowed money and his library on the fledgling institution but wasn't *the* founder; and sculptor Daniel Chester French's model reputedly was either a descendant of Harvard's or a student, but not Harvard himself.

Boston Attractions

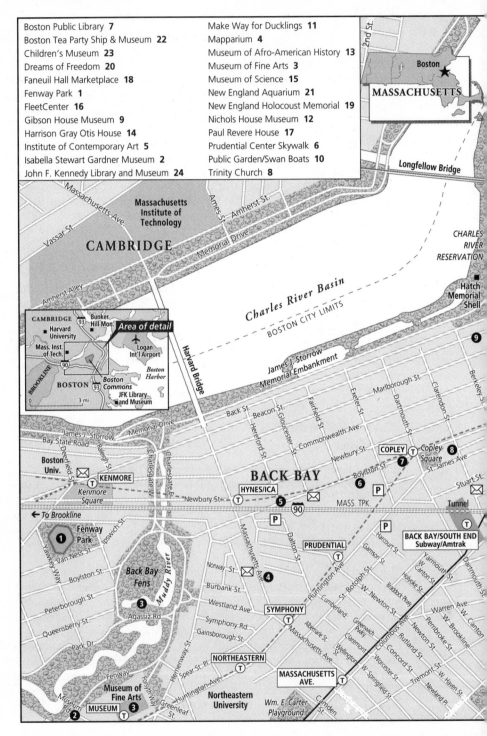

Boston Public Library **7**
Boston Tea Party Ship & Museum **22**
Children's Museum **23**
Dreams of Freedom **20**
Faneuil Hall Marketplace **18**
Fenway Park **1**
FleetCenter **16**
Gibson House Museum **9**
Harrison Gray Otis House **14**
Institute of Contemporary Art **5**
Isabella Stewart Gardner Museum **2**
John F. Kennedy Library and Museum **24**

Make Way for Ducklings **11**
Mapparium **4**
Museum of Afro-American History **13**
Museum of Fine Arts **3**
Museum of Science **15**
New England Aquarium **21**
New England Holocaust Memorial **19**
Nichols House Museum **12**
Paul Revere House **17**
Prudential Center Skywalk **6**
Public Garden/Swan Boats **10**
Trinity Church **8**

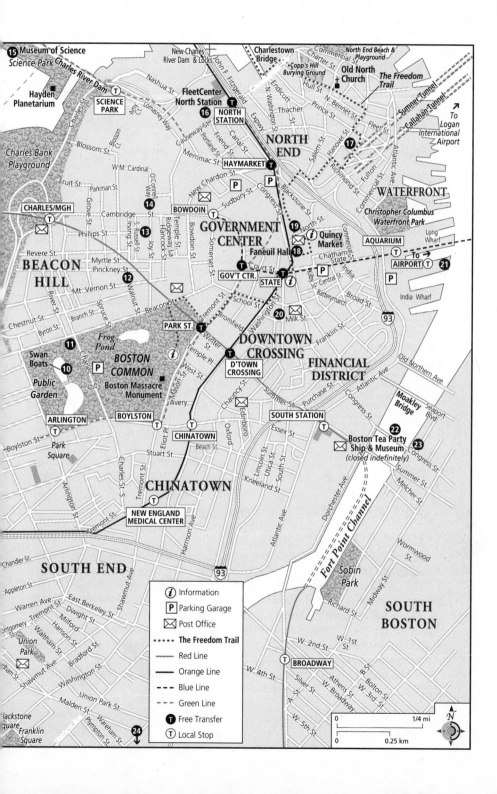

15 Museum of Science
Science Park
Charles River Dam
Hayden
Planetarium

New Charles
River Dam & Locks

Charlestown
Bridge

Charter St.
Copp's Hill
Burying Ground

North End Beach &
Playground

Old North
Church

The Freedom
Trail

SCIENCE
PARK

FleetCenter
North Station

16 NORTH
STATION

NORTH
END

Sumner Tunnel

Callahan Tunnel

To
Logan
International
Airport

Charles
Bank
Playground

HAYMARKET

17

WATERFRONT

CHARLES/MGH

BOWDOIN

14

13

GOVERNMENT
CENTER

19

Quincy
Market

Christopher Columbus
Waterfront Park

Long
Wharf

AQUARIUM

To
AIRPORT

21

BEACON
HILL

12

Faneuil Hall

18

GOV'T CTR.

STATE

India Wharf

P

20

PARK ST.

DOWNTOWN
CROSSING

FINANCIAL
DISTRICT

Old Northern Ave.

11

Frog
Pond

Swan
Boats

10

BOSTON
COMMON

Public
Garden

Boston Massacre
Monument

D'TOWN
CROSSING

Moakley
Bridge

22

ARLINGTON

BOYLSTON

SOUTH STATION

Boston Tea Party
Ship & Museum
(closed indefinitely)

23

CHINATOWN

CHINATOWN

NEW ENGLAND
MEDICAL CENTER

Fort Point Channel

Sobin
Park

SOUTH END

SOUTH
BOSTON

Union
Park

24

BROADWAY

i Information
P Parking Garage
✉ Post Office
····· **The Freedom Trail**
—— Red Line
—— Orange Line
- - - Blue Line
- - - Green Line
T Free Transfer
Ⓣ Local Stop

0   1/4 mi
0   0.25 km

N

Across Mass. Ave., the Information Center distributes maps and self-guided tour directions and has a bulletin board that lists campus activities. You may also want to visit the university's art and science museums; see Chapter 17 for more information.

Information Center: Holyoke Center, 1350 Mass. Ave. ☎ 617-495-1573. Internet: www.harvard.edu. T: Harvard (Red Line). Open: Information Center Mon–Sat 9 a.m.–5 p.m.; Sun noon to 5 p.m. Free guided tours five times a day Mon–Sat during the summer; during school year (except vacations), twice a day on weekdays and once on Sat. Call for exact times; reservations aren't necessary.

Isabella Stewart Gardner Museum
Fenway

Arts patron Isabella Stewart Gardner (1840–1924) designed this magnificent home in the style of a 15th-century Venetian palace. After Gardner's death, the home became a gorgeous museum — and a testament to the timeless judgment of a fascinating, iconoclastic woman. The collections include European, American, and Asian painting and sculpture, and furniture and architectural details from European churches and palaces. Allow at least two hours to peruse works by Titian, Botticelli, Raphael, Rembrandt, Matisse, James McNeill Whistler, and John Singer Sargent. Under the terms ofGardner's will, the arrangement of the galleries does not change, but special shows go up in a separate space two or three times a year.

280 The Fenway (at Museum Road, off Huntington Avenue). ☎ 617-566-1401. Internet: www.gardnermuseum.org. T: Museum (Green Line E); walk two blocks straight ahead (away from Huntington Avenue, with the Museum of Fine Arts on your right). Admission: $11 adults weekends, $10 adults weekdays, $7 seniors, $5 college students with ID, and free for children under 18. Open: Tues–Sun 11 a.m.–5 p.m. and some Mon holidays. Closed Jan 1, Thanksgiving, and Dec 25.

John F. Kennedy Library and Museum
Dorchester

A magnificent building designed by I. M. Pei, the Kennedy Library celebrates the life and legacy of the 35th president. History buffs will want to spend at least 90 minutes exploring exhibits that recall "Camelot." The displays include audio and video recordings, replicas of the Oval Office and the office of the attorney general under JFK (Robert F. Kennedy), a film about the Cuban missile crisis, and imaginatively displayed documents and memorabilia. A 17-minute film about Kennedy's early life introduces the museum, which regularly updates displays and schedules special exhibits, lectures, and other events. Allow for travel time — 30 minutes from or to downtown Boston.

Columbia Point (off Morrissey Boulevard). ☎ 877-616-4599 or 617-929-4500. Internet: www.jfklibrary.org. T: JFK/UMass (Red Line); then take the free shuttle bus, which runs every 20 minutes. By car: Take I-93/Route 3 south to Exit 15 (Morrissey Boulevard/JFK Library), turn left onto Columbia Road, and follow the signs to the free parking lot. Admission: $8 adults, $6 seniors and students with ID, $4 children 13–17, and free for children under 13. Open: Daily 9 a.m.–5 p.m. (last film at 3:55). Closed Jan 1, Thanksgiving, and Dec 25.

Mapparium
Back Bay

One of the most unusual attractions anywhere, the Mapparium is a hollow glass globe 30 feet across. The 608 stained-glass panels show our world as things were in 1935. Visitors walk through the globe on a bridge below the equator, enjoying the view and the unusual acoustics. The Mapparium is part of the new Mary Baker Eddy Library, a research center that includes two floors of exhibits.

World Headquarters of the First Church of Christ, Scientist, 200 Mass. Ave. (between Clearway Street and Westland Avenue). ☎ *617-450-7000. Internet:* www.marybakereddy.org. *T: Symphony (Green Line E) or Mass. Ave. (Orange Line). Or Hynes/ICA (Green Line B, C, or D); turn left at exit and walk four blocks. Admission (includes library exhibits): Adults $5; seniors, students and children 6–17 $3; children under 6 free. Open: Tues–Fri 10 a.m.–9 p.m.; Sat 10 a.m.–5 p.m.; Sun 11 a.m.–5 p.m.*

Museum of Fine Arts
Fenway

Out-of-towners typically hear about the MFA because of special exhibitions and traveling shows, not because of the real appeal: an unbeatable combination of the familiar and the unexpected. The galleries contain so many classic pieces that you'll probably feel as if you've bumped into an old friend at least once during your visit. The collections span the centuries and the globe — from Old Kingdom Egyptian collections (that means mummies, kids) to contemporary photography. The celebrated impressionist paintings include 43 Monets. And you'll always run across something, ancient or modern, that leaves you glad you made the trip.

Schedule at least half a day to explore; art fiends should allow more time. The best way to get an overview is to take a free **guided tour.** These tours start on weekdays (except Monday holidays) at 10:30 a.m. and 1:30 p.m.; Wednesdays at 6:15 p.m.; and Saturdays at 10:30 a.m. and 1:00 p.m. If you prefer to explore the sprawling galleries on your own, pick up a floor plan or family activity booklet at the information desk. Check ahead for special family- and child-friendly activities, which take place year-round.

The MFA is one of the most expensive museums in the country; if your plans allow, a Boston CityPass can be a great investment.

Cambridge Attractions

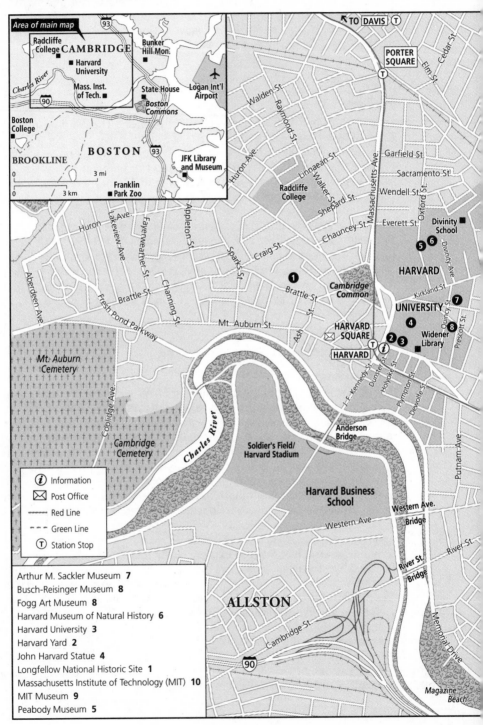

Area of main map

93
Radcliffe College CAMBRIDGE
Bunker Hill Mon.
Harvard University
Charles River
Mass. Inst. of Tech.
90
State House
Logan Int'l Airport
Boston Commons
Boston College
BROOKLINE
BOSTON
93
JFK Library and Museum
Franklin Park Zoo

0   3 mi
0   3 km

TO DAVIS
PORTER SQUARE
Cedar St.
Elm St.
Walden St.
Raymond St.
Garfield St.
Sacramento St.
Wendell St.
Oxford St.
Huron Ave.
Linnaean St.
Walker St.
Shepard St.
Radcliffe College
Everett St.
Divinity School
Chauncey St.
HARVARD
Huron Ave.
Lakeview Ave.
Fayerweather St.
Appleton St.
Craig St.
Sparks St.
Brattle St.
Cambridge Common
Kirkland St.
UNIVERSITY
Quincy St.
Prescott St.
Aberdeen Ave.
Brattle St.
Channing St.
Mt. Auburn St.
Ash St.
HARVARD SQUARE
Widener Library
HARVARD
Fresh Pond Parkway
Mt. Auburn Cemetery
Coolidge Ave.
Cambridge Cemetery
Charles River
Anderson Bridge
Soldier's Field/ Harvard Stadium
J.F. Kennedy St.
Dunster St.
Holyoke St.
Plympton St.
DeWolfe St.
Putnam Ave.
Harvard Business School
Western Ave.
Western Ave.
Bridge
ALLSTON
River St.
River St.
Bridge
Cambridge St.
90
Memorial Drive
Magazine Beach

(i) Information
✉ Post Office
Red Line
Green Line
T Station Stop

Arthur M. Sackler Museum **7**
Busch-Reisinger Museum **8**
Fogg Art Museum **8**
Harvard Museum of Natural History **6**
Harvard University **3**
Harvard Yard **2**
John Harvard Statue **4**
Longfellow National Historic Site **1**
Massachusetts Institute of Technology (MIT) **10**
MIT Museum **9**
Peabody Museum **5**

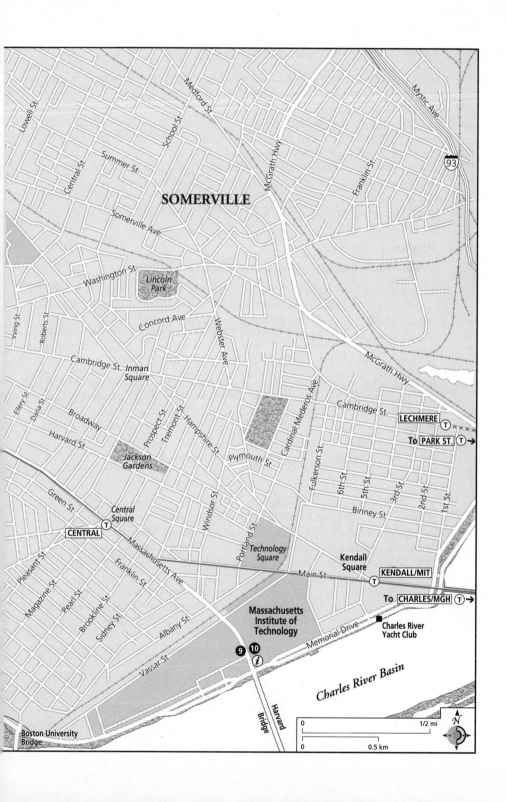

Ongoing renovation and construction sometimes mean certain galleries are closed. If you have a particular interest, double-check before visiting that the galleries you want to see are open.

465 Huntington Ave. (at Museum Road). ☎ *617-267-9300. Internet:* www.mfa.org. *T: Museum (Green Line E). Or Ruggles (Orange Line); walk two blocks on Ruggles Street. Admission, good for 2 visits within 30 days of purchase: Adults $15 entire museum, $13 when only West Wing is open; students and seniors $13 entire museum, $12 when only West Wing is open. Children 7–17 $5 on school days before 3 p.m., otherwise free. Voluntary contribution ($14 suggested), Wed 4:00–9:45 p.m. Surcharges may apply for special exhibitions. No fee to visit only shop, library, or auditoriums. Open: Entire museum Mon–Tues 10:00 a.m.–4:45 p.m.; Wed 10:00 a.m.–9:45 p.m.; Thurs–Fri 10 a.m.–5 p.m.; Sat–Sun 10:00 a.m.–5:45 p.m. Open: West Wing only Thurs–Fri 5:00–9:45 p.m. Closed Thanksgiving, Dec 25.*

Museum of Science
Science Park (between Boston and East Cambridge)

A superb destination for children and adults, the Museum of Science introduces principles and theories so painlessly that the intro is almost sneaky. Hands-on displays and exhibits explore every scientific field you can imagine, but — I can't emphasize this enough — always in a fun, accessible way.

Allow at least a couple of hours; if you plan to take in a show (see the next paragraph), you may want to set aside a day. The Virtual FishTank, acquired when the science museum joined forces with the Computer Museum, is one of the most popular exhibits. You can "build" your fish using your home computer (visit www.virtualfishtank.com) or on the scene, then watch as your new pet interacts with other people's creations.

A show at one of the museum's theaters, which charge separate admission, is well worth your time. The Mugar Omni Theater shows IMAX movies on a five-story domed screen; the Charles Hayden Planetarium schedules daily star shows, weekend rock-music laser extravaganzas, and shows on special astronomical topics.

Buy all tickets at once, not only because the price is cheaper but because shows sell out. You can buy tickets in person and order them in advance (subject to a service charge) over the phone or online using a credit card.

Science Park (off Route 28). ☎ *617-723-2500. Internet:* www.mos.org; *for tickets,* http://tickets.mos.org. *T: Science Park (Green Line); follow signs along elevated walkway onto bridge. Admission: Exhibit halls $12 adults, $10 seniors, $9 children 3–11, free for children under 3. Mugar Omni Theater, Hayden Planetarium, or laser shows $8 adults, $6 seniors and children 3–11, free for* children under 3. Discounted admission tickets for two or three attraction combinations. Open: Museum July 5–Labor Day Sat–Thurs 9 a.m.–7 p.m., Fri 9 a.m.–9 p.m.; day after Labor Day–July 4 Sat–Thurs 9 a.m.–5 p.m., Fri 9 a.m.–9 p.m. Shows during museum hours and some evenings; call or check the Web site for the schedule. Closed Thanksgiving, Dec 25.

New England Aquarium
Waterfront

A sprawling complex, the Aquarium has grown more popular since adding a 3D IMAX theater in 2001. The exhibits contain more than 7,000 fish and aquatic mammals, including sea lions that perform every 90 minutes in the floating pavilion Discovery. The centerpiece is the 187,000-gallon Giant Ocean Tank; other exhibits focus on local ecology, the Aquarium medical center, and a roster of regularly changing special topics. Allow at least two and a half hours for the Aquarium, plus an hour or so if you plan to take in a film in the state-of-the-art Simons IMAX Theatre.

"Science at Sea" harbor tours operate daily in the spring, summer, and fall. Tickets are $13 for adults, $10 for seniors and college students with ID, $9 for youths 12 to 18, and $8.50 for children under 12. IMAX tickets cost $8 for adults, $6 for seniors and children 3 to 11. Discounts are available when you combine a visit to the aquarium with a harbor tour, an IMAX movie, or a whale watch (see Chapter 18).

At busy times, the Aquarium can be uncomfortably crowded and the lines unbearably long. The Boston CityPass is a good option — in time even more than money — on hot summer days when having a ticket allows you to go straight to the entrance. Seriously consider investing in the pass, especially if you're traveling with restless children. If you don't buy a pass, try to make this your first stop of the day, and arrive when the doors open.

Central Wharf (off Atlantic Avenue at State Street). ☎ *617-973-5200. Internet:* www.neaq.org. *T: Aquarium (Blue Line). Admission: $13.50 adults, $11.50 seniors, $7.50 children 3–11, free for children under 3. No fee to visit outdoor exhibits, cafe, and gift shop. Open: July–Labor Day Mon–Tues and Fri 9 a.m.–6 p.m.; Wed–Thurs 9 a.m.–8 p.m.; Sat–Sun and holidays 9 a.m.–7 p.m. Day after Labor Day–June Mon–Fri 9 a.m.–5 p.m.; Sat–Sun and holidays 9 a.m.–6 p.m. Closed Thanksgiving, Dec 25, and until noon Jan 1.*

Prudential Center Skywalk
Back Bay

The 50-story Prudential Tower boasts Boston's only 360-degree view. The displays are reasonably interesting, and the panorama can't be beat. Visit at twilight on slightly overcast days to enjoy spectacular sunsets. The

52nd floor holds the Top of the Hub restaurant and lounge (see Chapters 14 and 23).

Note: The John Hancock Tower, formerly the Skywalk's only competition, closed permanently in 2001.

800 Boylston St. (at Fairfield Street). ☎ *617-859-0648. T: Prudential (Green Line E) or Copley (Green Line B, C, or D); walk toward tower. Admission: $7 adults, $4 seniors and children 2–10. Open: Daily 10 a.m.–10 p.m.*

Public Garden/Swan Boats
Back Bay

One of the most pleasant spots in the city, the Public Garden is eight square blocks of peaceful greenery surrounding an agreeable body of water. The oldest botanical garden in the country boasts thriving blooms from spring through late fall, and the action on the lagoon is always diverting. Children love to feed the geese, ducks, and swans. Adults get a kick out of the sculptures and monuments, which commemorate George Washington, the first use of ether as an anesthetic, and other apparently random people and events.

The **swan boats** have been synonymous with Boston since 1877. Still operated by the same family, the fiberglass birds on pedal boats (the attendants pedal, not the passengers) make a great low-tech break. Fans of *The Trumpet of the Swan,* by E. B. White, can't miss these vessels. Allow 30 minutes.

Near the corner of Charles and Beacon streets, nine little bronze figures immortalize Robert McCloskey's book *Make Way for Ducklings.* Nancy Schön's renderings of Mrs. Mallard and her babies inspire delighted shrieks from small visitors.

Between Arlington, Boylston, Charles, and Beacon streets. T: Arlington (Green Line). Or Charles/MGH (Red Line); follow Charles Street five blocks to Beacon Street. Open: Daily year-round. As in any park, be careful at night, especially if you're alone.

Swan boats ☎ *617-522-1966. Internet:* www.swanboats.com. *Admission: $2 adults, $1.50 seniors, $1 children 2–15. Open: Daily, third Mon of April–mid-Sept. Summer 10 a.m.–5 p.m.; spring 10 a.m.–4 p.m.; fall weekdays noon to 4 p.m., weekends 10 a.m.–4 p.m.*

The Freedom Trail

You get no sense of the Freedom Trail's role for visitors if you just say "16 historic sights make up the 3-mile trail" (Internet: www. thefreedomtrail.org). Not only are the attractions interesting, but the trail — a line of bricks or red paint on the sidewalk from Boston Common to Charlestown — makes finding your way around downtown considerably less confusing than would otherwise be the case.

This section lists the stops along the trail, starting with Boston Common and ending with the Bunker Hill Monument. This is the order that usually appears in pamphlets, maps, and other publications, but you don't have to speed-walk from one end to the other, go in exact order, or even see everything. Start in Charlestown and work backward, skip a stop or two, or even get "lost" — this area is too small for you to go too far astray. I insist on just one thing: Wear comfortable walking shoes.

The Freedom Trail takes at least two hours, even if you don't linger too long at any one stop. If that's too much time, consider a free 90-minute walking tour of the "heart" of the trail with a National Park Service ranger (see Chapter 17). To head out on your own, start at the Visitor Information Center at 146 Tremont St., on Boston Common. Take the T to Park Street (Red or Green Line).

Boston Common
Downtown/Beacon Hill

In 1634, Boston bought what's now the country's oldest park. In 1640, the land became common ground; serving as a cow pasture (until 1830), military camp, and all-purpose municipal gathering place. Plaques and memorials abound. One of the loveliest is up the hill from the T station, on Beacon Street across from the State House. Augustus Saint-Gaudens designed the bas-relief **Robert Gould Shaw Memorial,** which honors Colonel Shaw and the Union Army's 54th Massachusetts Colored Regiment, which fought in the Civil War. (The 1989 movie *Glory,* with Matthew Broderick and Denzel Washington, told the story of the first American army unit made up of free black soldiers.)

Between Beacon, Park, Tremont, Boylston, and Charles streets. Visitors Information Center ☎ 800-SEE-BOSTON or 617-536-4100. T: Park Street (Red or Green Line).

Massachusetts State House
Beacon Hill

Governor Samuel Adams laid the cornerstone of the state capitol in 1795. The great Federal-era architect Charles Bulfinch designed the imposing central building and landmark golden dome. Free tours — guided and self-guided — leave from the second floor. Visit the rear of the building, off Bowdoin Street, to see a 60-foot monument that illustrates the hill's original height (material from the top went into 19th-century landfill projects).

Beacon St. (at Park Street). ☎ 617-727-3676. T: Park Street (Red or Green Line); walk up Park Street one block. Admission: Free. Open: Weekdays 9 a.m.–5 p.m.; Sat 10 a.m.–4 p.m. Tours Mon–Sat 10:00 a.m.–3:30 p.m.

Park Street Church
Downtown/Beacon Hill

Henry James described this 1809 structure as "the most interesting mass of bricks and mortar in America." Plaques arrayed around the entrance describe the storied history, which includes the first public performance of "America" ("My Country 'Tis of Thee") on July 4, 1831.

1 Park St. (at Tremont Street). ☎ 617-523-3383. T: Park Street (Red or Green Line). Admission: Free. Open: Late June–Aug Tues–Sat 9:30 a.m.–4:00 p.m. Year-round services Sun 9:00 a.m., 10:45 a.m., 5:30 p.m.

Old Granary Burying Ground
Downtown

This cemetery, which dates to 1660, was once part of Boston Common. The graveyard contains the final resting places of patriots Samuel Adams, Paul Revere, John Hancock, and James Otis; merchant Peter Faneuil (spelled "FUNAL"); the victims of the Boston Massacre; and Benjamin Franklin's parents. The wife of Isaac Vergoose, whom historians believe was "Mother Goose" of nursery-rhyme fame, is also buried here.

Gravestone rubbing is *illegal* in Boston's historic cemeteries (and pretty bad karma, if you ask me).

Tremont St. (at Bromfield Street). T: Park Street (Red or Green Line); walk one block on Tremont Street. Open: Daily 8 a.m.–5 p.m. (until 3 p.m. in the winter).

King's Chapel and Burying Ground
Downtown

A squat granite structure, King's Chapel is historically and architecturally interesting. The first Anglican church in Boston, the chapel replaced a wooden one and construction (from 1749 to 1754) went on *around* the previous building. After the Revolution, in a rejection of the royal religion, King's Chapel became the first Unitarian church in America.

The **burying ground,** on Tremont Street, is the oldest in the city (1630). Elaborate colonial headstones dot the graveyard, which is the final resting place of John Winthrop, the first governor of the Massachusetts Bay Colony; William Dawes, who rode with Paul Revere; and Mary Chilton, the first female colonist to step ashore on Plymouth Rock.

58 Tremont St. (at School Street). ☎ 617-523-1749. T: Government Center (Green or Blue Line); walk one block on Tremont Street. Open: Chapel summer daily 9:30 a.m.–1:00 p.m.; winter Sat 10 a.m.–2 p.m. Services Wed 12:15 p.m., Sun 11:00 a.m. Burying ground daily 8:00 a.m.–5:30 p.m. (until 3:00 p.m. in winter).

The Freedom Trail

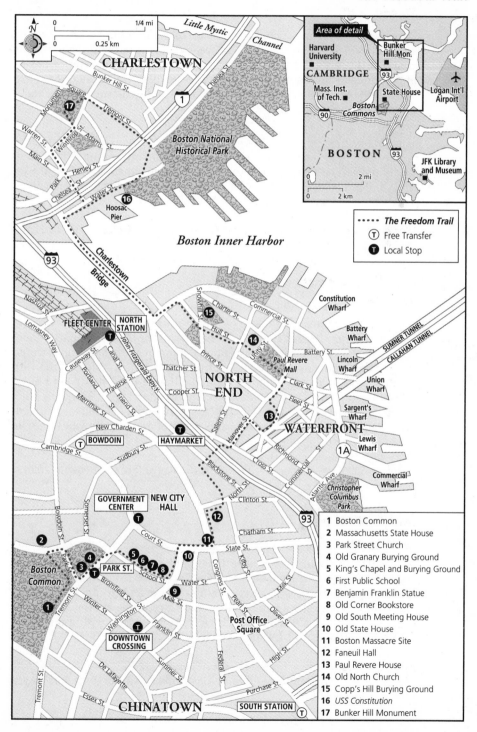

The Freedom Trail

- (T) Free Transfer
- (T) Local Stop

1   Boston Common
2   Massachusetts State House
3   Park Street Church
4   Old Granary Burying Ground
5   King's Chapel and Burying Ground
6   First Public School
7   Benjamin Franklin Statue
8   Old Corner Bookstore
9   Old South Meeting House
10 Old State House
11 Boston Massacre Site
12 Faneuil Hall
13 Paul Revere House
14 Old North Church
15 Copp's Hill Burying Ground
16 *USS Constitution*
17 Bunker Hill Monument

First Public School/Benjamin Franklin Statue
Downtown

A colorful folk-art mosaic marks the site of the first public school in the country, which opened in 1634 (two years before Harvard). The school's illustrious alumni include John Hancock, Benjamin Franklin, Charles Bulfinch, Ralph Waldo Emerson, George Santayana, and Leonard Bernstein. Now called Boston Latin School, the structure still exists in the Fenway neighborhood.

A statue of Boston native **Benjamin Franklin** (1706–1790) is inside the fence. The plaques on the base describe Franklin's numerous accomplishments. The elegant granite building behind the statue is **Old City Hall,** built in 1865 and designed in Second Empire style by Arthur Gilman (who laid out the Back Bay) and Gridley J. F. Bryant.

School St. (at Province Street). T: State (Orange or Blue Line); walk two blocks on Washington Street and turn right.

Old Corner Bookstore
Downtown

This land once held the home of religious reformer Anne Hutchinson, who wasted no time in ticking off church authorities — in 1638, a mere eight years after the establishment of Boston, leaders excommunicated Hutchinson, who also was expelled from town. In the middle of the 19th century, the little brick building (which dates to 1712) held the publishing house of Ticknor & Fields. Publisher James "Jamie" Fields's wide circle of friends included Henry Wadsworth Longfellow, Henry David Thoreau, Ralph Waldo Emerson, Nathaniel Hawthorne, and Harriet Beecher Stowe.

3 School St. (at Washington Street). T: State (Orange or Blue Line); walk two blocks up Washington Street.

Old South Meeting House
Downtown

The Boston Tea Party started in this building, which remains a religious and political gathering place today. On December 16, 1773, revolutionaries protesting the royal tea tax assembled here and wound up dumping the cargo of three ships into the harbor. An interactive multimedia exhibit tells the building's fascinating story. This structure, with a landmark clock tower, dates to 1729; the original went up in 1670.

310 Washington St. ☎ *617-482-6439. Internet:* www.oldsouthmeeting house.org. *T: State (Orange or Blue Line); walk three blocks up Washington*

Street. Admission: $5 adults, $4 seniors and students, $1 children 6–18, free for children under 6. Open: Daily April–Oct 9:00 a.m.–5:30 p.m.; Nov–March weekdays 10 a.m.–4 p.m., weekends 10 a.m.–5 p.m.

Old State House
Downtown

Built in 1713, the Old State House served as the seat of the colony's government before the Revolution and as the state capitol until 1797. The gilded lion and unicorn that adorn the exterior are replicas — the original symbols of British rule went into a bonfire on July 18, 1776, the day Bostonians first heard the Declaration of Independence read from the balcony. Inside you'll find the Bostonian Society's **museum of the city's history.** Displays include an introductory video on the history of the building, and changing exhibits that showcase the society's enormous collection of documents, photographs, and artifacts. Plan on at least 45 minutes if you enjoy history, considerably less if you're more interested in architecture (or in getting to Faneuil Hall Marketplace for some shopping and eating).

206 Washington St. (at State Street). ☎ *617-720-3290. Internet:* www.boston history.org. *T: State (Blue or Orange Line). Admission: $5 adults, $4 seniors and students, $1 children 6–18, free for children under 6. Open: Daily 9 a.m.–5 p.m.*

Boston Massacre Site
Downtown

Look for the ring of cobblestones on the traffic island in the middle of State Street behind the Old State House. This spot marks the approximate site of the Boston Massacre, a conflict that took place March 5, 1770, and helped launch the colonial rebellion. Angered at the presence of royal troops in Boston, colonists threw snowballs, garbage, rocks, and other debris at a group of soldiers. The redcoats panicked and fired into the crowd, killing five men, who lie in the Old Granary Burying Ground.

State Street at Devonshire Street. T: State (Blue or Orange Line).

Faneuil Hall
Downtown

The "Cradle of Liberty" was a gift to the city from prosperous merchant Peter Faneuil. Built in 1742, the site grew to more than twice the original size in 1805, using a Charles Bulfinch design. Note the statue on the Congress Street side of Samuel Adams (yes, as in the beer), one of the countless orators whose declamations shook the building in the years before the Revolution. Faneuil Hall also played host to advocates of abolition, temperance, and women's suffrage. Under the terms of Faneuil's will, the building remains a public meeting (and sometimes concert) hall, and the ground floor holds retail space. National Park Service rangers give free 20-minute talks every half-hour in the second-floor auditorium and operate a visitor center on the first floor.

The French Huguenot name "Faneuil" more or less rhymes with "Daniel," though *Fan*-yoo-ul is another pronunciation.

Across North Street on Union Street, you'll see a series of glass towers in a small park; this is the **New England Holocaust Memorial.** Built in 1995, this memorial is a moving reminder, in the midst of attractions that celebrate freedom, of the consequences of a world without freedom. The pattern on the glass is 6 million random numbers, one for each Jew who died during the Holocaust.

Dock Square (Congress Street off North Street). ☎ *617-242-5675. T: Government Center (Green or Blue Line) or Haymarket (Orange Line). Admission: Free. Open: Second floor daily 9 a.m.–5 p.m.; ground floor Mon–Sat 10 a.m.–9 p.m., Sun noon to 6 p.m.*

Paul Revere House
North End

Remember "Listen, my children, and you shall hear/Of the midnight ride of Paul Revere"? Paul Revere's ride started here, in what's now one of the most enjoyable stops on the Freedom Trail. On April 18, 1775, Revere set out for Lexington and Concord and into the American imagination (courtesy of Henry Wadsworth Longfellow) from his home, which he had bought in 1770. The oldest house in downtown Boston, Revere's home dates to around 1680. The self-guided tour permits a glimpse of 18th-century life and many family heirlooms.

19 North Square (at North Street between Richmond and Prince streets). ☎ *617-523-2338. Internet:* www.paulreverehouse.org. *T: Haymarket (Green or Orange Line). Cross under the elevated highway and follow the Freedom Trail. Admission: $2.50 adults, $2 seniors and students, $1 children 5–17. Open: Daily April 15–Oct 9:30 a.m.–5:15 p.m., Nov–April 14 9:30 a.m.–4:15 p.m. Closed Mon Jan–March, Jan 1, Thanksgiving, Dec 25.*

Old North Church
North End

Formally named Christ Church, this is the oldest church in Boston, dating to 1723. In the original steeple, sexton Robert Newman hung two lanterns on the night of April 18, 1775, alerting Paul Revere to the movement of British troops. The second beacon told Revere the redcoats were crossing the Charles River by boat, not on foot ("One if by land, two if by sea"). Markers and plaques dot the building and gardens; note the bust of

George Washington, reputedly the first memorial to the first president. The quirky gift shop and museum (☎ 617-523-4848), in a former chapel, is open daily from 9 a.m. to 5 p.m., and all proceeds go to support the church.

Robert Newman was a great-grandson of George Burroughs, one of the victims of the Salem witch trials of 1692.

193 Salem St. (at Hull Street). ☎ 617-523-6676. Internet: www.oldnorth.com. T: Haymarket (Green or Orange Line); cross under the elevated highway and walk six blocks on Salem Street. Admission: Free; donations appreciated. Open: Daily 9 a.m.–5 p.m. Services (Episcopal) Sun 9 a.m., 11 a.m., 4 p.m.

Neighborhood watch

Boston and Cambridge are famous for neighborhoods that make good destinations for out-of-towners interested in exploring beyond the usual attractions. I particularly enjoy these three locations (two in Boston, one in Cambridge), but if you're visiting friends who want to explore an area you've never heard of, jump at the chance — this is one of the best ways to get to know a new city.

✔ **Beacon Hill,** west and north of the golden dome of the State House, is one of the city's oldest neighborhoods, a festival of brick and brownstone that looks the way you probably think Boston "should." Wander downhill toward Charles Street, making sure to explore the lovely side streets and tiny parks. One of the oldest black churches in the country, the African Meeting House, is at 8 Smith Court.

Between Beacon Street, Embankment Road, Cambridge Street, and Park Street. T: Charles/MGH (Red Line) or Park Street (Green Line).

✔ **The North End,** traditionally an Italian-American neighborhood, today is more than half newcomers, but the area retains an Italian flavor. You'll see Italian restaurants, *caffès,* bakeries, pastry shops, and food stores. This detour is easy from the Freedom Trail, and worth more than just a quick trip for a pasta dinner. Hanover and Salem streets are the main drags; you'll find plenty of action on the side streets, too.

Between I-93, Commercial Street, and North Washington Street. T: Haymarket (Green or Orange Line); cross under the elevated highway.

✔ **Harvard Square,** Cambridge's best-known intersection, attracts a kaleidoscopic assortment of students, shoppers, street musicians, and sightseers. This area is a retail playground (see Chapter 19) that's especially lively on weekend afternoons. Stop at the information booth near the main T entrance (☎ 617-497-1630; open Monday through Saturday 9 a.m. to 5 p.m., Sunday 1 to 5 p.m.), visit Harvard University (see the listing under "The Top Attractions" in this chapter), or explore on your own. The area's three main thoroughfares and the connecting side streets make great places for wandering.

Intersection of Mass. Ave., John F. Kennedy Street, and Brattle Street. T: Harvard (Red Line).

Copp's Hill Burying Ground
North End

The Mather family of Puritan ministers, Robert Newman, and Prince Hall lie in the second-oldest graveyard (1659) in the city. Hall, a prominent member of the free black community that occupied the hill's north slope in colonial times, fought at Bunker Hill and established the first black Masonic lodge. The highest point in the North End enjoys a great view of the Inner Harbor, the northern part of the Big Dig construction, and Charlestown (look for the masts of the USS *Constitution*).

Between Hull, Snowhill, and Charter streets. T: North Station (Green or Orange Line). Follow Causeway Street to North Washington Street, where it becomes Commercial Street. Walk two blocks, turn right, and climb the hill. Open: Daily 9 a.m.–5 p.m. (until 3 p.m. in winter).

USS Constitution
Charlestown

In modern terms, "Old Ironsides" retired undefeated. Launched in 1797 as one of the U.S. Navy's six original frigates, the USS *Constitution* never lost a battle. The tour guides are active-duty sailors in 1812 dress uniforms, honoring the ship's prominent role in the War of 1812. The frigate earned the nickname during an engagement on August 19, 1812, with the French warship *Guerriere,* whose shots bounced off Old Ironsides' thick oak hull as if the hull were iron. The ship sailed under its own power in 1997 for the first time since 1881, drawing international attention. Tugs tow the Constitution into the harbor every Fourth of July.

The nearby **Constitution Museum** (☎ **617-426-1812;** Internet: www.uss constitutionmuseum.org) contains participatory exhibits that illustrate the history and operation of the ship. Also at the navy yard, National Park Service rangers (☎ **617-242-5601**) staff an information booth and give free one-hour guided tours of the base.

Charlestown Navy Yard (off Constitution Road). ☎ 617-242-5670. T: North Station (Green or Orange Line); follow Causeway Street to North Washington Street, turn left, and cross the bridge. Total walking time: About 15 minutes. Admission for tours and museum: Free. Open: Museum daily May–Oct 9 a.m.–6 p.m.; Nov–April 10 a.m.–4 p.m. Constitution tours daily 9:30 a.m.–3:50 p.m. Closed Jan 1, Thanksgiving, Dec 25.

Bunker Hill Monument
Charlestown

One of Boston's best-known landmarks, this 221-foot granite obelisk honors the colonists who died in the Battle of Bunker Hill on June 17,

1775. The win was a costly victory for the other side. Half of the British troops died or were injured. The battle led to the British decision to abandon Boston nine months later. A flight of 294 stairs leads to the top — there's no elevator, and the windows are small, but the view affords a look at the Charles River–end of the Big Dig. The ranger-staffed lodge at the base holds dioramas and exhibits.

Monument Square (at Tremont Street). ☎ *617-242-5644. T: Ferry between Long Wharf or North Station and navy yard, then follow the Freedom Trail up the hill. Or Community College (Orange Line); cross Rutherford Avenue and walk toward the monument. Or Number 92 or 93 bus along Main Street (foot of the hill) to and from Haymarket. Admission: Free. Open: Monument daily 9:00 a.m.–4:30 p.m.; visitor center daily 9 a.m.–5 p.m.*

Index of Top Attractions by Neighborhood

Back Bay
Beacon Hill
Boston Common
Mapparium
Massachusetts State House
Park Street Church
Prudential Center Skywalk
Public Garden/Swan Boats
Robert Gould Shaw Memorial

Cambridge
Harvard University/John Harvard
   Statue

Charlestown
Bunker Hill Monument
USS *Constitution*/Charlestown
   Navy Yard

Dorchester
John F. Kennedy Library and Museum

Downtown
Benjamin Franklin Statue
Boston Massacre Site
Dreams of Freedom/Benjamin
   Franklin's Birthplace

First Public School Site
King's Chapel and Burying Ground
Old City Hall
Old Corner Bookstore
Old Granary Burying Ground
Old South Meeting House
Old State House

Faneuil Hall Marketplace
Faneuil Hall
New England Holocaust Memorial

Fenway
Isabella Stewart Gardner Museum
Museum of Fine Arts

North End
Copp's Hill Burying Ground
Old North Church
Paul Revere House

Science Park
Museum of Science

Waterfront
New England Aquarium

Index of Top Attractions by Type

Churches and Burying Grounds
Copp's Hill Burying Ground
King's Chapel and Burying Ground
Old Granary Burying Ground
Old North Church
Park Street Church

Gardens
Boston Common
Public Garden/Swan Boats

Historic Buildings and Sites
Benjamin Franklin Statue
Boston Massacre Site
Bunker Hill Monument
Faneuil Hall
First Public School Site
Massachusetts State House
Old City Hall
Old Corner Bookstore
Old State House
Old South Meeting House

Paul Revere House
USS *Constitution*

Memorials
New England Holocaust Memorial
Robert Gould Shaw Memorial

Museums and Cultural Centers
Dreams of Freedom
Isabella Steward Gardner Museum
John F. Kennedy Library and Museum
Mapparium
Museum of Fine Arts
Museum of Science
New England Aquarium

Observation Areas
Prudential Center Skywalk

Universities
Harvard University

Chapter 17

More Cool Things to See and Do

• •

In This Chapter

▶ Entertaining the kids

▶ Finding special-interest attractions and activities

▶ Getting into the swing: sports

• •

*W*ell-known, high-profile attractions are great — that's why they're so popular, right? But when you get comfortable with Boston, you may feel ready for something more offbeat. The sights and activities in this chapter don't have the same broad appeal as those in Chapter 16, but this group is equally fun. In fact, if you're particularly interested, these may even be *more* fun. Here you'll find suggestions for keeping the kids (small and large) happy, entertaining travelers with specific interests, and captivating sports fans.

For locations of the various attractions described in this chapter, see the "Boston Attractions" and "Cambridge Attractions" maps in Chapter 16, unless otherwise noted.

Especially for Kids

Nearly every attraction in the Boston area appeals to children, and I'm not just saying that — kids clearly have fun all over town. That doesn't mean everyone loves every destination, however. For instance, the little ones feeding the birds at the Public Garden may find the Museum of Science overwhelming, while an older sibling may be more interested in the New England Aquarium.

Make sure you know what your kids are looking forward to and that they know what to expect in Boston. The Web is a great tool for this — a virtual visit from home can make a new destination feel more familiar.

The **Boston Tea Party Ship & Museum** (☎ 617-338-1773; Internet: www.
bostonteapartyship.com), long a fixture on the family-sightseeing
circuit, closed indefinitely after a devastating fire in 2001. A full-scale
replica of one of the three merchant ships used in the pivotal pre-
Revolutionary uprising, this was a fun stop on the way to or from the
Children's Museum. Check ahead to see whether this has reopened.

Children's Museum
Waterfront/Museum Wharf

Visitors under 10 or so usually have a great time here, and most older
travelers admit the attraction is fun, too. The novelty of raising your
voice in a place with *museum* in the name is just the beginning; the
exhibits combine recreation and education to good effect. The displays
include "Science Playground," where everyday objects such as golf balls
and soap bubbles illustrate principles of physics; "Boats Afloat," where
kids operate model vessels on a giant water tank; the "Dress-Up Shop,"
with enough costumes for any aspiring thespian; and the "New Balance
Climb," a kids-only two-story maze. A room is reserved for toddlers, and
the gift shop is tremendous. Allow at least two hours plus travel time
(the route from South Station passes some entertaining construction
equipment).

Museum Wharf, 300 Congress St. (at Fort Point Channel). ☎ *617-426-8855. Internet:
www.bostonkids.org. T: South Station (Red Line); walk north on Atlantic
Avenue one block (past the Federal Reserve Bank), turn right onto Congress Street,
follow it one long block, and cross the bridge. Admission: $7 adults, $6 children age
2–15 and seniors, $2 children age 1, free for children under 1; Fri 5–9 p.m. $1 for all.
Open: June–Aug Mon–Thurs 10 a.m.–7 p.m., Fri 10 a.m.–9 p.m., Sat–Sun
10 a.m.–5 p.m.; Sept–June Sat–Thurs 10 a.m.–5 p.m., Fri 10 a.m.–9 p.m. Closed Jan 1,
Thanksgiving, and Dec 25.*

Especially for Teens

Occupying teenagers can be tricky, but keeping the lines of communi-
cation open can pay off for everyone. If the adolescents in your group
cheerfully go anywhere, count yourselves among the lucky. (Humbly
grin at the jealous parents of the disgruntled teens at the next table.)
But is your child committed to sightseeing or more open to different
types of attractions if one of the sights is in a mall or club? Does a
campus tour count as fun or as pressure? Talk things out.

Shopping options abound. Two excellent malls — the **Shops at
Prudential Center** and **Copley Place** — connect through a skybridge,
so you don't need to go outside. The **CambridgeSide Galleria** mall
offers almost nothing unusual but is about five minutes on foot from
the Museum of Science. For information on these places and other
stores, see Chapter 19.

The shopping in **Harvard Square** also tends toward the generic, but with plenty of unconventional items, too. And the neighborhood scene, especially in "the Pit," near the main T entrance, is always, well, let's just call things eye-opening. For more information, see Chapter 19.

Nightlife may not be the first thing that springs to mind when you're thinking about teen diversions, but a trip to a theme restaurant or the theater can be a great family excursion. Kids love the food and music at the **House of Blues** and **Hard Rock Cafe,** and the interactive theater of *Shear Madness* and **Blue Man Group.** During the day (kids are not allowed at night), teens also enjoy the high-tech games at **Jillian's Boston,** a top destination for video-game fans and pool players. For family-oriented nightlife suggestions, turn to Part VI and look for the Kid Friendly icon.

Finally, consider a **campus tour.** The Boston area is home to dozens of schools. Most admissions offices are eager to show you around, and every college-oriented high-school student knows where to find a few top choices on the Web. Tours are fun, free, and potentially inspirational for the younger kids in your party. Among the many schools in the Boston area are Bentley College, Boston College, Boston University, Brandeis University, Emerson College, Harvard University, Lesley University, the Massachusetts Institute of Technology (MIT), Northeastern University, Simmons College, Suffolk University, Tufts University, the University of Massachusetts, and Wellesley College.

Especially for Sports Fans

The future of Fenway Park, the oldest facility in Major League Baseball (constructed in 1912), is a hot Boston sports topic. Plans to replace the legendary park were on hold after the franchise changed hands in 2002, but antique architecture and modern commerce may still be on a collision course. The team won the 1918 World Series and then took a long break (continuing through press time), which only adds to the aura. For diehard fans who want to see the old Fenway, there really is no time like the present.

Boston's sports scene offers more than just the Red Sox. Included here are a few other teams and places to round out your sports tour.

Fenway Park
Kenmore Square

The **Red Sox** play from April until at least early October. Tickets go on sale in January; the highest prices in baseball start at $18 for the bleachers. Just about every seat in the place is narrow, cramped, and delightfully close to the action. If you failed to plan your trip months in advance, not to worry: Check with the ticket office when you arrive in town, or visit on the day of the game you want to see. A limited number of standing-room tickets go on sale the day of the game, and ticket holders sometimes return unused ones. Your concierge may be able to lend a hand, too.

Given a choice between a right-field grandstand seat (in sections 1 through 11 or so) and the bleachers, go for the slightly less expensive bleachers and the better view.

You can also take a **tour of Fenway Park,** which includes a walk on the warning track. From May to September, tours begin on weekdays only at 10 a.m., 11 a.m., noon, and 1 p.m. No tours operate on holidays or before day games. Admission is $5 for adults, $4 for seniors, $3 for children under 16. Call ☎ **617-236-6666** for more information.

Red Sox ticket office, 4 Yawkey Way (near the corner of Brookline Avenue, in the park). ☎ *617-267-8661 for information; 617-267-1700 for tickets; 617-482-4SOX for touch-tone ticketing. Internet:* www.redsox.com. *T: Fenway (Green Line D) or Kenmore (Green Line B, C, or D). Games usually begin at 6 or 7 p.m. on weeknights, 1 or 3 p.m. on weekends.*

FleetCenter
North Station

The FleetCenter is home to two professional teams and a museum. The NBA's **Celtics** (www.bostonceltics.com) play from early October to April or May. Prices start as low as $10 for some games. Tickets to the NHL **Bruins** (www.bostonbruins.com) games sometimes sell out despite being among the most expensive in the league ($37 and up).

Also at "the Fleet," you can get a sense of how the Boston area earned the reputation as a sports paradise. The **Sports Museum of New England** (☎ **617-624-1234**) occupies the arena's fifth- and sixth-level concourses. This museum offers a specialized collection, most appealing for devoted fans of regional sports. Admission is $5 for adults; $4 for seniors, students, and children 6 to 17. Hours (subject to change during events) are Tuesday to Saturday 10 a.m. to 5 p.m. and Sunday noon to 5 p.m.

Off Causeway Street at North Station. ☎ *617-624-1000 for general information for every event. Internet:* www.fleetcenter.com. *T: Green or Orange Line.*

Gillette Stadium
Foxboro

The 2002 Super Bowl champion **New England Patriots** (☎ **800-543-1776;** Internet: www.patriots.com) sell out most games at Gillette Stadium, which opened in 2002 (replacing Foxboro Stadium). Plan as far ahead as possible. The team plays from August through December or January. If you're lucky enough to land one, tickets start at $49. In warm weather,

Gillette Stadium is the home field of Major League Soccer's New England Revolution (☎ **877-438-7325;** Internet: www.nerevolution.com) as well as a major concert venue.

Route 1. Call the Patriots' number or check the Web site, both listed in the preceding paragraph, for stadium information. Special commuter rail service runs from Boston and Providence before and after games. You may also be able to catch a bus from South Station or the Riverside Green Line T station to the stadium (call ☎ 800-23LOGAN for information about the bus).

College sports are much less expensive than their pro counterparts, and they're loads of fun. Ice hockey is the most hotly contested of the dozens of sports in which local teams compete. Check the papers to see what's up during your visit, then call to check ticket availability. The Division I schools are **Boston College** (☎ **617-552-3000**), **Boston University** (☎ **617-353-3838**), **Harvard University** (☎ **617-495-2211**), and **Northeastern University** (☎ **617-373-4700**).

Especially for Art Lovers

Art galleries cluster on **Newbury Street** in the Back Bay and dot many other Boston and Cambridge neighborhoods. If you enjoy seeing workspaces as well as the final product, check the Friday, Saturday, or Sunday *Globe* when you arrive to see if one of the area's artist-intensive neighborhoods has scheduled "open studios" during your visit. Or just head to Newbury Street; the big names tend to be near the Public Garden end, but the whole street is worth wandering. At your first stop, pick up a copy of the free *Gallery Guide.* When strolling along Newbury Street, remember to look above the first floor, where you're sure to find many more galleries. For a preview, visit www.newbury-st.com.

Institute of Contemporary Art
Back Bay

This museum has no permanent collection, so the treasures may be different every time you visit. The rotating exhibits concentrate on 20th- and 21st-century art. The broad-minded curatorial approach doesn't confine the shows to one medium or era, or even to what most people typically consider art. For example, a recent installation focused on classic automobiles: "Customized: Art Inspired by Hot Rods, Low Riders & American Car Culture."

The ICA has commissioned a new building for a site on the South Boston waterfront, near the federal courthouse on Fan Pier. The up-and-coming firm of Diller + Scofidio won an international competition with a striking design. Check at this location for updates on the construction, including architectural diagrams and models.

955 Boylston St. ☎ *617-266-5152. Internet:* www.icaboston.org. *T: Hynes/ICA (Green Line B, C, or D); turn left onto Mass. Ave. and left onto Boylston Street, then go one long block. Admission: $7 for adults, $5 for students and seniors, free for children under 12; free to all Thurs after 5 p.m. Open: Wed and weekends noon to 5 p.m.; Thurs noon to 9 p.m.; Fri noon to 7 p.m.*

Harvard University Art Museums
Cambridge

Harvard is home to three art museums, which house some 150,000 works. The **Fogg Art Museum** consists of 19 rooms, which concentrate on topics that range from 17th-century Dutch landscapes to contemporary sculpture. The **Busch-Reisinger Museum** is the only museum in North America devoted to the art of northern and central Europe — specifically Germany. The **Arthur M. Sackler Museum** houses the university's collections of Asian, ancient, and Islamic art.

The "Harvard Hot Ticket" includes admission to the art museums, the natural history museums (see "Some Specialty Museums," in this chapter), and the Semitic Museum (which is free anyway). The ticket costs $10 for adults, $8 for seniors and college students, and is good for one year from the date of purchase. Tickets are available at the museums and at the Harvard Collections store in Holyoke Center, 1350 Mass. Ave.

Fogg Art Museum, 32 Quincy St. (near Broadway); Busch-Reisinger Museum, enter through the Fogg; Arthur M. Sackler Museum, 485 Broadway (at Quincy Street). ☎ *617-495-9400. Internet:* www.artmuseums.harvard.edu. *T: Harvard (Red Line); cross Harvard Yard diagonally, and then cross Quincy Street. Or turn your back on the Coop and follow Mass. Ave. to Quincy Street, and then turn left. Admission (covers all three museums): $6.50 for adults, $5 for seniors and students, and free for children under 18; free to all on Sat before noon. Open: Mon–Sat 10 a.m.–5 p.m.; Sun 1–5 p.m. Closed: All major holidays.*

Some Specialty Museums

Museum of Afro-American History
Beacon Hill

This museum highlights the history of blacks in Boston and Massachusetts with fascinating displays and interactive exhibits. The complex includes the **African Meeting House,** 8 Smith Court, also known as the "Black Faneuil Hall." This place of worship is the oldest standing black church in the United States (1806).

46 Joy St. ☎ *617-742-1854. Internet:* www.afroammuseum.org. *T: Park Street (Red or Green Line); climb the hill, walk around the State House to the left, and follow Joy Street 3½ blocks. Admission: Free. Open: Mon–Sat 10 a.m.–4 p.m.*

Harvard Museum of Natural History and Peabody Museum of Archaeology & Ethnology
Cambridge

These museums house world-famous collections of items related to the natural world. The natural history museum comprises three collections: botanical, zoological (from insects to dinosaurs), and mineralogical. The Glass Flowers exhibit, 3,000 eerily lifelike models of more than 840 plant species, is the best known display. The Peabody mounts great displays on international people and cultures; the Native American collections are especially noteworthy.

The "Harvard Hot Ticket" includes admission to the natural history museums, the art museums (see "Especially for Art Lovers," in this chapter), and the Semitic Museum (which is free anyway). The ticket costs $10 for adults, $8 for seniors and college students, and is good for one year from the date of purchase. The ticket is available at the museums and at the Harvard Collections store in Holyoke Center, 1350 Mass. Ave.

Museum of Natural History, 26 Oxford St. ☎ *617-495-3045. Internet:* www.hmnh.harvard.edu. *Peabody Museum, 11 Divinity Ave.* ☎ *617-496-1027. Internet:* www.peabody.harvard.edu. *T: Harvard (Red Line); cross Harvard Yard, keeping the John Harvard statue on your right, turn right at the Science Center, and take the first left onto Oxford Street. Admission (covers both museums): $6.50 adults, $5 students and seniors, $4 children 3–18, children under 3 free; free to all on Sun before noon and Wed 3–5 p.m. during the school year. Open: Daily 9 a.m.–5 p.m.; Sun 1–5 p.m. Closed: Jan 1, July 4, Thanksgiving, and December 25.*

Architectural Highlights

Sheer variety makes Boston a unique treat for architecture buffs. Some areas boast fairly consistent style — notably Beacon Hill, where Federal-era construction abounds (and draconian zoning keeps things that way), and the Back Bay, which didn't exist until the 1830s and remains a 19th-century showpiece. Elsewhere in Boston and Cambridge, the most enjoyable feature is the juxtaposition of classic and cutting-edge.

Here's a convenient twist: Two of the city's architectural gems face each other across Copley Square.

Boston Public Library
Copley Square

This library is home to a museum-quality art collection — and that's just in the main entrance. The 1895 building, an Italian Renaissance–style design by Charles F. McKim, overflows with gorgeous doors, murals, frescoes, sculptures, and paintings. Pick up a brochure or take a free **Art and Architecture Tour.** The 30-minute excursions focus on the McKim building, which boasts ornamentation by such end-of-the-19th-century giants as John Singer Sargent, Daniel Chester French, and Pierre Puvis de Chavannes.

700 Boylston St. ☎ *617-536-5400. Internet:* www.bpl.org. *T: Copley (Green Line) or Back Bay (Orange Line). Admission: Free. Open: Mon–Thurs 9 a.m.–9 p.m.; Fri–Sat 9 a.m.–5 p.m.; Sun (Oct–May only) 1–5 p.m. Tours: Mon 2:30 p.m.; Tues and Wed 6:30 p.m.; Thurs and Sat 11 a.m.; Sun (Sept–May only) 2 p.m.*

Trinity Church
Copley Square

This Romanesque masterwork by H. H. Richardson sits across the square from the Boston Public Library. Completed in 1877, the church rests on a foundation of 4,502 vertical supports called *pilings* (remember, most of the Back Bay is landfill). Brochures and guides can direct you around the building, one of the finest examples of American church architecture. On Fridays, you can enjoy an organ recital, beginning at 12:15 p.m.

545 Boylston St. ☎ *617-536-0944. Admission: Free. Open: Daily 8 a.m.–6 p.m. Sunday services (Episcopal): 8 a.m., 9 a.m., 11 a.m., 6 p.m.*

Historic Houses

The **Paul Revere House** (see the Freedom Trail listings in Chapter 16) is the foremost example but hardly the only one. Charles Bulfinch, the renowned Federal-era architect, designed two Beacon Hill houses that are open for tours; another residence nearby offers a look at a later era. You must take a tour to visit these house museums. Across the river, you can walk in the footsteps of one of the most famous American poets. A tour is not mandatory but greatly enhances the experience.

Harrison Gray Otis House
Beacon Hill

Charles Bulfinch designed this house in 1796 for a promising lawyer who was later mayor of Boston. The historic furnishings and anecdote-laden tour give a sense of the life of a prosperous family in the young republic.

141 Cambridge St. ☎ *617-227-3956. Internet:* www.spnea.org. *T: Charles/MGH (Red Line); follow Cambridge Street away from the river. Tour charges: $5 adults, $4 seniors, $2.50 students. Tours: Wed–Sun hourly 11 a.m.–4 p.m.*

Longfellow National Historic Site
Cambridge/Harvard Square

The books and furnishings at Henry Wadsworth Longfellow's longtime home have remained intact since the legendary poet died in 1882. The house was already famous: When the British laid seige to Boston in the winter of 1775 and 1776, General George Washington made camp here. The ranger-led tour tells the story of the lovely house and famous occupants. The site reopened to visitors after extensive refurbishment in 2002; call ahead to confirm open days and hours.

105 Brattle St., Cambridge ☎ *617-876-4491. Internet:* www.nps.gov/long. *T: Harvard (Red Line); exit toward back of Alewife-bound train and follow Brattle Street six blocks. Admission: Free: Tour charges: $3 for adults, free for children under 17. Open: Wed–Sun 10:00 a.m.–4:30 p.m. Tour schedule varies seasonally; call ahead.*

Nichols House Museum
Beacon Hill

The furnishings and fine art at the 1804 house reflect the taste of several generations of the Nichols family. Charles Bulfinch designed the building (and the neighboring one at Number 57), which was a family home before becoming a museum in 1960. This is a singular chance to see how the upper crust lived and the neighborhood's only private-house museum.

55 Mount Vernon St. ☎ *617-227-6993. T: Park St. (Red or Green Line); climb the hill, walk around the State House to the left, follow Joy Street one long block, and turn left. Tour charge: $5. Tours: May–Oct Tues–Sat; Nov–April Mon, Wed, and Sat (open days may vary; call ahead); every half-hour 12:15– 4:15 p.m.*

Gibson House Museum
Back Bay

This 1859 house overflows with elaborate decorations that personify the word *Victorian.* To modern eyes, that seems synonymous with "over the top." The only design element more outrageous than the ornamentation is the accessories — including a little pink pagoda for the cat.

137 Beacon St. ☎ *617-267-6338. T: Arlington (Green Line); follow Arlington Street past the Public Garden and turn left on Beacon Street. Tour charges: $5. Tours: May–Oct Wed–Sun 1 p.m., 2 p.m., 3 p.m.; Nov–April weekends only 1 p.m., 2 p.m., 3 p.m. Closed: Major holidays.*

A Famous Park

The **Public Garden** (see Chapter 16) will probably satisfy most horticultural cravings. The garden's gorgeous seasonal plantings (which change as soon as specimens start looking tired) complement a variety of trees and shrubs arranged to allow aimless strolling and quiet contemplation. Nature fans can also visit the following attraction.

Arnold Arboretum
Jamaica Plain

Devoted green thumbs may want to set aside half a day for a trip to this botanical garden. Founded in 1872, this is one of the country's oldest parks, with about 15,000 ornamental trees, shrubs, and vines from all over the world, set upon 265 acres.

125 The Arborway (Jamaica Plain is southwest of downtown Boston). ☎ *617-524-1718. Internet:* www.arboretum.harvard.edu. *T: Forest Hills (Orange Line); follow signs to the entrance. Admission: Free. Open: Daily sunrise to sunset. Visitor center open: Weekdays 9 a.m.–4 p.m.; weekends noon to 4 p.m.*

More Cambridge Destinations

Massachusetts Institute of Technology (MIT)
Cambridge

MIT is the most prestigious technical college in . . . well, anywhere that doesn't have a Cal Tech alum nearby. Science gets top billing, but the techies care about more than just practical matters. Picasso, Alexander Calder, Eero Saarinen, and I. M. Pei are among the big names represented in the school's outdoor sculpture collection and architecture. Stop by the Information Center to take a free tour or pick up maps and brochures. The campus of MIT lies a mile or so down Mass. Ave. from Harvard Square, across the Charles River from Beacon Hill and the Back Bay.

MIT Information Center, 77 Mass. Ave. ☎ *617-253-4795. Internet:* http://web.mit.edu. *Tours: Weekdays 10 a.m., 2 p.m.*

MIT Museum
Cambridge

This museum shows holography and more conventional works. Exhibits don't always have an MIT connection, but some of the most interesting — for example, an interactive installation on artificial intelligence, and a look at the work of pioneering photographer Harold "Doc" Edgerton — come straight from campus.

265 Mass. Ave. ☎ *617-253-4444. Internet:* http://web.mit.edu/museum. *T: No. 1 (Dudley-Harvard) bus; exit at first stop across bridge. Or Kendall/MIT (Red Line); follow the campus map at street level. Admission: $5 adults; $2 students, seniors, and children 5–18; chidren under 5 free. Open: Tues–Fri 10 a.m.–5 p.m.; weekends noon to 5 p.m. Closed: Major holidays.*

Whale Watching

The waters off New England are choice whale-migration territory, and Boston is a center of whale watching. The magnificent mammals seek out the feeding grounds of **Stellwagen Bank,** which extend from Gloucester to Provincetown about 27 miles east of Boston. The most common species are the finback and humpback, but you may also see minke whales and rare right whales. The aquatic mammals often perform for spectators by jumping out of the water, and dolphins sometimes join the show. Trained naturalists serve as tour guides, identifying animals and interpreting activities.

The trip to the bank is long. (Children who are accustomed to immediate gratification may not appreciate the journey.) The tedium vanishes in an instant when the first whale appears.

Dress in plenty of layers to fend off the cool sea air, and add sunglasses, a hat, and rubber-soled shoes. Don't forget sunscreen and, of course, a camera. If you tend to get motion sickness, take precautions before you leave the dock.

New England Aquarium whale-watching expeditions (☎ 617-973-5281; Internet: www.neaq.org) operate daily from May through mid-October and on weekends in April and late October. On-board hands-on exhibits help pass the time and prepare passengers for spotting duty. The trips take four to five hours; check departure times when you make reservations. Tickets are $28.35 for adults, $22.58 for seniors and college students, $20.48 for youths 12 to 18, and $17.85 for children 3 to 11. Children must be 3 years old and at least 30 inches tall. Reservations are strongly recommended. The T stop is Aquarium (Blue Line). For information on attractions at the aquarium, see Chapter 16.

If the Aquarium whale watches are booked, try **Boston Harbor Cruises** (☎ 617-227-4321; Internet: www.bostonharborcruises.com) or **Beantown Whale Watch** (☎ 617-542-8000; Internet: www.beantownwhalewatch.com).

Chapter 18

Seeing Boston by Guided Tour

. . . .

In This Chapter

▶ Deciding whether to take a guided tour

▶ Seeing the sights on land, water, and (wow!) both

▶ Investigating special interests

. . . .

The most important question about guided tours is "Why?" If your time is limited, you have trouble getting around, or you haven't a clue what to expect from Boston, a general tour may be right for you. Visitors interested in a particular topic often want a guide who knows the details cold. And if you crave something offbeat, Boston has tours that cover land *and* water.

"Why not?" is an equally good question. Maybe a day trundling off and on a trolley sounds touristy, or you can't bear the cookie-cutter sameness of standard tours. Don't let that turn you off all tours, though — a special-interest walking tour may be perfect. One thing to note: Don't waste money on a tour ticket that covers a whole day if you think one circuit of a trolley is all you need (or can stand). You'll be cheating yourself out of the rich experiences you can only enjoy at ground level.

Boston offers four main types of guided tours: walking, trolley (a bus with a trolley-style body), cruise, and duck.

✔ **Walking tours** place you face-to-face with the city. Boston abounds with small pleasures — a whiff of ocean air, sunlight through a blown-glass window — and walking tours put you in touch with both. But they don't cover everything. Most are brief and tiring. And most regularly scheduled walking tours don't run in winter.

✔ For an overview, a narrated **trolley tour** can be a reasonable option. You can choose specific attractions on which to focus, or take advantage of the all-day pass to visit as many places as you can. Some trolley stops, especially in the North End, lie some distance from the attractions. And piling off a trolley with a little sticker on your shirt, which allows you to reboard, is very much a "typical tourist" thing. But these tours operate year-round.

✔ **Sightseeing cruises** offer sensational scenery and an unusual vantage point. Tours on the Inner Harbor pass the airport (a hit with aviation buffs), include some maritime history, and make pleasant alternatives to walking or driving. But these generally pricey tours aren't comprehensive or long lasting, and they close for the winter.

✔ **Boston Duck Tours,** the only amphibious operation in town, offers a great deal of fun for a fair amount of money. These, too, shut down in cold weather.

Walking Tours

Check the Thursday *Globe* "Calendar" section when you arrive to see whether any operators are offering special-interest or one-shot tours to coincide with events or anniversaries during your visit.

Free 90-minute Freedom Trail walking tours with **National Park Service** rangers as guides start as often as four times a day during busy periods, once daily in the winter. These tours cover the "heart" of the trail (see Chapter 16) — from the Old South Meeting House to the Old North Church. Schedules change seasonally. You don't need reservations but try to arrive 30 minutes prior to the start of the tour, especially during busy times; groups are 30 or less. Tours depart from the Visitor Center, 15 State St. (T: State [Orange or Blue Line]; ☎ 617-242-5642; Internet: www.nps.gov/bost), off Washington Street across from the Old State House. Call to check on tour times and schedules.

The best private walking tour provider is the nonprofit organization **Boston by Foot** (☎ 617-367-2345, or 617-367-3766 for recorded information; Internet: www.bostonbyfoot.com). From May through October, this company offers historical and architectural tours that concentrate on certain neighborhoods and topics. The volunteer guides love the subjects and welcome questions. The 90-minute tours run rain or shine; you don't need reservations. Buy tickets ($9) from the guide. Excursions that leave from Faneuil Hall meet at the statue of Samuel Adams on Congress Street. The regularly scheduled tours include the following:

✔ The **"Heart of the Freedom Trail"** tour starts at Faneuil Hall Tuesday through Saturday at 10 a.m.

✔ The **Beacon Hill** tour starts at the foot of the State House steps on Beacon Street weekdays at 5:30 p.m., Saturday at 10:00 a.m., and Sunday at 2:00 p.m.

✔ The **Victorian Back Bay** tour starts at the steps of Trinity Church at 10 a.m. Friday and Saturday.

✔ The **North End** tour starts at Faneuil Hall on Saturday at 2 p.m.

✔ The **"Boston Underground"** tour includes crypts, the subway, and the Central Artery construction. This tour starts at Faneuil Hall Sunday at 2 p.m.

✔ The **South End** tour starts at Southwest Corridor Park, on Dartmouth Street opposite Back Bay Station, at 10 a.m. on Saturday and Sunday.

The **Society for the Preservation of New England Antiquities** (☎ **617-227-3956**; Internet: www.spnea.org) offers a two-hour tour that focuses on life in the upstairs-downstairs world of Beacon Hill in 1800. "Magnificent and Modest" ($10) starts at the Harrison Gray Otis House, 141 Cambridge St. (see Chapter 17), at 11 a.m. on Saturdays and Sundays from May through October. The price includes a tour of the Otis House; reservations are recommended.

The **Boston Park Rangers** (☎ **617-635-7383**; Internet: www.ci.boston. ma.us/parks) offer free tours of the "Emerald Necklace," pioneering landscape architect Frederick Law Olmsted's loop of green spaces. The tours include Boston Common, Public Garden, Commonwealth Avenue Mall, Muddy River in the Fenway, Olmsted Park, Jamaica Pond, Arnold Arboretum, and Franklin Park. The full six-hour walk happens only a few times a year; one-hour tours that highlight a location or theme take place year-round. Check ahead for topics and schedules.

Trolley Tours

These tours are popular and an easy way to "see" everything without getting a good sense of what Boston is like. Don't fall into that trap — if you can manage the journey, climb down and look around.

The cutthroat competition between operators makes offerings virtually indistinguishable. Each has slightly different stops, but all cover the major attractions. The 90- to 120-minute tours usually include a map and all-day reboarding (so you don't have to do it all at once).

The guide makes or breaks the tour; if you have time, shop around to find one you particularly like before you pay (ask for a tryout). Local news outlets periodically "break" the story that guides are embellishing the facts in narratives (a whole summer of reciting the same stories would probably get to you, too), but most are on the level. And some of the most improbable-sounding stories are actually true. (For instance, the story of a woman and her lover buried alive by her husband inspired Edgar Allan Poe's "The Cask of Amontillado.")

Trolley tickets cost $19 to $24 for adults, $12 or less for kids. Stops usually are at hotels, attractions, and tourist information centers. To start, look for busy waiting areas where you can check out the guides and see if you click with one. Trolleys line up near the New England Aquarium and near the corner of Boylston Street and Charles Street South, where the Common meets the Public Garden.

Each company has cars painted a different color. Orange-and-green **Old Town Trolleys** (☎ 617-269-7150; Internet: www.historictours. com) are the most numerous. Minuteman Tours' **Boston Trolley Tours** (☎ 617-867-5539; Internet: www.historictours.com) are blue, and **Beantown Trolleys,** also known as Brush Hill Tours (☎ 800-343-1328 or 781-986-6100; Internet: www.bostontrolley.com) are red. **CityView Trolley** (☎ 617-363-7899; Internet: www.cityviewtrolley.com) operates silver trolleys. The **Discover Boston Multilingual Trolley Tours** (☎ 617-742-1440) vehicle is white; these tours are conducted in Japanese, Spanish, French, German, and Italian.

Sightseeing Cruises

Seeing Boston from the water gives you a sense of the city's maritime history — and confirms that (except in winter) the water is cooler than the land. On a sweaty summer day, a breezy cruise makes an enjoyable break from a march along the tourist track. The new perspective will help you remember that the city remains an active port, and the sheer number of sailboats will make you wonder if every office in the city is empty.

The season for narrated cruises runs April through October, with spring and fall offerings usually on weekends only. If you get seasick, check the size of the vessel before you pay; larger boats are more comfortable.

See Chapter 17 for information on whale watching.

Boston Harbor Cruises, 1 Long Wharf (☎ 617-227-4321; Internet: www. bostonharborcruises.com), operates 90-minute historic tours of the Inner and Outer Harbor at 11 a.m., 1 p.m., 3 p.m., and 6 or 7 p.m. (the sunset cruise). Tickets are $17 for adults, $14 for seniors, $12 for children under 12. The 45-minute *Constitution* round-trip cruise takes you around the Inner Harbor and docks at the Charlestown Navy Yard so you can go ashore and visit "Old Ironsides." Tours start every hour on the half-hour from 10:30 a.m. to 4:30 p.m., and leave the navy yard on the hour from 11 a.m. to 5 p.m. Tickets are $10 for adults, $9 for seniors, $8 for children. Trips leave from Long Wharf, off Atlantic Avenue between the New England Aquarium and the Marriott.

The **Charles Riverboat Company** (☎ 617-621-3001; Internet: www. charlesriverboat.com) operates out of the CambridgeSide Galleria mall, on First Street in East Cambridge. From the Charles, you can enjoy a panoramic view of Boston (including the towers of the Back Bay) and Cambridge (the landmark dome indicates that you're approaching MIT). The 55-minute cruises depart seven times a day.

Cruises run daily in June, July, and August, and on weekends only in April, May, and September. Tickets are $9 for adults, $8 for seniors, $6 for children 2 to 12. When there's enough demand, there's a sunset cruise Thursday through Saturday. Those tickets cost $10 for adults, $7 for seniors and children.

The cheapest "cruise" is the $1.25 ferry ride from Long Wharf to the Charlestown Navy Yard. The MBTA visitor pass (see Chapter 11) covers the ferry, which makes a great way to finish the Freedom Trail. Another route, also included in the pass, runs from the World Trade Center on Northern Avenue to Lovejoy Wharf, behind North Station.

Duck Tours

The most unusual excursions in town are 80-minute **Boston Duck Tours** (☎ **800-226-7442** or 617-723-DUCK; Internet: www.bostonducktours. com), which operate from April through November. The tours are relatively expensive, but you're paying for a novelty that's worth the money. The vehicles are reconditioned World War II amphibious landing craft known as *ducks* — and like the real thing, the vehicles move easily between land and water. The duck cruises around Boston, passing most of the major sights, and then heads to the Charles River dam and right into the water for a turn around the basin.

Tickets cost $23 for adults, $20 for seniors and students, $13 for children 4 to 12, and 25¢ for children under 4. Tours run every 30 minutes from 9 a.m. to 1 hour before sunset. Reservations are not accepted for groups of 15 or less, and tickets usually sell out, especially on weekends. Try to buy same-day tickets early in the day, or ask about the tickets available two days ahead. There are no tours from December through March.

At press time, the city and the company were negotiating to move the pick-up area for the Duck Tours. Boarding was on the Boylston Street side of the Prudential Center (also known as the "Pru"); that may remain in the neighborhood, but call ahead for the exact location.

Special-Interest Tours

Boston by Foot targets 6- to 12-year-olds (who must be accompanied by an adult) with **Boston by Little Feet.** The 60-minute walking tour concentrates on the architecture along the Freedom Trail and on Boston's role in the American Revolution. The price ($6 per person) includes a map. Tours run from May through October. Meet at the statue of Samuel Adams on the Congress Street side of Faneuil Hall on Saturday at 10 a.m., Sunday at 2 p.m., and Monday at 10 a.m. — rain or shine.

The **Historic Neighborhoods Foundation** (☎ 617-426-1885) offers a 90-minute "Make Way for Ducklings" tour. It follows the path of the Mallard family described in Robert McCloskey's book of the same name, ending at the Public Garden. The price is $7 for adults, $5 for children over 4, free for younger children. Call for schedules.

The **Boston History Collaborative** (☎ 617-574-5950; Internet: www. bostonhistorycollaborative.org), a nonprofit group created to promote historic tourism, coordinates several heritage trails that focus on subjects significant to local history. This group's offerings range from simple (a downloadable self-guided tour route) to elaborate (a 90-minute cruise or 5-hour trolley excursion). Each Web site links to the others. Check ahead for information about **Boston by Sea: The Maritime Trail** (www.bostonbysea.org), the **Literary Trail** (www.Lit-Trail.org), **Boston Family History** (www.BostonFamilyHistory. org), and the **Innovation Trail** (www.innovationtrail.org).

National Park Service rangers lead free two-hour walking tours of the **Black Heritage Trail,** a 1.6-mile route on Beacon Hill that includes stations of the Underground Railroad, homes of famous citizens, and the first integrated public school. Tours leave from the Visitor Center, 46 Joy St. (☎ 617-742-5415; Internet: www.nps.gov/boaf); check ahead for schedules. To explore on your own, pick up a brochure from the Visitor Center; these brochures include maps and descriptions of the buildings.

The **Boston Women's Heritage Trail** creates walking tours that include homes, churches, and social and political institutions associated with influential women. You can buy a guide (make sure you get the most recent, from 1999) at the National Park Service Visitor Center at 15 State St.; you can also check local bookstores and historic sites for these guides. For more detailed information, call ☎ 617-522-2872 or visit www.bwht.org.

Old Town Trolley (☎ 617-269-7150; Internet: www.historictours. com) offers specialty tours on a wide and changing variety of subjects. These tours include "JFK's Boston," which visits sights related to the former president; a brew pub tour; a chocolate-tasting tour; and a seafood tour. Tickets usually cost at least $22 for adults, more if the tour includes refreshments. Call for information, schedules, and reservations.

Chapter 19

A Shop-'Til-You-Drop Guide to Boston

. . . .

In This Chapter

▶ Checking out the big names and other famous labels

▶ Exploring the main shopping areas

▶ Finding the right place for what you want

. . . .

*B*efore you feel guilty about shopping when there's still so much sightseeing to do, consider this: Visitors to Boston consistently list the city's stores as favorite destinations, even ahead of the city's museums. Retail outlets of every description await you, from unusual boutiques to indistinguishable chain stores. In this chapter, I concentrate on the offbeat destinations, with plenty of attention to big national names and retail-intensive neighborhoods. All over town, you'll also find tons of businesses you recognize from the mall at home.

Unless otherwise noted, see the "Boston Shopping" map in this chapter for the locations of the stores I mention.

The Shopping Scene

 The first thing to know is that the 5% Massachusetts sales tax does not apply to clothing priced below $175 or to food items. If you buy an article of clothing for $175 or more, the tax applies only to the amount over $175. But if you're shipping merchandise to a state where the store has a branch, the sales tax for that state usually applies; check before celebrating a bargain that isn't.

Stores usually open at 9:30 or 10:00 a.m. and close at around 6 or 7 p.m. A few don't open on Sunday, but most do, from noon to 5 or 6 p.m. Exceptions include shopping malls, which stay open later; art galleries, which typically don't open until 11 a.m., and close on Monday; and smaller shops, which often have differing hours. When in doubt, call ahead.

Boston Shopping

Abercrombie & Fitch **21**
Ann Taylor **6, 21**
Anthropologie **1**
Artful Hand Gallery **6**
Barnes & Noble **3, 19**
Black Ink **14**
Borders **20**
Boston City Store **21**
Brattle Book Shop **15**
Caswell-Massey **6**
Coach **21**
Copley Place **6**
Crate & Barrel **21**
Dairy Fresh Candies **22**

Disney Store **21**
FAO Schwarz **8**
Filene's **17**
Filene's Basement **18**
The Gap **21**
Globe Corner Bookstore **7**
Gucci **6**
Hermès of Paris **11**
Koo De Kir **12**
Legal Seafoods **3, 6**
Lord & Taylor **5**
Louis Vuitton **6**
Macy's **16**
The Magic Hat **21**

Museum of Fine Arts **6, 21**
Neiman Marcus **6**
Newbury Comics **21**
Restoration Hardware **2**
Rockport **21**
Saks Fifth Avenue **4**
Salumeria Italiana **23**
Shop at the Union **9**
Shops at Prudential Center **3**
Shreve, Crump & Low **10**
Thomas Pink **6**
Tiffany & Co. **6**
Upstairs Downstairs Antiques **13**
Williams-Sonoma **6, 21**

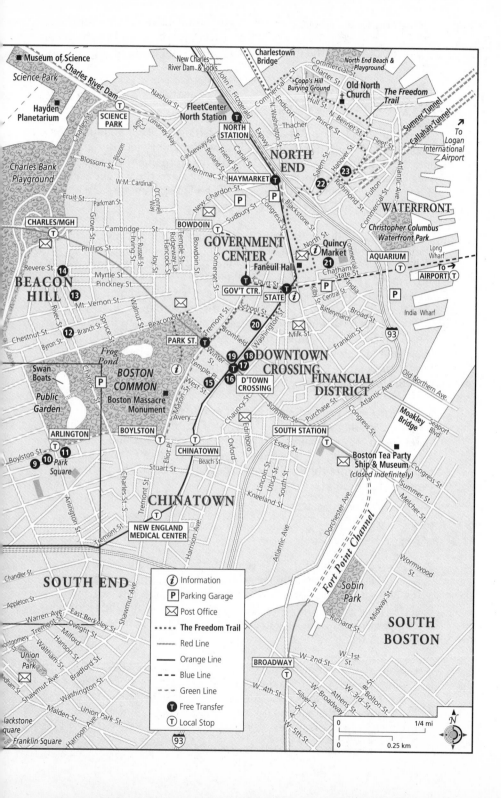

■ Museum of Science

Science Park

Hayden Planetarium

SCIENCE PARK

New Charles River Dam & Locks

Charles River Dam

Charlestown Bridge

North End Beach & Playground

Commercial St.

Copp's Hill Burying Ground

Old North Church

The Freedom Trail

Charles Bank Playground

Nashua St.

FleetCenter North Station

NORTH STATION

N. Washington St.

Endicott

N. Bennet St.

Prince St.

Hanover St.

To Logan International Airport

Sumner Tunnel

Callahan Tunnel

Blossom St.

Blossom Ct.

W.M. Cardinal

Causeway St.

Portland St.

Friend St.

Canal St.

Merrimac St.

HAYMARKET

Thacher

Fleet St.

WATERFRONT

Fruit St.

Parkman St.

O'Connell Way

New Chardon St.

Sudbury St.

Congress St.

Blackstone St.

North St.

Richmond St.

Fulton

Atlantic Ave.

Commercial St.

Christopher Columbus Waterfront Park

CHARLES/MGH

Cambridge St.

BOWDOIN

Temple St.

Hancock St.

Ridgeway La.

GOVERNMENT CENTER

North St.

Quincy Market

Long Wharf

Phillips St.

Revere St.

Grove St.

Irving St.

S. Russell St.

Joy St.

Somerset St.

Faneuil Hall

Chatham State St.

AQUARIUM

To AIRPORT

Myrtle St.

Pinckney St.

BEACON HILL

Mt. Vernon St.

GOV'T CTR.

Court St.

STATE

India St.

Central St.

India Wharf

Chestnut St.

Byron St.

Branch St.

Beacon St.

Tremont St.

School St.

Washington St.

Battenmarch

Broad St.

Milk St.

Franklin St.

93

Frog Pond

PARK ST.

Bromfield

Winter St.

DOWNTOWN CROSSING

Old Northern Ave.

Swan Boats

BOSTON COMMON

Temple Pl.

West St.

D'TOWN CROSSING

FINANCIAL DISTRICT

Atlantic Ave.

Congress St.

Moakley Bridge

Seaport Blvd.

Public Garden

Boston Massacre Monument

Mason St.

Avery

Chauncy St.

Edinboro

Summer St.

Purchase St.

ARLINGTON

BOYLSTON

SOUTH STATION

Boston Tea Party Ship & Museum (closed indefinitely)

Summer St.

Melcher St.

Boylston St.

Park Square

CHINATOWN

Eliot Pl.

Oxford

Beach St.

Essex St.

Lincoln St.

Utica St.

South St.

Kneeland St.

Stuart St.

Arlington St.

CHINATOWN

Charles St. S.

Tremont St.

NEW ENGLAND MEDICAL CENTER

Harrison Ave.

Atlantic Ave.

Dorchester Ave.

Fort Point Channel

Wormwood St.

Midway St.

SOUTH BOSTON

Chandler St.

SOUTH END

Richard St.

Sobin Park

Appleton St.

Warren Ave.

East Berkeley St.

Dwight St.

Milford St.

Shawmut Ave.

Tremont St.

Montgomery St.

Waltham St.

Hanson St.

Bradford St.

BROADWAY

W. 1st St.

W. 2nd St.

Union Park

Washington St.

Union Park St.

W. 3rd St.

W. 4th St.

Silver St.

W. Broadway

Athens St.

B. Bolton St.

Malden St.

Shawmut Ave.

blackstone quare

Franklin Square

Harrison Ave.

93

W. 5th St.

(i) Information

P Parking Garage

✉ Post Office

••••• **The Freedom Trail**

Red Line

Orange Line

Blue Line

Green Line

● Free Transfer

Ⓣ Local Stop

0 — 1/4 mi

0 — 0.25 km

N

Always check out the gift shop when you visit a museum or other attraction (see Chapters 16 and 17). Prices are competitive, and the merchandise often draws on the museum's collections in design or inspiration.

The Biggest Name

That would be **Filene's Basement,** 426 Washington St., at Summer Street. After a period when the store's well-known bargains were harder to sniff out, "the Basement" (now part of the Midwestern chain Value City) is back on track. Somehow the store has maintained the cachet accumulated in nearly a century of great deals on men's, women's, and children's clothing and accessories.

The legendary "automatic markdown" policy applies only at this store. After merchandise has been on the racks for two weeks, the price drops by 25%. Boards hanging from the ceiling bear the all-important dates; the original sale date is on the back of the price tag. Prices continue to fall until, after five weeks (and 75% off), everything remaining goes to charity. To fit in with the locals, be aggressive and don't be shy about telling people how much — how little, really — you paid for that stunning designer outfit. And if you can't make up your mind about something, just buy the item. You can always return merchandise, but you can't always come back and find that special number the next day. Yes, this is the voice of experience talking.

The store is open weekdays 9:30 a.m. to 7:30 p.m., Saturday 9:00 a.m. to 7:30 p.m., Sunday 11:00 a.m. to 7:00 p.m. Crowds can be huge at lunch and after work, especially during special sales; try to shop in the morning or mid-afternoon. T: Downtown Crossing (Red or Orange Line); enter directly from the station or through Filene's, the department store upstairs.

The Big Names

People complain about the rise of chain stores, but when the same people really need a wedding present, off they trot to Crate & Barrel. Many of Boston's high-profile retailers are branches, often of chains based in New York. I single out a few in the neighborhood descriptions that appear later in this chapter; for that only-in-Boston feeling, check out the following:

✔ **Shreve, Crump & Low,** 330 Boylston St. (☎ **617-267-9100**), is the oldest jewelry store in the country (in business since 1796), selling legendary diamonds, traditional silver baby presents, and even antiques on the second floor. Call it "Shreve's," and remember to check out the estate jewelry.

✔ The **Museum of Fine Arts** operates gift shops at Copley Place (☎ 617-536-8818) and in the South Market Building at Faneuil Hall Marketplace (☎ 617-720-1266). The well-stocked satellites can't replace the real thing, but these other locations make a fine substitute.

✔ **Filene's,** 426 Washington St., at Summer Street, Downtown Crossing (☎ 617-357-2100), and CambridgeSide Galleria, East Cambridge (☎ 617-621-3800), is part of a national department-store conglomerate but with a fine old New England name (fie-*leen's*). *Note:* This is not Filene's Basement (see the preceding section, "The Biggest Name"), which is below Filene's and no longer the same company.

✔ **Newbury Comics** is a local chain of fantastic music stores that also stock gifts and comics. There are three handy locations: 332 Newbury St., Back Bay (☎ 617-236-4930); 1 Washington Mall, Washington Street off State Street, Downtown Crossing (☎ 617-248-9992); and 36 John F. Kennedy St., in the Garage mall, Harvard Square, Cambridge (☎ 617-491-0337).

Great Shopping Neighborhoods

Here I zero in on some consumer-friendly areas and single out some favorite stops. By no means does that mean these areas are the only parts of town worth trolling, or that the shops I mention are the only ones you should visit. You know what you like, and you can probably track down your favorite stuff. Hey, you turned straight to the shopping chapter (go on, confess) — trust your instincts.

The Back Bay

From name-dropping socialites to skateboarders in droopy pants, everyone shops in the Back Bay. The main shopping streets are Newbury and Boylston (T: Arlington [Green Line]).

For locations of shops on Newbury Street, see the "Newbury Street Shopping" map in this chapter.

Newbury Street is the Rodeo Drive of New England. Known as the home of the area's toniest boutiques and art galleries, Newbury runs from **Chanel** and **Burberrys** (at Arlington Street) to the **Virgin Megastore** and **Urban Outfitters** (at Mass. Ave.). The street even has a Web site (www.newbury-st.com). You'll see **Brooks Brothers,** two **Armani** outlets, the alarmingly huge **Niketown,** and an assortment of other famous names, including **Kiehl's** (cosmetics) and **Diptyque** (fancy French candles).

I tend to seek out the smaller retailers who celebrate specialties in an attitude-free parallel universe: for exquisite jewelry, **John Lewis, Inc.,** 97 Newbury St. (☎ 617-266-6665); for museum-quality artisan work, the **Society of Arts and Crafts,** 175 Newbury St. (☎ 617-266-1810; Internet: www.societyofcrafts.org); for gothic home accessories (not as far-out as this sounds), **Gargoyles, Grotesques & Chimeras,** 262 Newbury St. (☎ 617-536-2362). Fine cosmetics and friendly service appeal equally at **E6 Apothecary,** 167 Newbury St. (☎ 800-664-6635 or 617-236-8138; Internet: www.e6apothecary.com); the **International Poster Gallery,** 205 Newbury St. (☎ 617-375-0076; Internet: www. internationalposter.com), offers an agreeable mix of art and commerce; and **Avenue Victor Hugo Bookshop,** 339 Newbury St. (☎ 617-266-7746; Internet: www.avenuevictorhugobooks.com), is an old-time independent bookseller. That's six. I promise you can find a dozen more with hardly any effort.

Dozens of art galleries are Newbury Street's other claim to fame. Pick up a copy of the free *Gallery Guide* (at any gallery and many other businesses), or start at Arlington Street and work your way west. Remember that some of the most interesting collections are above ground level. Don't be afraid to ask questions — the people hanging around the gallery, who often include the manager, love to talk about the art.

Boylston Street gets going at Arlington Street, with **Hermès of Paris** and **Shreve, Crump & Low** (see "The Big Names" earlier in this chapter), and extends past the entrance to the **Shops at Prudential Center** (see later in this section). This street is where you'll find **FAO Schwarz, Restoration Hardware, Anthropologie,** and **Lord & Taylor.**

The **Shop at the Union,** 356 Boylston St. (☎ 617-536-5651; Internet: www.weiu.org) is one exceptional destination. The shop carries a dizzying variety of top-quality gifts, clothing, home accessories, and jewelry — not cheap but practically guilt free. Proceeds go to the non-profit Women's Educational and Industrial Union, an educational and social-service organization founded in 1877.

Boylston Street also holds one entrance to the giant consumer wonderland of the **Shops at Prudential Center,** 800 Boylston St. (T: Prudential [Green Line E] or Back Bay [Orange Line]; ☎ 800-SHOP-PRU or 617-267-1002), and **Copley Place,** 100 Huntington Ave. (☎ 617-375-4400). Skybridges link the malls, which incorporate dozens of national chains that allow you to pretend you've never left home, plus a smattering of unique boutiques.

The "Pru" contains a food court, a **Legal Sea Foods** (☎ 617-266-6800) restaurant (see Chapter 14), a huge **Barnes & Noble,** dozens of shops, an entrance to **Saks Fifth Avenue,** and various pushcarts that sell souvenirs, crafts, and accessories. The **Greater Boston Convention & Visitors Bureau** (☎ 800-SEE-BOSTON or 617-536-4100; Internet: www. bostonusa.com) operates the information booth.

Newbury Street Shopping

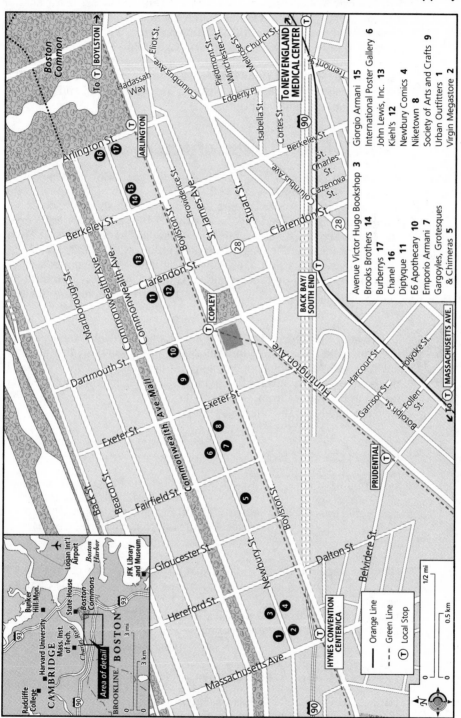

Giorgio Armani **15**
International Poster Gallery **6**
John Lewis, Inc. **13**
Kiehl's **12**
Newbury Comics **4**
Niketown **8**
Society of Arts and Crafts **9**
Urban Outfitters **1**
Virgin Megastore **2**

Avenue Victor Hugo Bookshop **3**
Brooks Brothers **14**
Burberrys **17**
Chanel **16**
Diptyque **11**
E6 Apothecary **10**
Emporio Armani **7**
Gargoyles, Grotesques
& Chimeras **5**

Copley Place is a more upscale complex — Tiffany & Co. is one of the first stores you see entering from the Pru. **Neiman Marcus** is the anchor and the store's neighbors include such big names as **Gucci, Louis Vuitton,** and London haberdasher **Thomas Pink. Williams-Sonoma, Caswell-Massey,** and **Legal Sea Foods** (☎ 617-266-7775) also are here. Independent retailers tend not to thrive in this location; a welcome exception is the **Artful Hand Gallery,** Copley Place (☎ 617-262-9601), which carries a discriminating selection of jewelry, wood and glass pieces, ceramics, and sculpture.

Faneuil Hall Marketplace

Boston's top attraction, Faneuil Hall Marketplace (T: Government Center [Green or Blue Line]; ☎ 617-338-2323) draws much of its appeal from abundant consumer enticements. Most street-level shops are chain outlets such as **Ann Taylor, Coach, Crate & Barrel,** the **Disney Store,** and **Rockport;** there's also a huge, free-standing **Abercrombie & Fitch.** Exceptions include **The Magic Hat,** Marketplace Center (☎ 617-439-8840), which stocks all the trappings to satisfy would-be magicians. Second-floor shops (not including the **Gap** and **Williams-Sonoma**) tend to be quirkier independents, as do the pushcarts that cluster between the North Market Building and Quincy Market.

The **Boston City Store** (☎ 617-635-3606), on the lower level of Faneuil Hall, is a must if you enjoy unpredictability. At press time, this fun and unusual destination was open by appointment only; call ahead to see if that's changed. City surplus doesn't sound all that exciting, but the funky merchandise ranges from T-shirts to mounted-police horseshoes to old street signs — and the offerings change regularly.

Charles Street

Beacon Hill's main street is both a neighborhood hangout and a gift-shopper magnet. Charles Street (T: Charles/MGH [Red Line]) is also home to some excellent antiques shops and a curiously refined 7-Eleven — thanks to the strict zoning laws that cover the landmark district.

Head for a specific destination, or just stroll up one side of the street and down the other. My favorite gift shops are **Koo De Kir,** 34 Charles St. (☎ 617-723-8111), and **Black Ink,** 101 Charles St. (☎ 617-723-3883). **Upstairs Downstairs Antiques,** 93 Charles St. (☎ 617-367-1950) is a good place to start antique hunting.

Downtown Crossing

Filene's, Macy's, and **Filene's Basement** occupy the corner of Washington and Summer streets, the busiest stretch of the pedestrian mall at the center of Downtown Crossing (T: Downtown Crossing [Red or Orange Line]). The shopping here isn't as highfalutin as in the Back Bay or as touristy as at Faneuil Hall Marketplace. Downtown Crossing is where the locals shop.

Washington and Winter streets overflow with discount clothing and shoe stores, souvenir carts, and places for office workers to grab a quick lunch. Another necessity for real Bostonians is a well-stocked bookstore, and Downtown Crossing has three. **Barnes & Noble** and **Borders** carry a predictably huge range of books. The stock at the **Brattle Book Shop,** 9 West St. (off Washington Street; ☎ 800-447-9595 or 617-542-0210; Internet: www.brattlebookshop.com), is an unpredictably huge assortment of used, rare, and out-of-print titles.

The North End

You already know you'll be coming here for a pasta dinner. If you want to make your own, the North End (T: Haymarket [Green or Orange Line]) is the place to stock up.

Italian groceries and fresh meats and cheeses cram the tiny **Salumeria Italiana,** 151 Richmond St. (☎ 617-523-8743). Your sweet tooth can lead you to **Dairy Fresh Candies,** 57 Salem St. (☎ 800-336-5536 or 617-742-2639).

Cambridge

Harvard Square (T: Harvard [Red Line]) grows less individualized by the day, but this area is still worth a trip if you know where to look. Bookstore enthusiasts and T-shirt collectors will be particularly happy here. (For locations of stores in this section, see the "Harvard Square Shopping" map in this chapter.)

Agreeable chain stores in the neighborhood include **Urban Outfitters, Barnes & Noble** (which runs the book operation at the **Harvard Coop**), **Crate & Barrel,** and **Tower Records.**

"The Square" is great for window-shopping, and the best displays are at **Calliope,** 33 Brattle St. (☎ 617-876-4149), a terrific children's clothing and toy store. **Colonial Drug,** 49 Brattle St. (☎ 617-864-2222), a family business that specializes in hard-to-find fragrances, is one block away. At **Beadworks,** 23 Church St. (☎ 617-868-9777), you'll find everything you need to make your own jewelry — an excellent activity if kids are along, and even if not.

If something at one of the Harvard museums catches your eye, visit **Harvard Collections,** in Holyoke Center, 1350 Mass. Ave. (☎ 617-496-0700), for pieces copied from or inspired by objects in the university's vast stores of art and artifacts — an excellent, unusual souvenir.

Join the crowd: College bookstores

Anything big enough to hold a college logo is for sale somewhere, and Boston offers a breathtaking variety. The big name is Harvard, of course, but savvy sight-seers may prefer something less predictable. If that's you, check out the following:

✔ **Barnes & Noble** at Boston University, 660 Beacon St., Kenmore Square (☎ 617-267-8484)

✔ **Emerson College Book Store,** 80 Boylston St., Theater District (☎ 617-728-7700)

✔ **MIT Coop,** 3 Cambridge Center, Kendall Square (☎ 617-499-3200)

✔ **Northeastern University Bookstore,** 360 Huntington Ave., Fenway (between Symphony Hall and the Museum of Fine Arts; ☎ 617-373-2286)

✔ **Suffolk University Bookstore,** 148 Cambridge St., Beacon Hill (☎ 617-227-4085)

For Harvard paraphernalia, try the following, all in Harvard Square:

✔ **Harvard Coop,** 1400 Mass. Ave. (☎ 617-499-2000)

✔ **Harvard Shop,** 52 John F. Kennedy St. (☎ 617-864-3000)

✔ **J. August & Co.,** 1320 Mass. Ave. (☎ 617-864-6650)

Now, how about those bookstores? Two of the area's best general-interest stores are here: **WordsWorth Books,** 30 Brattle St. (☎ 800-899-2202 or 617-354-5201; Internet: www.wordsworth.com); and the **Harvard Book Store,** 1256 Mass. Ave. (☎ 800-542-READ outside the 617 area code, or 617-661-1515; Internet: www.harvard.com). Words-Worth discounts everything except textbooks at least 10%, and the basement of the Harvard Book Store overflows with discounted and used books.

Two worthwhile special-interest bookstores are **Curious George Goes to WordsWorth,** 1 John F. Kennedy St. (☎ 617-498-0062; Internet: www.wordsworth.com), an excellent children's store, and the **Globe Corner Bookstore,** 28 Church St. (☎ 617-497-6277; Internet: www.globecorner.com), where you'll find travel books, maps, narratives, and atlases.

Harvard Square also makes a good starting point for a shopping stroll. **Mass. Ave.** runs north to **Porter Square** (T: Porter [Red Line]) through boutique country and southeast toward funkier **Central Square** (T: Central [Red Line]). Heading toward Porter, be sure to leave time for a stop at **Abodeon,** 1713 Mass. Ave. (☎ 617-497-0137), a quirky home-furnishings store, and **Joie de Vivre,** 1792 Mass. Ave. (☎ 617-864-8188), a superb gift shop with a great kaleidoscope collection. On the way to Central Square, you'll pass **Bowl & Board,** 1063 Mass. Ave. (☎ 617-661-0350), which specializes in upscale home accessories, and a **Crate & Barrel** furniture store. Just outside Central Square,

Harvard Square Shopping

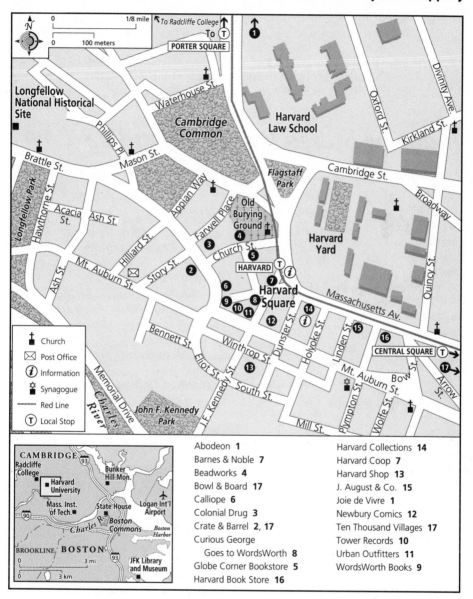

Abodeon **1**
Barnes & Noble **7**
Beadworks **4**
Bowl & Board **17**
Calliope **6**
Colonial Drug **3**
Crate & Barrel **2, 17**
Curious George
  Goes to WordsWorth **8**
Globe Corner Bookstore **5**
Harvard Book Store **16**

Harvard Collections **14**
Harvard Coop **7**
Harvard Shop **13**
J. August & Co. **15**
Joie de Vivre **1**
Newbury Comics **12**
Ten Thousand Villages **17**
Tower Records **10**
Urban Outfitters **11**
WordsWorth Books **9**

Ten Thousand Villages, 694 Mass. Ave. (☎ **617-876-2414**) is a non-profit craft and gift shop that a friend of mine fondly calls "the Third World tchotchke emporium."

In **East Cambridge,** the **CambridgeSide Galleria,** 100 CambridgeSide Place (☎ **617-621-8666**), is a three-level mall with more than

100 specialty stores, including a huge **J. Crew** store, a branch of **Borders,** several restaurants, and a food court. Part of the appeal is how astonishingly generic this place is; the Galleria may be just the bargaining chip you need to lure your teenagers to the nearby Museum of Science. T: Lechmere (Green Line), then walk two blocks. Or Kendall/ MIT (Red Line), then the free shuttle bus, which runs every 10 to 20 minutes Monday through Saturday from 10:00 a.m. to 9:30 p.m. and Sunday from 11:00 a.m. to 7:00 p.m.

Index of Stores by Merchandise

Antiques
Upstairs Downstairs Antiques

Art and Posters
International Poster Gallery

Books
Avenue Victor Hugo Bookshop
Barnes & Noble
Borders
Brattle Book Shop
Curious George Goes to WordsWorth
Globe Corner Bookstore
Harvard Book Store
Harvard Coop
WordsWorth Books

Clothing and Accessories
Abercrombie & Fitch
Ann Taylor
Armani
Burberrys
Brooks Brothers
Chanel
Coach
The Gap
Gucci
Hermès of Paris
J. Crew
Louis Vuitton
Thomas Pink
Urban Outfitters

Cosmetics and Perfume
Caswell-Massey
Colonial Drug

E6 Apothecary
Kiehl's

Crafts
Artful Hand Gallery
Society of Arts and Crafts

Department Stores
Filene's
Lord & Taylor
Macy's
Neiman Marcus
Saks Fifth Avenue

Discount Clothing
Filene's Basement

Food and Candy
Dairy Fresh Candies
Salumeria Italiana

Footwear
Niketown
Rockport

Gifts and Toys
Anthropologie
Black Ink
Boston City Store
Calliope
Disney Store
FAO Schwarz
Joie de Vivre
Koo De Kir
The Magic Hat

Museum of Fine Arts gift shops
The Shop at the Union
Urban Outfitters

Home Accessories
Abodeon
Bowl & Board
Crate & Barrel
Diptyque
Gargoyles, Grotesques & Chimeras
Restoration Hardware
Williams-Sonoma

Jewelry
Beadworks
John Lewis, Inc.

Shreve, Crump & Low
Tiffany & Co.

Malls
CambridgeSide Galleria
Copley Place
Shops at Prudential Center

Music
Newbury Comics
Tower Records
Virgin Megastore

Chapter 20

Five Great Boston Itineraries

● ●

In This Chapter

▶ Plotting one-, three-, and five-day adventures

▶ Keeping the kids entertained

▶ Dabbling in the art world

▶ Organizing your time

● ●

*F*rom the moment you land in a new destination, you can almost hear the clock ticking. The unfamiliar place offers so much for you to see, and you never seem to have enough time to explore all the possibilities.

Relax and consider two things: First, Boston is a compact place; you can get a good sense of the city in a few days. Second, you can't master *any* destination of appreciable size in a short time, so the pressure is off. Yes, you can see six or eight places in a day, but what does that get you? A mediocre-to-unsatisfying trip and exhaustion, that's what.

Do what you want with the time you have. In this chapter, I suggest outlines for trips of certain durations or focuses; feel free to mix and match as you see fit.

Boston in One Day

Two itineraries leap to mind if you can spend only one day in Boston: You can concentrate on one attraction (such as the Museum of Fine Arts, Harvard Square, Newbury Street, or the Museum of Science) without the smallest pang about not doing more, or you can try to sample enough of the city to get a sense that you've actually been here, not just *seen* everything. Here I offer suggestions for the latter. This itinerary works in a loop — you can start at the beginning in the morning, or pick things up in the middle and go from there.

Start with an hour or less at **Filene's Basement** (see Chapter 19). Be there when it opens at 9:30 a.m., or earlier if the store is offering a special sale — check the newspapers when you arrive. Then follow the **Freedom Trail** from **Boston Common** to **Faneuil Hall Marketplace,** or take a 90-minute National Park Service ranger tour (see Chapter 18).

Have lunch at the marketplace (see Day 1 in the next itinerary, "Boston in Three Days") as you evaluate your options for what to do after lunch. Pick one of these four: Finish the Freedom Trail, take a **sightseeing cruise** (see Chapter 18), explore the **New England Aquarium** (see Chapter 16), or head to the **Children's Museum** (see Chapter 17). In the late afternoon, make your way to the Back Bay and enjoy the view from the **Prudential Center Skywalk.** Sunset is the perfect time to visit; let your appetite and the time of year determine whether you eat dinner before or after. If you can't leave town without a lobster, there are three branches of **Legal Sea Foods** close by. If you'd rather stay downtown, enjoy dinner at the waterfront Legal's, and then head to the lounge at the 33rd-floor **Bay Tower** (see Chapter 23) for drinks, dessert, and dancing.

Boston in Three Days

Day 1: In the morning, follow at least part of the **Freedom Trail** (see Chapter 16). The trail officially starts at Boston Common, but you can start in Charlestown, somewhere in the middle, or at the National Park Service Visitor Center with a ranger tour (see Chapter 18). The trail takes at least two hours. On the first section, consider a shopping detour to **Filene's Basement,** especially if you can get there before the lunch rush. See the first map in Chapter 19 for the location. Break for coffee, snacks, or lunch at **Faneuil Hall Marketplace,** where takeout counters and sit-down restaurants satisfy nearly every taste. **Durgin-Park** (see Chapter 14) is a good choice for the latter. If the weather is fine, take a picnic — stock up in the Quincy Market food court — across Atlantic Avenue to the end of Long Wharf (past the Marriott) or to Christopher Columbus Park.

In the afternoon, push on to the **North End.** Between the Paul Revere House and the Old North Church, pause on **Hanover Street** for espresso or cappuccino and a pastry at a *caffè* (see Chapter 15). If you opt to finish the trail — and I'm *not* saying you have to — return downtown on the MBTA **ferry** to Long Wharf from the Charlestown Navy Yard. When you arrive at Long Wharf, look for a branch of **Legal Sea Foods** across the street from the ferry dock; you can grab some dinner here (but first you may decide to visit your hotel to rest and wash up — the people at the next table certainly will appreciate your rejuvenated cleanliness). If all this sounds exhausting, pick a restaurant near your hotel instead. If you're still up for more, make evening plans that include a trip to the **Prudential Center Skywalk** or back to Faneuil Hall Marketplace before or after dinner.

Day 2: This is museum day. Be there when the doors open at the **Museum of Fine Arts (MFA)** at 10 a.m., or the **Museum of Science** at 9 a.m., and plan to stay at least through midday — both museums offer decent options for lunch. If art is your interest, consider spending

part of the afternoon at the **Isabella Stewart Gardner Museum,** up
the street from the MFA. From the science museum, a strenuous but
rewarding walk leads to the **Bunker Hill Monument** (the last stop on
the Freedom Trail, in case you didn't get there on Day 1). The walk
takes about 30 minutes; that's not long for some, but most of the trip
is uphill.

If none of that appeals to you, start the day at the **John F. Kennedy
Library and Museum** or the **Children's Museum.** Any of these options
can land you in the Back Bay by midafternoon, the perfect time for
a **Duck Tour, swan boat** ride, or just some downtime in the **Public
Garden.** Collect yourself and do a little **shopping** on Newbury or
Boylston Street (see Chapter 19). Freshen up (again, remember new-
found friends at the adjoining tables), and head to the **North End** for
a hearty Italian dinner. Follow with dessert and people-watching in a
Hanover Street *caffè* (especially if you didn't indulge on Day 1). Or plan
a visit to a bar or club — maybe the **Comedy Connection, Cheers,** or
the **Black Rose,** all at Faneuil Hall Marketplace, or Cambridge's **House
of Blues** (see Chapter 23).

Check the forecast when you arrive; inclement weather may mean
scheduling your museum-visiting day to coincide with nasty conditions.

Day 3: Now you're off to **Cambridge.** This area can occupy a whole
day or just half (if the latter, use the extra time to further explore one
of the options on the Day 1 or 2 itineraries earlier in this section). Start
with breakfast in the heart of **Harvard Square** — continental at **Au Bon
Pain,** 1360 Mass. Ave. (☎ **617-497-9797**), or full at the **Greenhouse
Coffee Shop,** 3 Brattle St. (☎ **617-354-3184**). Then tour the Harvard
campus (see Chapter 16), visit one or more of the **university museums**
(see Chapter 17), or do some **shopping** (see Chapter 19). Stroll along
picturesque Brattle Street to the **Longfellow National Historic Site**
(see Chapter 17). For lunch, follow the students to **Mr. Bartley's Burger
Cottage** (see Chapter 14), or picnic by the river on something tasty
from **Formaggio's Deli** (see Chapter 15). In the afternoon, continue to
explore or shop in Cambridge, or head back to Boston. Spend this time
hitting **Filene's Basement** if you haven't yet (or even if you have). For
the evening, consider activities that don't strain your budget, starting
with dinner at one of Boston's neighborhood restaurants (see Chapter
14). Follow with a student play or performance or a free concert or film.
If you're up for another big night out, consider a **Boston Symphony
Orchestra** performance or a pre- or post-Broadway play (see Chapter 22).

Boston in Five Days

If you have five days in Boston, follow the itinerary in the preceding
section for the first three days, and then continue with the following:

Day 4: Road trip! Turn to Chapter 21 and pick a town or two where you can spend the day. Explore **Lexington, Concord, Salem, Marblehead, Gloucester, Rockport, Plymouth,** or some sensible combination thereof. You don't need to rent a car for this, but you may want to; at busy times, book the car when you reserve your flight and hotel. Have dinner at your day-trip destination, or return to Boston or Cambridge. Afterward, you can hear jazz at the **Regattabar** in Cambridge or **Scullers** in Boston, or barely hear yourself think at a loud-mouth **club** in Cambridge, Somerville, or Boston (see Chapter 23).

Day 5: Today you tie up loose ends that would have left you saying, "If only we'd had time for (fill in the blank)." Leaf through Chapters 16, 17, and 18 to refresh your memory about places that sounded good — a **historic house?** The **New England Aquarium?** The **Freedom Trail** stops you skipped? A special-interest **walking tour?** One of the **museums** you couldn't fit in on Day 2? In the evening, check out a **sporting event,** one of the earlier nightlife suggestions, or your room (you need to pack, right?).

Boston with Kids

Here's an outline of a single kid-centric day in Boston. This itinerary is designed for warm weather; at colder times of the year, you may want to concentrate on indoor destinations such as museums and, if you must, malls. This is flexible enough to allow lingering at some stops and trimming (or even eliminating) others, and the schedule cries out to be personalized. Take the parts that help you keep the peace, and integrate these with adult-oriented activities to create family harmony. At all times, make sure the children are allowed to make suggestions before you finalize anything.

Order extra unbuttered toast at breakfast, or hang on to that extra half-bagel; you'll need the snack later.

Start with a **Boston Duck Tour** (see Chapter 18). Buy tickets at the Prudential Center (Pru) when the booth opens (no later than 9 a.m.), or be compulsive and snap up some of the limited allotment that goes on sale two days ahead. If you face a wait before your tour, wander around the shopping plaza or check out the **Christian Science Center reflecting pool,** across the street from the back of the Pru. (At press time, Duck Tours was negotiating to stay in the Back Bay; if that didn't happen, ask the person who answers the phone to suggest a kid-friendly place to spend time.)

Later, use the Boylston Street exit at the front of the Pru, turn right, and walk three blocks to Copley Square. The square contains a fountain, benches, and *The Tortoise and Hare at Copley Square,* a two-piece sculpture by Nancy Schön. Where's that camera? Follow Boylston

Street two blocks to the giant teddy bear in front of **FAO Schwarz.** *Before* you head inside, make sure everyone knows how much time and money the decision-makers consider acceptable.

Continue on Boylston Street two more blocks, and you come to the **Public Garden.** The **swan boats** make a good low-tech break. These vessels share the lagoon with live swans, ducks, and geese that want the rest of your breakfast. *Make Way for Ducklings,* another enchanting work by Nancy Schön, is near the corner of Beacon and Charles streets (diagonally across from where you enter the Garden).

Kids with liberal TV privileges may want to head across the street for lunch at **Cheers,** formerly the Bull & Finch Pub (see Chapter 23). Solid pub fare (including fine burgers) and a children's menu may make up for the fact that the real thing looks nothing like the set of the TV show. Alternatively, walk two blocks back on Boylston Street, turn left, and walk two and a half blocks to the **Hard Rock Cafe** (see Chapter 23).

In the afternoon, pick a museum or other learning experience: the **Children's Museum** for the younger set, the **Museum of Science** or the **New England Aquarium** for older kids.

For dinner, let the children name the restaurant — perhaps the Hard Rock Cafe if you had lunch elsewhere, a **North End** pasta place, or the multiple options at **Faneuil Hall Marketplace.** Finally, if this plan doesn't blow anyone's bedtime, spend the evening taking in a live performance of *Shear Madness* or **Blue Man Group** (see Chapter 22).

Boston for Art Lovers

Would-be artists and would-be art collectors flock to Boston for inspiration of all sorts in museums and galleries. From the dazzling Impressionist paintings at the Museum of Fine Arts to work by promising artists and craftspeople in cutting-edge Newbury Street galleries, the city abounds with aesthetic treats.

Check ahead for special museum shows. Short-term exhibits often require separate tickets, sometimes good only at a specific time.

For high-profile traveling exhibitions, many large hotels arrange packages that include museum tickets. Start investigating as soon as you hear about the show. You may not save money, but the tickets usually are valid at any time — an invaluable perk if your schedule is uncertain.

Stop one is the **Museum of Fine Arts (MFA),** which opens at 10 a.m. Take a free tour at 10:30 a.m. or help yourself to a floor plan and wander. I could cheerfully spend a day here, but you may not enjoy that kind of freedom with your vacation time. Go in with some sense of what you want to see; the Web site (www.mfa.org) is a great planning tool. When you've had your fill, move on (two blocks or so) to the **Isabella Stewart Gardner Museum.** Have lunch in the MFA's cafeteria, cafe, or restaurant (you may need a reservation), or the Gardner's cafe. Then hop on the Green Line and head for the Copley or Arlington stop. One block away is **Newbury Street,** home to more art galleries than you can possibly see in half a day — or even a whole day. If time allows, plan for an hour or so at one of the **historic houses** nearby (see Chapter 17) before or after you hit the galleries. Wind down with afternoon tea (see Chapter 15) or a drink (see Chapter 23) in the elegant confines of the **Four Seasons** or the **Ritz-Carlton, Boston** — or the tourist heaven known as **Cheers.** If you've kept your spending under control at the art galleries, you may want to have a little caviar with your tea.

Some Tips for Organizing Your Time

The most important advice I can offer is ridiculously simple: Be realistic. Trying to do too much wastes time, money, and the goodwill of your fellow travelers. For the record, scheduling more than three major destinations in a day is trying to do too much. Scheduling three of anything in one afternoon is madness, especially if you have dinner reservations.

How can you make your plans more practical? You can extend your trip, but it may be a bit late for that. If you travel with a group, you can split up. What you sacrifice in togetherness, you more than make up for in maximized satisfaction and minimized boredom. Plus, if you get together at dinner you can compare notes on your day's activities. Here are some other suggestions:

- ✔ **Double-check open hours and days.** Setting the alarm, scheduling an early breakfast, and driving your family nuts so you can be at a certain attraction at 9 a.m. sharp is no fun when you arrive and find that the attraction opens at 10.

- ✔ **Double-check a map.** Again, ridiculous — unless you forget. When you catch yourself before you go from Filene's Basement to the North End by way of the Public Garden (hint: not a straight line), this won't seem so silly. But backtracking may be a good idea if, say, your hotel is nearby, and you can drop off the spoils of your trip to the Basement instead of lugging your purchases all over town.

- ✔ **Double-check with the kids.** Offer everyone a chance to change his or her mind, even if that messes up your itinerary. The sights and attractions that were theoretical at home may hold more appeal in 3-D — or seem disappointing. Better to have the "I'd rather do something else" conversation at the hotel than at the entrance to a distant attraction that, for whatever reason, has lost its luster.

Chapter 21

Exploring Beyond Boston: Four Great Day-Trips

. . . .

In This Chapter

▶ Planning your getaway

▶ Leaving town

▶ Exploring and eating on the road

. . . .

*P*art of Boston's appeal is its proximity to other fascinating destinations. Seven municipalities lie within an hour or so of downtown — Lexington, Concord, Salem, Marblehead, Gloucester, Rockport, and Plymouth — and all make enjoyable day-trips. (For the locations of these towns in relation to Boston, see the map on the inside back cover of this book.) Each boasts abundant historic associations and excellent sightseeing, with enough shopping and dining opportunities to keep everyone happy.

In this chapter, I walk you through the process of planning a day-trip to each of the seven, and suggest ways to visit the cities or towns individually and (except Plymouth) in pairs. I start with general pointers, and then offer specific tips on getting there, making the most of your day, and planning sightseeing and dining.

General Pointers

Rental cars and overnight stays are two items that can inflate the cost of your day-trip. If your visit to the Boston area is relatively short, I suggest you skip the room but consider the car, because packing up and moving for the second time in just a few days is more disruptive than convenient, but having wheels increases your flexibility and touring range. That said, remember that reliable public transportation serves each of the towns in this chapter; if you don't want to deal with a car, you don't need to. (For information about the commuter rail and buses, contact the **T** at ☎ **800-392-6100** outside Massachusetts or 617-222-3200; Internet: www.mbta.com.)

If you want to plan an overnight stay, the chamber of commerce or other tourism authorities in each town will eagerly advise you. One good option is a bed-and-breakfast; see Chapter 6 for suggestions.

Summer and fall weekends are the day-trip version of rush hour. In pleasant weather, gridlock is a problem. If you can, try to schedule your trip for a weekday, preferably in the spring or fall, when car and pedestrian traffic are more manageable and the weather slightly more predictable. Some businesses and attractions close for the winter, but if you visit then, the open ones will be practically empty.

Finally, if you don't want to worry about details, consider a guided half- or full-day bus trip. For a good selection and fair prices, contact **Gray Line's Brush Hill Tours,** 435 High St., Randolph, MA 02368 (☎ **800-343-1328** or 781-986-6100; Internet: www.grayline.com).

Where to find out more

Information offices can assist walk-in visitors. To receive information in advance (a good way to involve kids in the planning), contact the following:

- ✔ **Massachusetts:** Massachusetts Office of Travel & Tourism, 10 Park Plaza, Suite 4510, Boston, MA 02116 (☎ **800-227-6277** or 617-973-8500; Internet: www.mass-vacation.com)

- ✔ **Lexington and Concord:** Lexington Chamber of Commerce, 1875 Massachusetts Ave., Lexington, MA 02421 (☎ **781-862-2480**; Internet: www.lexingtonchamber.org); Concord Chamber of Commerce, 155 Everett St., Concord, MA 01742 (☎ **978-369-3120**; Internet: www.concordmachamber.org); and Greater Merrimack Valley Convention & Visitors Bureau, 9 Central St., Suite 201, Lowell, MA 01582 (☎ **800-443-3332** or 978-459-6150; Internet: www.merrimackvalley.org)

- ✔ **Salem and Marblehead:** Destination Salem, 59 Wharf St., Salem, MA 01970 (☎ **877-SALEM-MA** or 978-744-3663; Internet: www.salem.org); Marblehead Chamber of Commerce, 62 Pleasant St., P.O. Box 76, Marblehead, MA 01945 (☎ **781-631-2868**; Internet: www.marbleheadchamber.org); and North of Boston Convention & Visitors Bureau, 17 Peabody Sq., Peabody, MA 01960 (☎ **800-742-5306** or 978-977-7760; Internet: www.northofboston.org)

- ✔ **Gloucester and Rockport:** Gloucester Tourism Commission, 22 Poplar St., Gloucester, MA 01930 (☎ **800-649-6839** or 978-281-8865; Internet: www.gloucesterma.com); Rockport Chamber of Commerce and Board of Trade, 3 Main St., Rockport MA 01966 (☎ **978-546-6575**; Internet: www.rockportusa.com); and Cape Ann Chamber of Commerce, 33 Commercial St., Gloucester, MA 01930 (☎ **800-321-0133** or 978-283-1601; Internet: www.capeannvacations.com)

- ✔ **Plymouth:** Destination Plymouth, 170 Water St., Suite 10C, Plymouth, MA 02360 (☎ **800-USA-1620** or 508-747-7533; Internet: www.visit-plymouth.com), and Plymouth County Convention & Visitors Bureau, 32 Court St., Plymouth, MA 02360 (☎ **508-747-0100**; Internet: www.plymouth-1620.com)

Lexington and Concord

The Revolutionary War started in these prosperous suburbs, which were then country villages. With an assist from a Henry Wadsworth Longfellow poem, the events of April 1775 vaulted Lexington and Concord into immortality. On your day-trip, you'll understand why.

A visit to both towns makes a reasonable one-day excursion. Lexington is a half-day trip; if Concord appeals to you, you can spend the whole day there. Some attractions close for the winter and reopen after Patriots' Day, the third Monday of April.

There is no public transportation available between Lexington and Concord.

Hit the Boston Public Library (Chapter 17) or the Old North Church gift shop (Chapter 16), and track down Longfellow's poem "Paul Revere's Ride," a classic but historically dubious account of Revere's journey on April 18 and 19, 1775. You'll hear about the poem all over Lexington and Concord, and you may already know a little (the first lines are "Listen, my children, and you shall hear/Of the midnight ride of Paul Revere").

Getting to Lexington

To drive from Boston (9 miles) or Cambridge (6 miles), take Soldiers Field Road or Memorial Drive west to Route 2. Exit at Route 4/225, and follow signs into the center of town. From Route 128 (I-95), use Exit 31A and proceed into town. Parking is available on Mass. Ave., and a public metered lot is near the corner of Mass. Ave. and Waltham Street. The National Heritage Museum and Minute Man National Historical Park have free parking lots.

Public transportation is more complicated. Start by riding the Red Line to the last stop, Alewife. From there, bus routes number 62 (Bedford) and 76 (Hanscom) serve Lexington. The buses run Monday through Saturday, hourly during the day, and every 30 minutes during rush hours. No service is available on Sunday. The bus trip takes about 25 minutes and costs 75¢ one-way.

Getting around Lexington

The **Liberty Ride** (☎ **781-862-0500,** ext. 702) connects the downtown attractions with the National Heritage Museum and Minute Man National Historical Park. At press time, the service ran July through October only. The fare is $10 for adults, $5 for students under 18, and free for children under 6. That's steep if you have a car, but a deal if you're using public transportation — and this ticket gets you discounts at businesses around town, including the Historical Society, which knocks 25% off admission to its houses.

Seeing the sights in Lexington

Pick up maps and other information at the **Chamber of Commerce Visitor Center,** 1875 Mass. Ave. (☎ 781-862-2480). The center is open mid-April through October daily from 9 a.m. to 5 p.m., and November through mid-April daily from 10 a.m. to 4 p.m. Displays include a diorama that illustrates the battle.

The visitor center is on the **Village Green** or Battle Green, site of the Revolution's first skirmish. The monuments and memorials include the Minuteman Statue (1900) of the militia commander, Captain John Parker, who instructed his troops, "Don't fire unless fired upon, but if they mean to have a war, let it begin here!" It takes about an hour to check out the center displays and outdoor sights on the Battle Green.

The Lexington Historical Society (Internet: www.lexingtonhistory.org) operates the town's most compelling attraction, the **Buckman Tavern,** 1 Bedford St. (☎ 781-862-5598). The tavern is the only remaining building that stood on the Green on April 19, 1775. Costumed guides lead an outstanding tour that describes the building's history, the battle, and details of colonial life. Even if time is short, don't miss this one.

Tours of the society's other two properties are well worth your time but are short of can't-miss experiences. The **Hancock-Clarke House,** 36 Hancock St. (☎ 781-861-0928), one-third of a mile from the Green, houses the Historical Society's museum of the Revolution. The 1690 **Munroe Tavern,** 1332 Mass. Ave. (☎ 781-674-9238), is about a mile from the Green in the other direction. During the battle, the tavern fell into British hands and became the headquarters and, later, field hospital.

To see the houses, you must take a guided tour, which lasts 30 to 45 minutes per house. Hours are Monday through Saturday 10 a.m. to 4 p.m. and Sunday 1 to 4 p.m. The Buckman Tavern is open from early March to late November; the Hancock-Clarke House and Munroe Tavern are open from April to October. Admission for adults is $5 per house, $8 for two, and $12 for all three; for seniors, $7 for two houses and $11 for three; for children 6 to 16, $3 per house and $5 for two or three. Group tours run by appointment only.

The other major attraction in Lexington is the **National Heritage Museum,** 33 Marrett Rd. (Route 2A), at Mass. Ave. (☎ 781-861-6559 or 781-861-9638; Internet: www.monh.org), which takes a fun approach, illustrating history with cultural artifacts. In recent years, the temporary exhibits have included circus posters, Navajo rugs, and displays on George Washington and Frank Lloyd Wright, to name a few. For another look at the Revolution, visit the permanent installation on the

Lexington

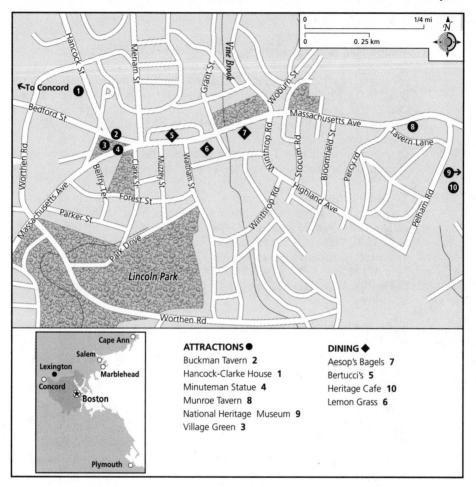

ATTRACTIONS ●

Buckman Tavern **2**
Hancock-Clarke House **1**
Minuteman Statue **4**
Munroe Tavern **8**
National Heritage Museum **9**
Village Green **3**

DINING ◆

Aesop's Bagels **7**
Bertucci's **5**
Heritage Cafe **10**
Lemon Grass **6**

Battle of Lexington. The Scottish Rite of Freemasonry sponsors the museum. Admission is free; the museum is open Monday through Saturday from 10 a.m. to 5 p.m. and Sunday from noon to 5 p.m.

Dining in Lexington

The center of town, near the intersection of Mass. Ave. and Waltham Street, offers a number of choices. If you're starting the day in Lexington, **Aesop's Bagels,** 1666 Mass. Ave. (☎ **781-674-2990**), is a good place for breakfast. For lunch, you may want to hold out until Concord. If you can't, try **Bertucci's,** 1777 Mass. Ave. (☎ **781-860-9000**), for pizza and pasta, or **Lemon Grass,** 1710 Mass. Ave. (☎ **781-862-3530**), for tasty Thai food. The **Heritage Cafe** at the National Heritage Museum is another popular spot.

Sights en route from Lexington to Concord

Minute Man National Historical Park (Internet: www.nps.gov/mima) spreads over 900 acres in Lexington, Concord, and Lincoln. The park encompasses the scene of the first Revolutionary War battle and a 4-mile piece of the road that the vanquished British troops used to retreat from Concord to Boston. Artwork and artifacts illustrate the displays at visitor centers in Lexington and Concord, either of which makes an excellent starting point. Visiting the park takes as little as half an hour (to see Concord's North Bridge) or as long as several hours, if you include stops at both visitor centers and maybe a ranger-led program.

The park is open daily, year-round. Admission is free; charges for special tours may apply. In Lexington, the **Minute Man Visitor Center** is off Route 2A, ½ mile west of I-95 (Massachusetts 128) Exit 33B (☎ 781-862-7753). The center is open daily from 9 a.m. to 5 p.m. (until 4 p.m. in winter). Concord's **North Bridge Visitor Center,** 174 Liberty St., off Monument Street (☎ 978-369-6993), overlooks the Concord River and the bridge. The center is open daily from 9 a.m. to 5 p.m. (until 4 p.m. in winter).

Walden Pond State Reservation, Route 126, Concord (☎ 978-369-3254; Internet: www.state.ma.us/dem/parks/wldn.htm), preserves the site of the cabin where Henry David Thoreau lived from 1845 to 1847. Besides being a literary pilgrimage site, this is popular with visitors who hike around the pond, picnic, swim, and fish. In fine weather, call before heading over to make sure the parking lot has space available (there's no additional parking); between Memorial Day and Labor Day, a parking fee (about $2) applies.

To get to Walden Pond State Reservation from Lexington, take Mass. Ave. west to Route 2A, bear left onto Route 2, and turn left onto Route 126. From Concord, take Walden Street (Route 126) south, away from Concord Center, cross Route 2, and look for signs pointing to the parking lot.

Getting to Concord

To drive from Lexington, take Mass. Ave. west, across Route 128, and pick up Route 2A. Pass through Lincoln and bear right onto Lexington Road in Concord. Follow HISTORIC CONCORD signs into the center of town. If you miss the turn-off, continue about ½ mile and take the next right onto Cambridge Turnpike, which runs into the center of town. To go straight to Walden Pond, take what's now Route 2/2A another mile or so and turn left onto Route 126. From Boston (18 miles) and Cambridge (15 miles), take Soldiers Field Road or Memorial Drive west to Route 2.

In Lincoln, stay in the right lane. Where the road makes a sharp left, go straight onto Cambridge Turnpike. Parking is available throughout town and at the attractions.

By public transportation, the commuter rail takes about 45 minutes from North Station in Boston, with a stop at Porter Square in Cambridge. The one-way fare is $4. (No public transportation is available between Lexington and Concord.) The station is about three-quarters of a mile from the town center. The attractions are accessible on foot but not all that close together; in hot or cold weather, make appropriate preparations (hats, water, sunscreen, and such).

If you want to fit in, pronounce it *conquered* (not *con*-cored).

Taking a tour of Concord

The **Chamber of Commerce** (☎ 978-369-3120; Internet: www.concord machamber.org) offers 90-minute tours from mid-April through October on Friday, Saturday, Sunday, and Monday holidays, and other days by appointment. These tours start at the information booth on Heywood Street, one block southeast of Monument Square. Also check to see whether Park Service rangers from the **North Bridge Visitor Center** (☎ 978-369-6993; Internet: www.nps.gov/mima) are leading tours during your visit.

Seeing the sights in Concord

The monuments and descriptions around and in the North Bridge Visitor Center give a good sense of Concord's best-known event — the Battle of Concord. The town is equally famous for literary associations, and indications of that abound, too. Visit **Sleepy Hollow Cemetery,** off Route 62 west (☎ 978-318-3233), and climb to Author's Ridge. In this area, you'll find the graves of Ralph Waldo Emerson, Nathaniel Hawthorne, and Henry David Thoreau, and Louisa May Alcott and her father, Bronson Alcott, among others. The cemetery is open daily from 7 a.m. to dusk and does not allow buses; call ahead for wheelchair access.

Concord Museum

The Concord Museum offers a fascinating, comprehensive look at the town's storied history. The best features of the galleries are not the abundant objects and artifacts, although these are impressive; the best features are the accompanying descriptions and interpretations that place the exhibits in context. For instance, you'll see one of the lanterns that signaled Paul Revere from the steeple of the Old North Church. This display includes just enough explanatory text to show why that's a big deal.

Concord

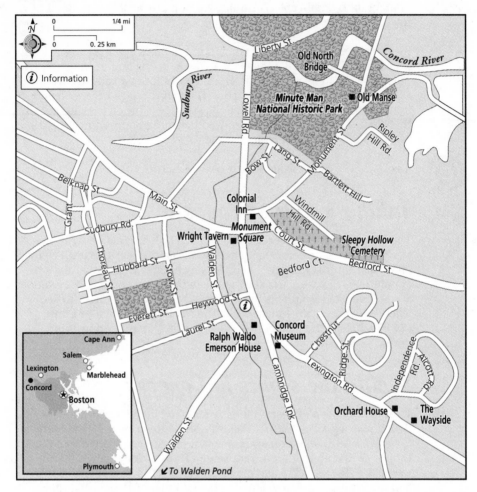

Lexington Road and Cambridge Turnpike. ☎ **978-369-9609** *(recorded info) or 978-369-9763. Internet:* www.concordmuseum.org. *Follow Lexington Road out of Concord Center and bear right at museum onto Cambridge Turnpike; entrance is on the left. Parking: In lot or on road. Admission: $7 adults, $6 seniors and students, $3 children under 16, $16 families. Open: April–Dec Mon–Sat 9 a.m.–5 p.m., Sun noon to 5 p.m.; Jan–March Mon–Sat 11 a.m.–4 p.m., Sun 1–4 p.m.*

The Old Manse

The Reverend William Emerson, Ralph Waldo Emerson's grandfather, built this house in 1770 and watched the Battle of Concord from the yard. For almost 170 years, the house was home to his widow, her second husband, their descendants, and (briefly) newlyweds Nathaniel and Sophia Peabody Hawthorne. The tour traces the history of the house and its occupants, using a rich trove of family memorabilia.

269 Monument St. (at North Bridge). ☎ ***978-369-3909.*** *Internet:* www.thetrustees.org. *From Concord Center, follow Monument Street until you see North Bridge parking lot on the right; the Old Manse is on the left. Guided tours: $7 adults, $6 seniors and students, $4.50 children 6–12, $20 families. Open: Mid-April–Oct Mon–Sat 10 a.m.–5 p.m.; Sun and holidays noon to 5 p.m. Last tour at 4:30 p.m. Closed Nov–mid-April.*

Orchard House

Louisa May Alcott lived and wrote at Orchard House, the setting for her best-known book, *Little Women* (1868). If you loved the book, don't leave town without seeing the house; if you don't understand what the fuss is about, this attraction may not be the best use of your time. The tour offers an intriguing look at 19th-century family life, overflowing with anecdotes and heirlooms. If you are or were a preadolescent girl, this stop may be one of the best parts of your trip.

399 Lexington Rd. ☎ ***978-369-4118.*** *Internet:* www.louisamayalcott.org. *Follow Lexington Road out of Concord Center past Concord Museum; the house is on the left. Parking: In lot; overflow parking lot is across the street. Guided tours: $7 adults, $6 seniors and students, $4 children 6–17, $16 families (up to 2 adults and 4 children). Open: April–Oct Mon–Sat 10:00 a.m.–4:30 p.m., Sun 1:00–4:30 p.m.; Nov–March Mon–Fri 11 a.m.–3 p.m., Sat 10:00 a.m.–4:30 p.m., Sun 1:00–4:30 p.m. Closed Jan 1–15.*

Ralph Waldo Emerson House

Emerson is a household name in Concord, where the man remains such a towering presence that guides at this attraction still call him "Mr. Emerson." The philosopher, essayist, and poet lived here from 1835 until he died, in 1882. The tour highlights Emerson's domestic life and the house's over-the-top Victorian decor.

28 Cambridge Turnpike. ☎ ***978-369-2236.*** *Take Cambridge Turnpike out of Concord Center; just before Concord Museum, house is on the right. Guided tours: $6 adults, $4 seniors and students; call to arrange group tours. Open: Mid-April–Oct Thurs–Sat 10:00 a.m.–4:30 p.m.; Sun 2:00–4:30 p.m. Closed Nov–mid-April.*

The Wayside

Nathaniel Hawthorne lived at the Wayside from 1852 until his death in 1864. The Alcott family lived here, too, as did Harriett Lothrop, who wrote the *Five Little Peppers* books under the pen name Margaret Sidney. This house is part of Minute Man National Historical Park; rangers lead the interesting tours, which explore the patchwork architecture and the lives and careers of the house's famous residents.

455 Lexington Rd. ☎ ***978-369-6975.*** *Internet:* www.nps.gov/mima/wayside. *Follow Lexington Road past Concord Museum and Orchard House; the Wayside is on the left. Guided tours: $4 adults; free for children under 17. Open: May–Oct Thurs–Tues 10:30 a.m.–4:30 p.m. Closed Nov–April.*

Dining in Concord

The **1716 Colonial Inn,** 48 Monument Sq. (☎ **978-369-2372;** Internet: www.concordscolonialinn.com), is a traditional establishment with a fine restaurant and two friendly lounges. The food is hardly adventurous, but you're here to soak up the atmosphere — the fact that the fare is also tasty is a bonus. The inn serves afternoon tea from Wednesday through Sunday (make a reservation).

In an off-the-tourist-track location, **Nashoba Brook Bakery & Cafe,** 152 Commonwealth Ave., West Concord (☎ **978-318-1999**), is a delightful soup-salad-sandwich place that also serves fantastic breads and desserts made in-house. From Concord Center, take Main Street west, cross Route 2, and proceed to the traffic light in front of the West Concord train station, bear right, go three blocks, and park on the street or in one of the handful of spots in the lot. The cafe is open Monday through Saturday from 8 a.m. to 8 p.m.

For picnic fixings, visit the **Cheese Shop,** 25–31 Walden St. (☎ 978-369-5778), near the town center.

Salem and Marblehead

The North Shore played a role in the Revolution and attained great prosperity by dominating the China trade in the early Federal era, but we know that's not why you flipped to this page. When you read "Salem," you thought, "Witches!"

The witch trials of 1692 left an indelible mark on Salem, which good-naturedly welcomes the association — while never forgetting that 20 people died in the unfounded hysteria. When you discover this pleasant city, you may want to hang around and find out about its rich maritime history. Salem shares that legacy with the affluent, picturesque town of Marblehead, which (Newport be hanged) is the self-proclaimed "Yachting Capital of America."

Much like Lexington and Concord, Salem and Marblehead together make a full day-trip. You easily can spend an entire day in either place.

Getting to Salem

To drive from Boston (17 miles), take the Callahan Tunnel to Route 1A north past the airport and into downtown Salem. Be careful in Lynn, where the road turns left and immediately right. Or take I-93 or Route 1 to Route 128, and then Route 114 into Salem. From Marblehead, follow Route 114 (Pleasant Street) west. Plenty of on-street parking is available, and a municipal garage is across from the National Park Service Visitor Center.

Bus route Number 450 runs from Haymarket (Green or Orange Line), and commuter trains operate from North Station (Green or Orange Line). The bus takes an hour, the train 30 to 35 minutes. The one-way fare is $2.75 for the bus, $3 for the train. For something more fun, check ahead to see whether ferries (☎ **617-227-4321;** Internet: www.boston harborcruises.com) are operating on the route from Boston's Long Wharf to the Blaney Street Ferry Terminal, off Derby Street, not far from downtown Salem. The trip takes about 75 minutes and costs about $10 for adults.

Taking a tour of Salem

The **Salem Trolley** (☎ **978-744-5469**) operates daily from 10 a.m. to 5 p.m. from April through October and on weekends in March and November. Tickets ($10 adults, $9 seniors, $5 children 5 to 12, $25 family) are good all day, and you can get off and on as much as you like at any of the 15 stops. The driver narrates a one-hour tour while making a loop around town; the first stop is at the Essex Street side of the National Park Service Visitor Center on New Liberty Street.

Seeing the sights in Salem

The **National Park Service Visitor Center,** 2 New Liberty St. (☎ **978-740-1650;** Internet: www.nps.gov/sama), distributes brochures and pamphlets, including one that describes a walking tour of the historic district. The center is open daily from 9 a.m. to 5 p.m. Architecture buffs will want to see Chestnut Street, a gorgeously preserved example of colonial style; the whole street is a registered National Historic Landmark.

The House of the Seven Gables

Nathaniel Hawthorne visited this house as a child, and legends about the building and its inhabitants inspired Hawthorne's 1851 novel of the same name. If you haven't read the book (or even if you have), watch the audio-visual program that tells the story before you start the tour. The six rooms of period furniture in the main house include pieces mentioned in the book, and a steep secret staircase. Costumed guides lead the tour (sometimes playing to the kids in the audience) and can answer just about any question about the novel, buildings, and artifacts.

*54 Turner St. ☎ **978-744-0991**. Internet: www.7gables.org. From downtown, follow Derby St. east three blocks past Derby Wharf. Guided tours: $9 adults, $8 seniors, $7 children 5–12, free for children under 5. Open: Mid-April–June and Nov–Dec daily 10 a.m.–5 p.m.; July–Oct daily 10 a.m.–7 p.m.; late Jan–mid-April Mon–Sat 10 a.m.–5 p.m., Sun noon to 5 p.m. Closed first three weeks of Jan.*

Salem

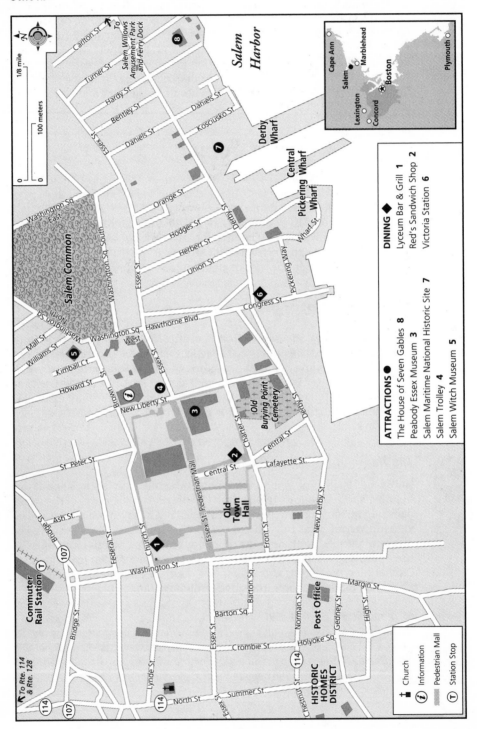

Salem Harbor

Inset map: Cape Ann, Marblehead, Boston, Salem, Lexington, Concord, Plymouth

DINING ◆
Lyceum Bar & Grill **1**
Red's Sandwich Shop **2**
Victoria Station **6**

ATTRACTIONS ●
The House of Seven Gables **8**
Peabody Essex Museum **3**
Salem Maritime National Historic Site **7**
Salem Trolley **4**
Salem Witch Museum **5**

✝ Church
ⓘ Information
Pedestrian Mall
Ⓣ Station Stop

Salem Common

Commuter Rail Station

Old Town Hall

Old Burying Point Cemetery

Post Office

HISTORIC HOMES DISTRICT

Derby Wharf
Central Wharf
Pickering Wharf

To Salem Willows Amusement Park and Ferry Dock

Peabody Essex Museum

This museum illustrates the history of Salem through displays of the objects and artifacts residents considered worth preserving — a fascinating approach that affords a look at treasures from around the world. The Peabody Museum began as a repository for the spoils of the China trade; the Essex Institute was the county historical society. Between the two, the sprawling collections encompass everything from toys to animal specimens to East Asian art. Visitors can tour a historic house or gallery, or take a self-guided tour using a pamphlet from about a dozen available on various topics.

The museum completed an extensive renovation and expansion project in 2002; check ahead for new exhibits and activities.

East India Square. ☎ *800-745-4054 or 978-745-9500. Internet:* www.pem.org. *Take Hawthorne Boulevard to Essex Street, following signs for Visitor Center, and enter on Essex or New Liberty Street. Admission: $10 adults, $8 seniors and students with ID, free for children under 17. House tour only, $6. Open: Mon–Sat 10 a.m.–5 p.m.; Sun noon to 5 p.m. Closed Mon Nov–March.*

Salem Maritime National Historic Site

The waterfront, before beginning to decay in the early 1800s, linked Salem to the world for many years. On this harborfront land, National Park Service buildings and displays recall the port's heyday. The most recent addition to the site is in the water alongside the orientation center: a full-size replica of a 1797 East Indiaman merchant vessel. The ranger-led tour includes the three-masted 171-footer *Friendship*.

174 Derby St. ☎ *978-740-1660. Internet:* www.nps.gov/sama. *Take Derby Street east, just past Pickering Wharf; the orientation center is on the right. Admission: Free; guided tours: $5 adults, $3 seniors and children 6–16. Open: Daily 9 a.m.–5 p.m.*

Salem Witch Museum

The Salem Witch Museum is so memorable that I'm fighting the urge to call the place "haunting" (oh, well). The informative and frightening museum's three-dimensional audiovisual presentation uses life-sized figures to illustrate the witchcraft trials and the accompanying hysteria. That sounds a little corny, but the 30-minute narration does a good job of explaining the historical context and consequences. (One "man" dies when others pile rocks onto a board on the man's chest — you may need to remind small children that this is not real.)

The "witch" on the traffic island across from the Witch Museum is Roger Conant, who founded Salem in 1626. Nice outfit, Roger.

19½ Washington Square. ☎ *978-744-1692. Internet:* www.salemwitch museum.com. *Follow Hawthorne Boulevard to the northwest corner of Salem Common. Admission: $7 adults, $6 seniors, $4.50 children 6–14. Open: July–Aug daily 10 a.m.–7 p.m.; Sept–June daily 10 a.m.–5 p.m.*

Dining in Salem

For a quick bite, try **Red's Sandwich Shop,** 15 Central St. (☎ **978-745-3527**). The fare's cheap, good, and served fast, but the shop doesn't take credit cards. **Victoria Station,** Pickering Wharf, at the corner of Derby and Congress streets (☎ **978-744-7644**), is part of a chain but offers a terrific view of the marina. The **Lyceum Bar & Grill,** 43 Church St. (at Washington St.; ☎ **978-745-7665;** Internet: www.lyceumsalem.com) is one of the best restaurants north of Boston. The bar and grill serves creative American fare at lunch on weekdays, dinner daily, and Sunday brunch. For any meal, make a reservation.

Getting to Marblehead

To drive from Boston (15 miles), take the Callahan Tunnel and follow Route 1A past the airport north through Revere and Lynn. Bear right where you see signs for Swampscott and Marblehead. Follow Lynn Shore Drive into Swampscott, bear left onto Route 129, and follow the road to Marblehead. Or take I-93 or Route 1 to Route 128, and then Route 114 through Salem into Marblehead. From Salem, take Route 114 east. Parking is limited — grab the first spot you see, and be sure you know your time limit.

Bus route Number 441/442 runs from Haymarket (Green or Orange Line) in Boston to downtown Marblehead. During rush periods on weekdays, the Number 448/449 connects Marblehead to Downtown Crossing (Red or Orange Line). The 441 and 448 buses detour to Vinnin Square shopping center in Swampscott; otherwise, the routes are the same. The trip takes about an hour and costs $2.75 one-way.

Seeing the sights in Marblehead

The **Marblehead Chamber of Commerce** operates an information booth on Pleasant Street near Spring Street. The booth is open daily from late May through October, 10 a.m. to 6 p.m. (In the off-season, visit the office at 62 Pleasant St., just up the hill.) You can pick up pamphlets and a map, but the town is ideal for wandering, especially around "Old Town," the historic district. Be sure to visit Crocker Park or Fort Sewall, on the harbor at opposite ends of Front Street; the view from either place is amazing.

Marblehead is a top-notch shopping destination. Shops, boutiques, and galleries dot Washington and Front streets, with another prime area on Atlantic Avenue.

Abbot Hall

The Selectmen's Meeting Room houses Archibald M. Willard's painting *The Spirit of '76*. That title may not ring a bell, but the painting will when you see the widely imitated drummer, drummer boy, and fife player. Cases in the halls contain objects and artifacts from the collections of the Marblehead Historical Society; a stop here takes five or ten minutes at most.

Washington Square. ☎ 781-631-0528. From the historic district, follow Washington Street up the hill toward the clock tower. Admission: Free. Open: Nov–April Mon, Tues, Thurs 8 a.m.–5 p.m., Wed 7:30 a.m.–7:30 p.m., Fri 8 a.m.–1 p.m.; May–Oct Mon, Tues, Thurs 8 a.m.–5 p.m., Fri 8 a.m.–5 p.m., Sat 9 a.m.–6 p.m., Sun 11 a.m.–6 p.m.

Jeremiah Lee Mansion

For a house with an apparently obscure claim to fame, the 1768 Lee Mansion is surprisingly appealing. The original hand-painted wallpaper is the headliner, and the house is an excellent example of pre-Revolutionary Georgian architecture. The Marblehead Historical Society's informative guides bring the history to life with stories about the home and its renovations. The society's headquarters, across the street at 170 Washington St., contains several galleries and is open year-round, Tuesday through Saturday 10 a.m. to 4 p.m.; admission is free.

161 Washington St. ☎ 781-631-1069. Follow Washington Street uphill toward Abbot Hall; the mansion is on the right. Guided tours: $5 adults, $4.50 seniors and students. Open: June–mid-Oct Mon–Sat 10 a.m.–4 p.m.; Sun 1–4 p.m. Closed Nov–mid-May.

King Hooper Mansion

Robert Hooper was a shipping magnate who earned his nickname by treating his sailors well. His 1728 mansion, which gained a Georgian addition in 1747, now contains period furnishings. Though these pieces aren't original to the home, the furnishings give a sense of upper-crust life in the 18th century. The building houses the Marblehead Arts Association, which stages monthly exhibits.

8 Hooper St. ☎ 781-631-2608. Look for the colorful sign off Washington Street at the foot of the hill near the Lee Mansion. Guided tours: Free; donations requested. Open: Mon–Sat 10 a.m.–4 p.m.; Sun 1–5 p.m. Call ahead; no tours during private parties.

Marblehead

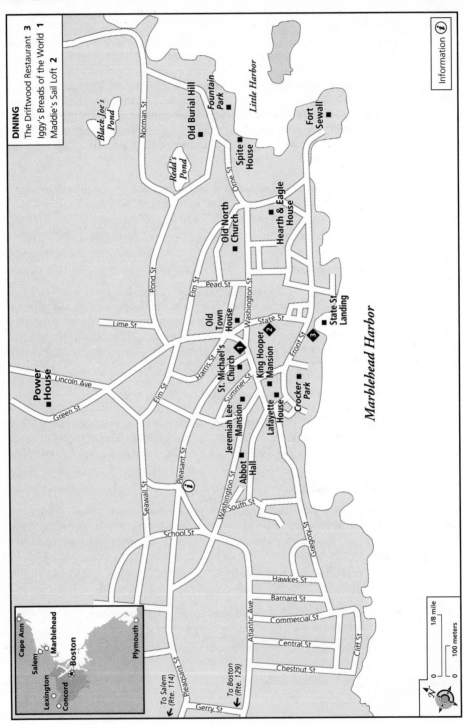

DINING

The Driftwood Restaurant **3**
Iggy's Breads of the World **1**
Maddie's Sail Loft **2**

Information ⓘ

Black Joe's Pond

Norman St.

Redd's Pond

Old Burial Hill

Fountain Park

Orne St.

Spite House

Little Harbor

Fort Sewall

Old North Church

Hearth & Eagle House

Pond St.

Elm St.

Pearl St.

Washington St.

Lime St.

Old Town House

State St.

Harris St.

St. Michael's Church **1**

King Hooper Mansion **2**

Front St.

State St. Landing **3**

Power House

Lincoln Ave.

Green St.

Elm St.

Summer St.

Jeremiah Lee Mansion

Lafayette House

Crocker Park

Marblehead Harbor

Pleasant St.

Washington St.

Abbot Hall

South St.

Seawall St.

School St.

Gregory St.

Hawkes St.

Barnard St.

Atlantic Ave.

Commercial St.

Central St.

Cliff St.

Chestnut St.

Pleasant St. (Rte. 114)
To Salem

To Boston (Rte. 129)

Gerry St.

Cape Ann
Salem
Lexington
Concord
Marblehead
Boston
Plymouth

N

0   1/8 mile
0   100 meters

Dining in Marblehead

Iggy's Bread of the World, 5 Pleasant St. (☎ 781-639-4717), serves coffee and some of the best baked goods in the Boston area. Iggy's is a great place to pick up a snack to enjoy while you watch the action on the harbor. The **Driftwood Restaurant,** 63 Front St. (☎ 781-631-1145), a diner-style neighborhood hangout, serves excellent fresh seafood at lunch, and breakfast all day (until 5 p.m. in the summer, 2 p.m. in the winter). The casual **Maddie's Sail Loft,** 15 State St. (☎ 781-631-9824), enjoys a well-deserved reputation for fresh seafood and strong drinks. The Loft serves lunch daily, dinner Monday through Saturday.

Gloucester and Rockport

Gloucester, Rockport, Essex, and Manchester-by-the-Sea make up Cape Ann, a dizzyingly beautiful peninsula that gained international attention with the 2000 release of the movie *The Perfect Storm.* Gloucester is a city in transition, a sightseeing and whale-watching center that's also one of the few commercial fishing ports remaining in New England. The fading industry traces its roots even further back than the city's first European settlement in 1623. Rockport, at the tip of the cape, is nearly as old but has a less hardscrabble history. Rockport enjoys a reputation as a summer community overflowing with gift shops and galleries.

The contrast of Gloucester and Rockport makes for an enjoyable one-day trip; exploring either can also fill a day.

Getting to Gloucester

To drive from Boston (33 miles), take I-93 or Route 1 to Route 128, which ends in Gloucester. Exit 14 puts you on Route 133, a longer but prettier approach to downtown than exits 11 and 9. Plenty of on-street parking is available, and a free lot is located on the causeway to Rocky Neck.

The commuter rail runs from North Station in Boston to Gloucester. The trip takes about an hour and costs $4.50 one-way. The **Cape Ann Transportation Authority (CATA)** (☎ 978-283-7916; Internet: www. canntran.com), runs buses on Cape Ann (from the Gloucester station to the waterfront, for example) and operates special routes during the summer; call for schedules.

Remember that *Gloucester* rhymes with *roster.*

Gloucester and Rockport

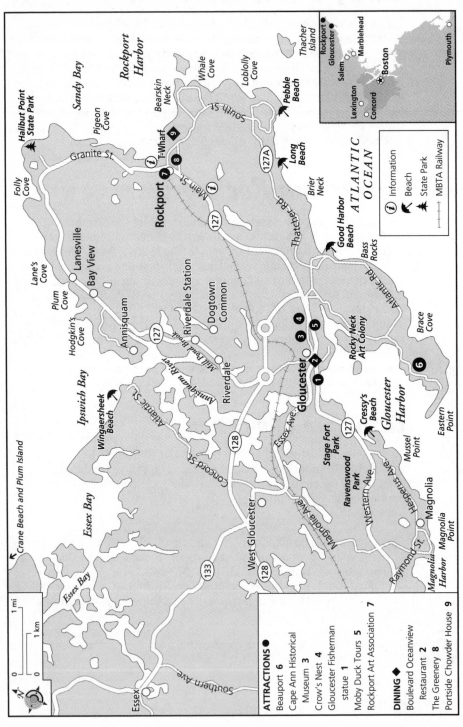

ATTRACTIONS ●
Beauport **6**
Cape Ann Historical
  Museum **3**
Crow's Nest **4**
Gloucester Fisherman
  statue **1**
Moby Duck Tours **5**
Rockport Art Association **7**

DINING ◆
Boulevard Oceanview
  Restaurant **2**
The Greenery **8**
Portside Chowder House **9**

Taking a tour of Gloucester

Pick up a *Gloucester Maritime Trail* brochure, which describes four excellent self-guided tours. You can find this brochure at the **Visitors Welcoming Center** (☎ 800-649-6839 or 978-281-8865), open summer only at Stage Fort Park, off Route 127 near the intersection with Route 133; or the **Cape Ann Chamber of Commerce,** 33 Commercial St. (☎ 800-321-0133 or 978-283-1601), open daily in summer and weekdays in winter.

Moby Duck Tours (☎ 978-281-3825; Internet: www.mobyduck.com) are 55-minute sightseeing excursions that travel on land before plunging into the water. The amphibious vehicles leave from Harbor Loop downtown. Tickets (cash only) cost $14 for adults, $12 for seniors, and $8 for children under 12. Tours run daily from Memorial Day through Labor Day, and on weekends in September.

Seeing the sights in Gloucester

On Stacy Boulevard just west of downtown, the statue that symbolizes the city testifies to the danger of the seafaring life. More than 10,000 fishermen lost their lives in Gloucester's first three centuries; Leonard Craske's bronze Gloucester Fisherman, *The Man at the Wheel,* memorializes the fishermen.

To reach East Gloucester, follow signs from downtown or use Exit 9 from Route 128. On East Main Street, follow signs to the Rocky Neck Art Colony, the oldest continuously operating art colony in the country. Park in the lot on the tiny causeway and follow the crowds to Rocky Neck Avenue and its studios, galleries, and restaurants. Most galleries are open daily in the summer from 10 a.m. to 10 p.m.

Just east of downtown is the **Crow's Nest,** 334 Main St. (☎ 978-281-2965), the fishermen's bar that gained fame through the book and movie of *The Perfect Storm.* The bar is a local hangout.

Beauport (Sleeper-McCann House)

Henry Davis Sleeper decorated this "fantasy house" to illustrate literary and historical themes, which you can learn about during the fascinating house tour. Sleeper, an interior designer, drew on huge collections of American and European art and antiques to create the home from 1907 to 1934. The entertaining tour visits 26 of the 40 rooms. Note that the house, operated by the Society for the Preservation of New England Antiquities, is not open on summer weekends.

75 Eastern Point Blvd. ☎ 978-283-0800. Internet: www.spnea.org. *Follow East Main Street south to Eastern Point Boulevard (a private road), drive ½ mile to house, and park on the left. Guided tours: $10 adults, $9 seniors, $5 students and children 6–12. Open: Tours on the hour May 15–Sept 14 Mon–Fri 10 a.m.–4 p.m.; Sept 15–Oct 15 daily 10 a.m.–4 p.m. Closed summer weekends and Oct 16–May 14.*

Cape Ann Historical Museum

Cape Ann's history and artists dominate the displays at this lovely museum. The American Luminist painter Fitz Hugh Lane, a Gloucester native, has a gorgeous gallery. Other spaces hold contemporary works, and the maritime and fisheries galleries contain fascinating exhibits, models, photographs, and even entire boats (you won't believe how small some of the boats are).

27 Pleasant St. ☎ 978-283-0455. Follow Main Street west through downtown and turn right onto Pleasant Street; the museum is one block up on the right. Parking: Metered street parking or in pay lot across street. Admission: $5 adults, $4.50 seniors, $3.50 students, free for children under 6. Open: March–Jan Tues–Sat 10 a.m.–5 p.m. Closed Feb.

Dining in Gloucester and nearby Essex

The **Boulevard Oceanview Restaurant,** 25 Western Ave., on Stacy Boulevard (☎ 978-281-2949), serves inexpensive sandwiches and ocean-fresh seafood, including superb Portuguese specialties, in a dinerlike atmosphere; you should make a reservation for dinner in the summer. Another dining option: Follow the locals to the Stage Fort Park snack bar, the **Cupboard**, for fried seafood and blue-plate specials.

Going to or leaving Cape Ann on Route 128, turn away from Gloucester on Route 133 and head west to Essex. This beautiful little town is an important culinary landmark: the birthplace of the fried clam. According to legend, that took place at **Woodman's of Essex,** Main Street (☎ 800-649-1773 or 978-768-6451). Woodman's draws locals and out-of-towners for lobster, steamers, onion rings, and, oh, yeah, fried clams. This dining spot is mobbed year-round, but the line moves quickly. An ATM is on the premises; no credit cards are accepted.

Getting to Rockport

By car from Boston (40 miles), take I-93 or Route 1 to Route 128. Just before Route 128 ends, follow signs to Route 127, and go north into Rockport. Or continue to the end (Exit 9), turn left onto Bass Avenue, and go about ½ mile to Route 127A north. From Gloucester, follow Main Street to Eastern Avenue (Route 127) or Bass Avenue. Route 127A is more scenic but longer than Route 127. In downtown Rockport, circle once to look for parking, and then try the back streets. Or use the parking lot on Upper Main Street (Route 127) on weekends. Parking is free; the shuttle bus downtown costs $1.

The commuter rail runs from North Station in Boston to Rockport. The 60- to 70-minute trip costs $5 one-way. The station is off Upper Main Street, less than a mile from the center of town.

The **Cape Ann Transportation Authority (CATA)** (☎ 978-283-7916; Internet: www.canntran.com), runs buses from town to town on Cape Ann.

Seeing the sights in Rockport

Pick up the pamphlet *Rockport: A Walking Guide* from **The Rockport Chamber of Commerce and Board of Trade**, 3 Main St. (☎ 978-546-6575; Internet: www.rockportusa.com). The chamber office is open daily in summer and weekdays in winter; the chamber operates an information booth from mid-May to mid-October about a mile from downtown on Upper Main Street (Route 127), just before the WELCOME TO ROCKPORT sign.

Rockport boasts no must-see attractions, but there's more to the town than knickknack shopping. The knickknack shopping *is* excellent, though — wander around downtown, making sure to detour onto Bearskin Neck, which has more gift shops than some whole cities. (And an interesting name — read the plaque at the entrance to the street to learn the story.) All over downtown, shops sell jewelry, gifts, toys, clothing, novelties, handmade crafts, paintings, and sculpture.

Opposite Bearskin Neck on the town wharf, you'll see a red wooden fish warehouse called Motif No. 1. The warehouse exerts a mysterious totemic power over Rockport residents — or is a testament to the fact that *anything* can become a tourist attraction. Motif No. 1 is famous for being famous. No, I don't know what the big deal is.

More than two dozen art galleries display the works of local and nationally known artists. In addition, the **Rockport Art Association,** 12 Main St. (☎ 978-546-6604), sponsors major exhibitions and special shows throughout the year. The association is open daily, year-round.

To get a sense of the power of the sea, take Route 127 north of town to the tip of Cape Ann. **Halibut Point State Park** (☎ 978-546-2997; Internet: www.state.ma.us/dem/parks/halb.htm) has a staffed visitor center, walking trails, tidal pools, and water-filled quarries — but no swimming. This park is great place to wander around and admire the scenery. On a clear day, you can see Maine.

Where to watch whales

Whale-watching is even more popular in Gloucester than in Boston (turn to Chapter 16 for a full description of whale watching). Prices run about $30 for adults, less for seniors and children; most tour companies will match any competitor's offer, including guaranteed sightings, AAA discounts, or coupons. Downtown, you'll find **Cape Ann Whale Watch** (☎ 800-877-5110 or 978-283-5110; Internet: www.caww.com), **Capt. Bill's Whale Watch** (☎ 800-33-WHALE or 978-283-6995; Internet: www.captainbillswhalewatch.com), and **Seven Seas Whale Watch** (☎ 800-238-1776 or 978-283-1776; Internet: www.7seas-whalewatch.com). At the Cape Ann Marina, off Route 133, is **Yankee Whale Watch** (☎ 800-WHALING or 508-283-0313; Internet: www.yankeewhalewatch.com).

Dining in Rockport

Woodman's of Essex (see "Dining in Gloucester and nearby Essex," earlier in this chapter) will serve you a drink, but Rockport is a dry town. I suggest a picnic, if the day is not too windy. Head to Halibut Point (see "Seeing the sights in Rockport"), the end of Bearskin Neck, or another agreeable spot. Stop for provisions at the **Greenery,** 15 Dock Sq. (☎ 978-546-9593), or the **Portside Chowder House,** Tuna Wharf, off Bearskin Neck (☎ 978-546-7045), and then sit back and admire the scenery.

Plymouth

The Pilgrims reside in our national memory, wearing tall black hats and buckled shoes. A visit to this town may cause elementary school flashbacks, but the trip may also leave you with a new sense of the difficulties those early settlers overcame. Best of all, you get a *real* sense — the attractions that are replicas are faithful reproductions, but many are genuine 17th-century relics.

Plymouth is a reasonable day trip that's especially popular with children. The town also makes a good stop between Boston and Cape Cod.

Getting there

By car from Boston (40 miles), follow I-93 south about 9 miles and bear left onto Route 3. Take Route 3 to Exit 6A (Route 44 east), and then follow signs to the historic attractions. Or continue on Route 3 to the Regional Information Complex at Exit 5 for maps, brochures, and information. To go directly to Plimoth Plantation, use Exit 4. The trip from Boston takes 45 to 60 minutes if you avoid rush hour. The downtown area is compact, so park where you can. The waterfront meters are particularly convenient.

The commuter rail serves Plymouth (at peak commuting times service is to nearby Kingston) from Boston's South Station during the day on week-days and all day on weekends; the trip takes one hour, and the one-way fare is $5. **Plymouth & Brockton buses** (☎ **617-773-9401** or 508-746-0378; Internet: www.p-b.com) leave from South Station and take about the same time. The bus is more expensive than the commuter rail ($9 one-way, $17 round-trip) but runs more often. The **Plymouth Area Link** bus (☎ **506-222-6106;** Internet: www.gatra.org/pal.htm) connects the train stations with downtown and other destinations. The fare is 75¢.

Taking a tour

A narrated tour with **Plymouth Rock Trolley** (☎ **508-747-3419;** Internet: www.plymouthrocktrolley.com) includes unlimited on-and-off privi-leges. The trolley operates daily from Memorial Day to October, and on weekends through Thanksgiving. Trolleys serve the plantation every hour and other stops every 20 minutes. Tickets cost $10 for adults, $9 for seniors and AAA members, and $8 for children 3 to 12.

To get a Pilgrim's perspective, take a 90-minute **Colonial Lantern Tour** (☎ **800-698-5636** or 508-747-4161; Internet: www.lanterntours.com). Participants carry pierced-tin lanterns as they walk around the original settlement under the direction of a knowledgeable guide. Tours run nightly from April through Thanksgiving. The standard history tour begins at 7:30 p.m. The "Ghostly Haunts and Legends" tour starts at 9 p.m. Call for reservations and meeting places. Tickets are $10 for adults and $8 for children.

Narrated cruises run from April or May through November. One-hour **Splashdown Amphibious Tours** (☎ **508-747-7658;** Internet: www.duck toursplymouth.com) take you around town on land and water. The trips leave from Harbor Place, on Water Street near the Governor Bradford motor inn. These tours cost $17 for adults, $10 for children under 12, and $3 for children under 3.

Seeing the sights

The **Visitor Center,** 130 Water Street (across from the town pier; ☎ **508-747-7525**), distributes information on Plymouth's attractions. The center is open seasonally (spring through Thanksgiving); in the winter, stop at the Regional Information Complex at Exit 5 off Route 3 before heading into town.

Plymouth

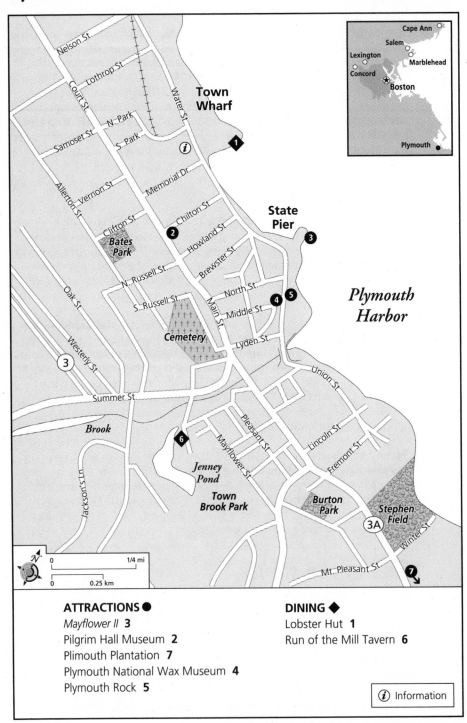

ATTRACTIONS ●
Mayflower II **3**
Pilgrim Hall Museum **2**
Plimouth Plantation **7**
Plymouth National Wax Museum **4**
Plymouth Rock **5**

DINING ◆
Lobster Hut **1**
Run of the Mill Tavern **6**

(i) Information

The sight to see is (ask the kids) Plymouth Rock, which history tells us was the landing place of the *Mayflower* passengers. Originally 15 feet long and 3 feet wide, the rock is now much smaller, having been moved (and broken) several times. Yes, this is just a rock, but the descriptions are absorbing, and a solemn sense of history surrounds the enclosure.

Mayflower II

A stone's throw from Plymouth Rock, *Mayflower II* is a full-scale reproduction of the type of vessel that brought the Pilgrims from England to Plymouth in 1620. Full scale is a mere 106½ feet — you may want to remind the kids that this is not a scaled-down model. Costumed guides provide first-person narratives about the voyage and the vessel, and displays illustrate the Pilgrims' experiences and the history of the ship, which was built in England from 1955 to 1957. Plan to spend at least an hour here.

State Pier. ☎ *508-746-1622. Internet:* www.plimoth.org. *Admission: $8 adults, $6 children 6–12, and free for children under 6. Admission for both Mayflower II and Plimoth Plantation: $22 adults, $20 seniors, $14 children 6–12, free for children under 6. Open: April–Nov daily 9 a.m.–5 p.m.*

Pilgrim Hall Museum

This museum illustrates the daily lives of Plymouth's first white residents with unbeatable props — original possessions of the Pilgrims and the Pilgrims' descendants. Displays include one of early settler Myles Standish's swords, an uncomfortable chair that belonged to the Pilgrim's original leader, William Brewster (you can sit on a modern-day model, not on the original), and Governor Bradford's Bible. Allow at least an hour.

75 Court St. ☎ *508-746-1620. Internet:* www.pilgrimhall.org. *From Plymouth Rock, walk north on Water Street and up the hill on Chilton Street. Admission: $5 adults, $4.50 seniors and AAA members, $3 children 5–17, free for children under 5. Open: Feb–Dec daily 9:30 a.m.–4:30 p.m. Closed Jan.*

Plimoth Plantation

Allow at least half a day to experience this re-creation of the 1627 Pilgrim village. The "settlers" are actors who assume the personalities of members of the original community; if you chat them up, the actors will pretend not to know anything contemporary, which many kids enjoy. The settlers also take part in typical activities, using only the tools and cookware available at the time; you may be able to join the cast in activities such as harvesting or witnessing a trial. Wear comfortable shoes, because you'll be walking all over, and the plantation isn't paved.

Route 3. ☎ *508-746-1622. Internet:* www.plimoth.org. *From Route 3, take Exit 4, "Plimoth Plantation Highway." Admission: $20 adults, $12 children 6–12, free for children under 6. Admission for both Plimoth Plantation and Mayflower II: $22 adults, $20 seniors, $14 children 6–17, free for children under 6. Open: April–Nov daily 9 a.m.–5 p.m. Closed Dec–March.*

Plymouth National Wax Museum

This museum illustrates the Pilgrim story in vivid detail that makes the experience informative and memorable. If time is tight and kids are along, this is the stop to make (after the Rock, of course). The galleries hold more than 180 life-sized figures, arranged in striking dramatic scenes, with soundtracks narrating the stories. The scenes include the Pilgrims' move to Holland, the harrowing trip to the New World, the first Thanksgiving, and the tale of Myles Standish, Priscilla Mullins, and John Alden, which you may remember from the Longfellow poem you studied in third grade social studies. Allow 60 to 90 minutes.

16 Carver St. ☎ 508-746-6468. From Plymouth Rock, turn around and walk up the hill or the steps. Admission: $6 adults, $5.50 seniors, $2.75 ages 5–12, free for children under 5. Open: March–June and Sept–Nov daily 9 a.m.–5 p.m.; July–Aug daily 9 a.m.–9 p.m. Closed Dec–Feb.

Dining

On Town Wharf, off Water Street, the **Lobster Hut** (☎ 508-746-2270) is a self-service seafood restaurant with a sensational view. Try the soups and the excellent "rolls" (hot dog buns with your choice of seafood filling). You can order beer and wine, but only with a meal. The **Run of the Mill Tavern** (☎ 508-830-1262) is near the water wheel at Jenney Grist Mill Village, in Town Brook Park off Summer Street. The tavern doesn't overlook the ocean but serves tasty bar fare and seafood in an attractive setting; the clam chowder is great.

Part VI

Living It Up after the Sun Goes Down: Boston Nightlife

The 5th Wave   By Rich Tennant

"For tonight's modern reinterpretation of Carmen, those in the front row are kindly requested to wear raincoats."

In this part . . .

*B*oston offers patrons of the performing arts a cornucopia: an internationally renowned symphony orchestra, the beloved Boston Pops, a top-notch ballet company, theater a step away from Broadway, and student performances of every imaginable type. The next two chapters outline your choices and steer you toward sources that can tell you more.

You may notice that I'm not rushing to tout the nightlife options, which are nowhere near as encyclopedic, though some can be just as entertaining. This city loves bars and embraces clubs that schedule everything from comedy to folk to jazz to rock. True, the post-midnight scene is sketchy, but that's not to say that you can't howl at the moon into the wee hours. You just may not have a lot of company.

- **Ticketmaster** (☎ 617-931-2000; Internet: www.ticketma
- **Next Ticketing** (☎ 617-423-NEXT or 617-423-6398; Ir nextticketing.com)
- **Tele-charge** (☎ 800-447-7400; Internet: www click "Across the USA")

Before you finalize your ticket order, be s
which will include a service charge and
charge can be hefty, and it applies
may change, double-check the re
credit card number.

Venues list major events
venues' Web sites; ch
company, or artist
tion in advance

The Sp

To take a broad look at what types of performing arts events Boston has to offer, check a general resource such as the *Boston Globe*'s Web site, **Boston.com** (http://ae.boston.com). Major pop and rock performers play at the **FleetCenter** (☎ 617-624-1000; Internet: www.fleetcenter. com). Many smaller venues, listed later in this chapter, operate Web sites that list upcoming shows. Also visit your favorite performer's or group's Web site to check schedules. If you already know who or what you want to see — a particular guest artist with the Boston Pops, say, or the Boston Ballet's *Nutcracker* — go right to the performing arts companies. See "The Performing Arts" later in this chapter for contact information on these and other companies.

A hotel package that includes tickets to a show can be a terrific conven- ience. The ticket price may not reflect a great savings, but knowing for sure that you have seats for *The Nutcracker* will save a lot of worrying.

Some companies and venues sell tickets by phone or on the Web; many use an agency. The major Boston ticketing agencies are

ter.com)

ternet: www.

telecharge.com,

re to ask for the total price,
possibly other fees. The service
er ticket, not per order. If your plans
und policy before you hand over your

months (sometimes years) in advance on the
eck ahead to see whether your favorite group,
is scheduled to play Boston. Knowing this informa-
may influence your travel plans.

r-of-the-Moment Approach

he "Calendar" section of the Thursday *Boston Globe,* the "Scene" section of the Friday *Boston Herald,* and the Sunday arts sections of both
papers overflow with possibilities. If you can handle a tiny bit of planning, call your hotel and ask the concierge or front desk to hang on to
"Calendar" for you. Other good resources are the weekly *Boston Phoenix*
and biweekly *Improper Bostonian* — available free from newspaper
boxes all over town.

When you find something appealing, call the box office to see whether
the event is sold out. If something jumps out at you and you're looking
for a deal, check at a BosTix booth (see "Saving Money on Tickets"
later in this chapter) for discounted same-day tickets. If a show sounds
great but is sold out, ask for help from your concierge, who may have
ticket connections. Finally — this is a long shot, but worth a try — visit
the box office in person. Patrons sometimes return tickets (good ones,
too), and some venues block seats before configuring the performance
space, and then release the extras.

Saving Money on Tickets

Perhaps the best arts resource in town is BosTix, which operates
booths at Faneuil Hall Marketplace (on the south side of Faneuil Hall)
and in Copley Square (at the corner of Boylston and Dartmouth streets).
BosTix sells same-day theater and concert tickets for half-price, subject
to availability. No credit cards, refunds, or exchanges are allowed.
Check the board or the Web site for the day's offerings.

Stepping out — Boston-style

Like your trip to Boston, your big evening out can turn into a festival of untied loose ends — if you let that happen. You already know where you're going, but that doesn't mean the planning is over. Here are a few other issues to address before heading out:

✔ **What to wear:** Just about anything clean and neat will suffice. You won't be out of place in something dressy, but for most events, anything short of a sweatsuit is fine. If you insist on wearing jeans to the symphony, theater, or ballet, I doubt I can stop you. But I will suggest that a big evening out feels a lot splashier if you're dressed for the occasion.

✔ **Where to dine:** Most restaurants in and near the Theater District can accommodate the beat-the-clock dining style of patrons with an 8 o'clock curtain to catch, but you must remember to alert (and, if necessary, remind) the staff. Two of my favorite destinations before or after a show are **Buddha's Delight,** 5 Beach St., 2nd floor (☎ **617-451-2395**), for vegetarian Vietnamese and Asian food, and **Finale,** 1 Columbus Ave. (☎ **617-423-3184**), which specializes in desserts. Turn to Chapters 14 and 15 for restaurant reviews.

✔ **When to arrive:** Be on time for the performance or bear the consequences. If you're not in your seat when the curtain goes up, you'll have to wait for a break in the action, and that may take a while.

✔ **How to get there:** Walk or take the T, especially if your destination is in the Theater District. If you take a cab or (heaven help you) drive, allow plenty of time, which you'll spend sitting in traffic. To reach the Theater District, go to Boylston or Arlington (Green Line), or New England Medical Center or Chinatown (Orange Line). South Station (Red Line) is about 15 minutes away on foot. Symphony Hall has a T stop: Symphony (Green Line E). Or get off at Hynes/ICA (Green Line B, C, or D), and then walk ten minutes on Mass. Ave. The FleetCenter is at North Station (Green or Orange Line).

BosTix (☎ **617-482-2849;** Internet: www.bostix.org) also sells full-price advance tickets and offers discounts on theater, music, and dance events. Half-price tickets go on sale at 11 a.m. The booths are open Tuesday through Saturday 10 a.m. to 6 p.m., and Sunday 11 a.m. to 4 p.m. The Copley Square booth is open Monday 10 a.m. to 6 p.m.

The Performing Arts

Before plunging into specifics of venues and companies, I want to recommend two eclectic series. The first is summer only, outdoors, and free. From early June to early September, the **Hatch Shell** amphitheater (T: Charles/MGH [Red Line] or Arlington [Green Line]; ☎ **617-727-9547,** ext. 450) on the Esplanade, located on the Boston side of the Charles River, between Storrow Drive and the water, books music and dance

Boston Performing Arts and Nightlife

Anchovies **11**
The Atrium **37**
Avalon **4**
Axis **3**
The Bar at the Ritz **30**
The Bay Tower **39**
Berklee College of Music **12**
The Black Rose **38**
Blue Man Group **22**
BosTix **14, 38**
Boston Ballet **25**
Boston Beer Works **2, 36**
Boston Center for the Arts **19**
Boston Pops **10**
Boston Symphony Orchestra **10**
Bristol Lounge **28**
Charles Playhouse **22**

Cheers **31, 38**
Club Café **17**
Colonial Theatre **27**
Comedy Connection
   at Faneuil Hall **38**
DeLux Café **18**
Emerson Majestic Theatre **26**
FleetBoston Pavilion **43**
FleetCenter **35**
Fritz **20**
The Good Life **41**
Hard Rock Café **16**
Hatch Shell **32**
Hill Tavern **34**
Huntington Theatre Company **9**
Isabella Stewart Gardner
   Museum **6**

Jacques **21**
Jillian's Boston **5**
Mr. Dooley's Boston Tavern **40**
Museum of Fine Arts **7**
New England
   Conservatory of Music **8**
Oak Bar **15**
Paradise Rock Club **1**
Parish Café and Bar **29**
Radius **42**
Sevens Ale House **33**
Shear Madness **22**
Shubert Theatre **23**
Symphony Hall **10**
Top of the Hub **13**
Wang Theatre **25**
Wilbur Theater **24**

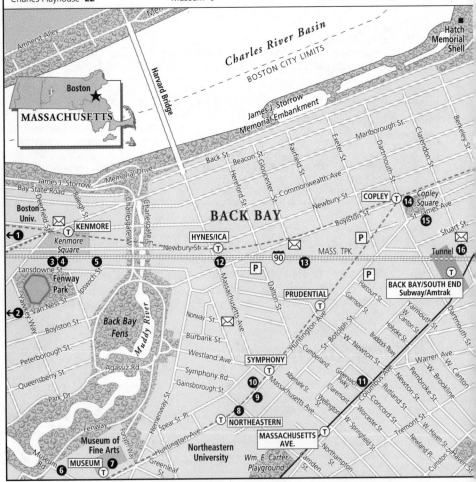

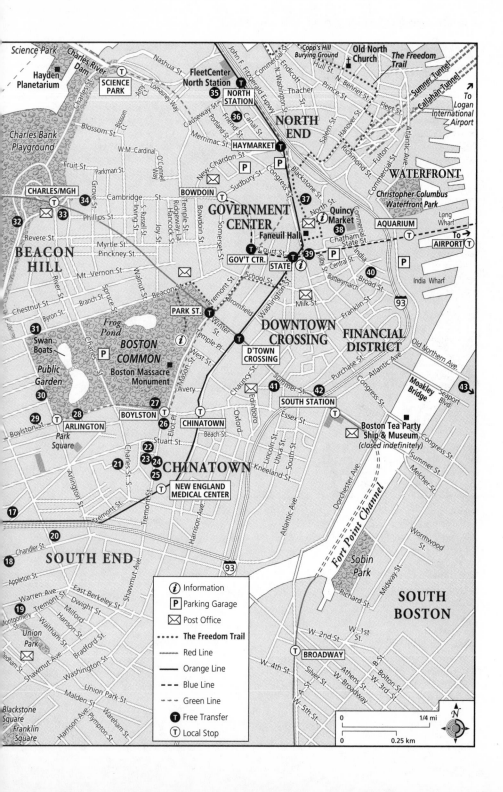

Science Park

Charles River Dam

Hayden Planetarium

Nashua St.

Copp's Hill Burying Ground

Old North Church

The Freedom Trail

John F. Fitzgerald Expwy.

Commercial St.

N. Endicott St.

Hull St.

N. Bennet St.

Prince St.

Thacher

Sumner Tunnel

Callahan Tunnel

To Logan International Airport

FleetCenter North Station

35

SCIENCE PARK

Amy Ct.

Lomasney Way

Causeway St.

Portland St.

Canal St.

Friend St.

NORTH STATION

36

Salem St.

Hanover St.

Fleet St.

Richmond St.

Fulton St.

Commercial St.

Atlantic Ave.

NORTH END

WATERFRONT

Charles Bank Playground

Blossom St.

Blossom Ct.

W.M. Cardinal

Merrimac St.

New Chardon St.

HAYMARKET

P

Blackstone St.

Congress St.

N. Washington St.

37

Christopher Columbus Waterfront Park

Fruit St.

Parkman St.

O'Connell Way

New Chardon St.

Sudbury St.

North St.

Commercial St.

Long Wharf

CHARLES/MGH

34

Cambridge St.

BOWDOIN

Bowdoin St.

GOVERNMENT CENTER

Quincy Market

38

State St.

Chatham

India St.

AQUARIUM

To AIRPORT

32

33

Phillips St.

Grove St.

S. Russell St.

Irving St.

Temple St.

Somerset St.

GOV'T CTR.

Faneuil Hall

39

Kilby St.

Central St.

Broad St.

India Wharf

BEACON HILL

Revere St.

Myrtle St.

Pinckney St.

Mt. Vernon St.

Joy St.

Bowdoin St.

School St.

STATE

Milk St.

Batterymarch

40

93

Chestnut St.

Byron St.

Branch St.

Spruce St.

Walnut St.

Beacon St.

Tremont St.

Bromfield

Washington St.

DOWNTOWN CROSSING

Franklin St.

FINANCIAL DISTRICT

Old Northern Ave.

Moakley Bridge

Seaport Blvd.

43

31

Swan Boats

Frog Pond

BOSTON COMMON

P

Boston Massacre Monument

PARK ST.

Winter St.

Temple Pl.

West St.

D'TOWN CROSSING

Chauncy St.

Summer St.

Purchase St.

Atlantic Ave.

Congress St.

Public Garden

30

Avery

Mason St.

27

26

BOYLSTON

CHINATOWN

Beach St.

Edinboro

Oxford

Essex St.

Lincoln St.

Utica St.

South St.

41

42

SOUTH STATION

Boston Tea Party Ship & Museum (closed indefinitely)

Summer St.

Melcher St.

29

28

ARLINGTON

Boylston St.

Park Square

Stuart St.

Eliot Pl.

CHINATOWN

Kneeland St.

Dorchester Ave.

Congress St.

22

23

24

25

21

Charles St. S.

Tremont St.

NEW ENGLAND MEDICAL CENTER

Harrison Ave.

Atlantic Ave.

Fort Point Channel

Wormwood St.

Midway St.

17

Arlington St.

Sobin Park

SOUTH BOSTON

20

SOUTH END

Chandler St.

Shawmut St.

93

Richard St.

W. 2nd St.

W. 1st St.

B. St.

18

Appleton St.

East Berkeley St.

W. 1st St.

19

Warren Ave.

Tremont St.

Dwight St.

Milford

Hanson St.

Bradford St.

BROADWAY

W. 4th St.

W. Broadway

Silver St.

Athens St.

W. 3rd St.

Bolton St.

Montgomery St.

Waltham St.

Union Park

Shawmut Ave.

Washington St.

Malden St.

Union Park St.

Plympton St.

W. 5th St.

Blackstone Square

Franklin Square

Harrison Ave.

Wareham St.

ⓘ Information

P Parking Garage

✉ Post Office

····· The Freedom Trail

─── Red Line

─── Orange Line

--- Blue Line

─ · ─ Green Line

🔵 Free Transfer

Ⓣ Local Stop

0   1/4 mi

0   0.25 km

N

Cambridge Performing Arts and Nightlife

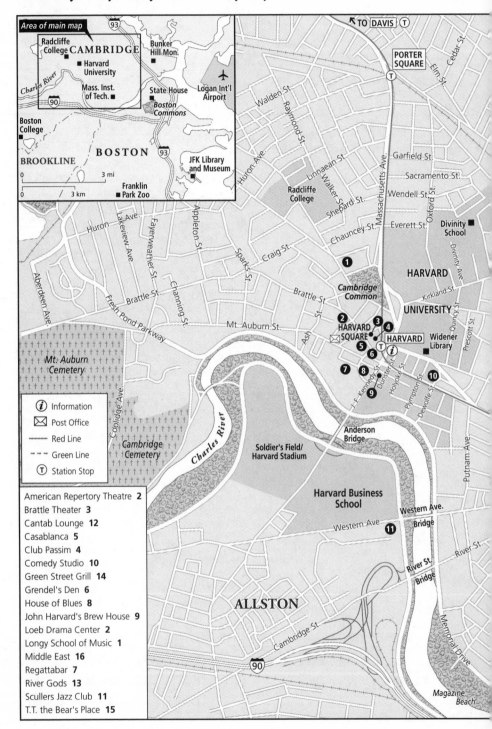

Area of main map

TO DAVIS

CAMBRIDGE
Radcliffe College
Harvard University
Mass. Inst. of Tech.
Charles River
BROOKLINE
Boston College
BOSTON
State House
Boston Commons
Logan Int'l Airport
JFK Library and Museum
Franklin Park Zoo

0   3 mi
0   3 km

PORTER SQUARE

Garfield St.
Sacramento St.
Wendell St.
Everett St.
Divinity School

Radcliffe College

HARVARD UNIVERSITY

Cambridge Common

HARVARD SQUARE

HARVARD

Widener Library

Mt. Auburn Cemetery

Cambridge Cemetery

Charles River

Soldier's Field/ Harvard Stadium

Anderson Bridge

Harvard Business School

Western Ave.
Western Ave.   Bridge

River St.
River St. Bridge

ALLSTON

Cambridge St.

Memorial Drive

Magazine Beach

Legend

(i) Information
✉ Post Office
——— Red Line
- - - Green Line
(T) Station Stop

American Repertory Theatre **2**
Brattle Theater **3**
Cantab Lounge **12**
Casablanca **5**
Club Passim **4**
Comedy Studio **10**
Green Street Grill **14**
Grendel's Den **6**
House of Blues **8**
John Harvard's Brew House **9**
Loeb Drama Center **2**
Longy School of Music **1**
Middle East **16**
Regattabar **7**
River Gods **13**
Scullers Jazz Club **11**
T.T. the Bear's Place **15**

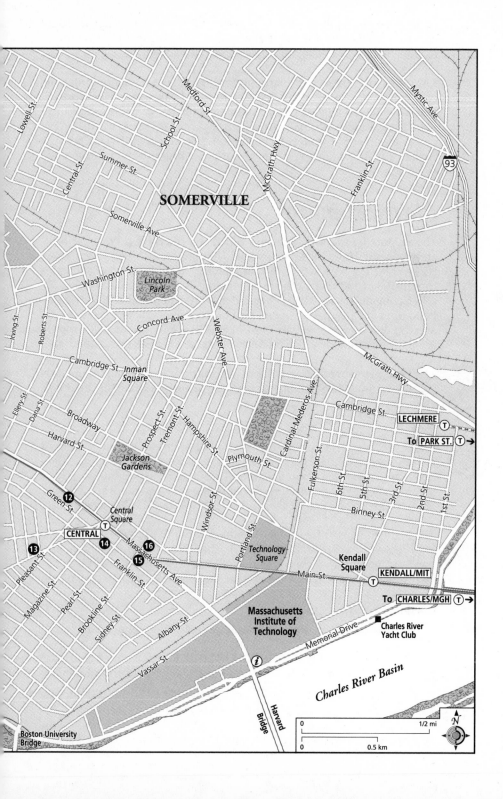

SOMERVILLE

Lowell St.
Central St.
Summer St.
Medford St.
School St.
McGrath Hwy
Mystic Ave.
Franklin St.
Somerville Ave.

Washington St.
Lincoln Park

Irving St.
Roberts St.
Concord Ave.
Webster Ave.
McGrath Hwy

Cambridge St.
Inman Square

Ellery St.
Dana St.
Broadway
Prospect St.
Tremont St.
Hampshire St.
Cambridge St.
Cardinal Mederos Ave.
LECHMERE Ⓣ
To **PARK ST.** Ⓣ →

Harvard St.
Jackson Gardens
Plymouth St.
Fulkerson St.
6th St.
5th St.
3rd St.
2nd St.
1st St.
Binney St.

Green St.
⑫
Central Square
CENTRAL Ⓣ
⑭
Massachusetts Ave.
⑯
Windsor St.
Portland St.
Technology Square
Kendall Square
KENDALL/MIT Ⓣ

⑬
Pleasant St.
⑮
Franklin St.
Main St.
To **CHARLES/MGH** Ⓣ →

Magazine St.
Pearl St.
Brookline St.
Sidney St.
Albany St.
Massachusetts Institute of Technology
Memorial Drive
Charles River Yacht Club

Vassar St.
ⓘ
Harvard Bridge

Charles River Basin

Boston University Bridge

0   1/2 mi
0   0.5 km
N

performances and films. (If you've seen the Boston Pops' Fourth of July concert on TV, you've seen the Hatch Shell.) Seating is on the grass or on a blanket, if you have one. Check ahead for schedules.

The other top series coordinates performances by international stars of classical music, dance, theater, jazz, and world music. The **FleetBoston Celebrity Series,** 20 Park Plaza, Boston, MA 02116 (☎ **617-482-2595,** or 617-482-6661 for Celebrity Charge; Internet: www.celebrityseries.org), takes place at venues throughout the Boston area. Tickets are available to individual performances or in packages to three or more events.

Classical music

The **Boston Symphony Orchestra (BSO)** and the **Boston Pops** perform at **Symphony Hall,** 301 Mass. Ave. (at Huntington Avenue; T: Symphony [Green Line E]). The hall, known around the world for perfect acoustics, turned 100 in 2000; when the main tenants are away, the hall books other companies. The BSO is in residence from September to April, the Pops from May to early July and part of December. Tickets start at $25 and top out around $90. Call ☎ **617-266-1492** or 617-CONCERT for program information, or 617-266-1200 for tickets; or check www.bso.org.

The Pops also schedules a week of *free* outdoor performances, including the renowned Fourth of July concert, in early summer at the Hatch Shell, and three weeks of holiday shows at Symphony Hall.

Visit the box office two hours before a BSO or Pops show time, when returns from subscribers go on sale (at full price). A limited number of symphony "rush" tickets (one per person, same-day only) go on sale for $8 at 9 a.m. Friday, and 5 p.m. on Tuesday and Thursday. Wednesday evening and Thursday morning rehearsals are sometimes open to the public; call to see if rehearsal tickets ($15) are available.

The highly regarded **Handel & Haydn Society** (☎ **617-266-3605;** Internet: www.handelandhaydn.org) schedules "historically informed" concerts, often with a choir, year-round. The ensemble uses period instruments and techniques in interpreting baroque and classical music.

Museum productions

For music with art, investigate these options at Boston museums:

- ✔ The **Museum of Fine Arts** (☎ **617-267-9300**) schedules courtyard concerts on Wednesday evenings from June through September.

- ✔ The **Isabella Stewart Gardner Museum** (☎ **617-734-1359**) books music on weekend afternoons from September through April.

You can also check out Chapter 16 for more information about these museums.

College concerts

Students and faculty members at three prestigious institutions perform frequently during the academic year; admission is usually free or cheap. Most area colleges schedule student performances, but these are the big three:

- ✔ **Berklee College of Music** (☎ 617-747-2261; Internet: www. berklee.edu)

- ✔ **New England Conservatory of Music** (☎ 617-585-1122; Internet: www.newenglandconservatory.edu)

- ✔ **Longy School of Music** (☎ 617-876-0956; Internet: www.longy.edu)

Pop and rock music

The **FleetCenter,** off Causeway Street (T: North Station [Orange or Green Line]; ☎ **617-624-1000;** Internet: www.fleetcenter.com), is the major arena for touring groups and artists. Built in 1995, FleetCenter is a top-of-the-line facility, but the seating is at a pretty shallow angle; bring binoculars.

The **FleetBoston Pavilion,** Wharf 8, off Northern Ave., South Boston (T: South Station [Red Line]; ☎ **617-374-9000;** Internet: www.fleet bostonpavilion.com), is a huge white tent open only in the summer. The pavilion books pop, jazz, folk, country, and some rock and rap artists. The airy outdoor setting makes this especially enjoyable. The venue is at least a 30-minute walk from the T station; call ahead for shuttle-bus and water-transportation information.

Turn to Chapter 23 for listings of smaller places to hear live rock and pop.

Dance

If you've heard of the **Boston Ballet** (☎ **617-695-6955;** Internet: www. bostonballet.org), that's probably because of *The Nutcracker* — an excellent reason, but not the only one. The company presents classic and modern works from October through May. Performances are at the Wang Theatre, 270 Tremont St.

Built as a movie palace in the 1920s, the Wang presents certain difficulties for the ballet audience — namely, awkward sight lines and the sensation that you're about to fall out of the balcony. Spend as much as you can on tickets for *The Nutcracker* (the highest price tops $70), especially if you're introducing your kids to this holiday spectacle. And remember your opera glasses.

The Theater Scene

Pre-Broadway tryouts still play in Boston, as do touring national companies of shows that do well in New York. The Theater District is a tiny area that centers on the intersection of Tremont and Stuart streets, between Chinatown and the Back Bay. Boston boasts a lively theater scene, and it's not unusual for shows to be up at every major professional stage. Two noted repertory companies and dozens of colleges also contribute to the buzz.

See "Saving Money on Tickets," earlier in this chapter, for information on BosTix and its same-day half-price-ticket operation. Full-price tickets for legitimate theaters seldom go for less than $20; smaller companies and college performances are considerably cheaper.

Big-time theater

Most Broadway shows play in the Theater District at the following locations:

- ✔ **Colonial Theatre,** 106 Boylston St. (☎ 617-426-9366)
- ✔ **Shubert Theatre,** 265 Tremont St. (☎ 617-482-9393)
- ✔ **Wang Theatre,** 270 Tremont St. (☎ 617-482-9393)
- ✔ **Wilbur Theater,** 246 Tremont St. (☎ 617-423-4008)

To reach the Theater District, take the T to Boylston or Arlington (Green Line), or New England Medical Center or Chinatown (Orange Line).

Repertory companies

Two university spaces are home to professional troupes. The **Huntington Theatre Company** plays at the Boston University Theatre, 264 Huntington Ave. (T: Symphony [Green Line E]; ☎ 617-266-0800; Internet: www.huntington.org). The **American Repertory Theatre (ART)** performs at Harvard University's Loeb Drama Center, 64 Brattle St., Cambridge (T: Harvard [Red Line]; ☎ 617-547-8300; Internet: www.amrep.org).

The Huntington and the ART tend to be more adventurous than Theater District counterparts; for something even more audacious, head to the South End. The **Boston Center for the Arts,** 539 Tremont St. (between Berkeley and Clarendon streets; T: Back Bay [Orange Line]; ☎ 617-426-2787; Internet: www.bcaonline.org), boasts five performance spaces, with more under construction, and an apparent willingness to try just about anything.

Family-friendly theater

Children old enough to be interested in the theater can enjoy a good introduction at either of two long-running shows: Blue Man Group and *Shear Madness.* How old should your child be to attend these shows? I'd say 10 or so — this is a lot of money to spend on someone who may not last until the curtain falls — but that's your call. **Blue Man Group** (Internet: www.blueman.com) consists of three cobalt-colored performance artists and a rock band. The show incorporates goofy props (including food), music, and willing spectators who become participants — one even gets painted. ***Shear Madness*** (Internet: www.shearmadness.com) is a "comic murder mystery" set in a hair salon. The audience helps solve the crime; the details have been different at every performance since the show opened in Boston in 1980.

Both shows run (on different stages) at the Charles Playhouse, 74 Warrenton St., off Stuart Street, in the Theater District. Tickets for Blue Man Group cost $43 and $53; *Shear Madness* tickets run $34. Buy tickets at the box office or through Ticketmaster.

At the Movies

Free Friday Flicks (☎ **617-727-9547,** ext. 450; Internet: www.wbz.com) projects films on a large screen in the amphitheater at the Hatch Shell on the Esplanade (T: Charles/MGH [Red Line] or Arlington [Green Line]). These are family movies, with a tendency to lean toward the last couple of Disney releases rather than the classics. However, the season is long — a couple of gems usually sneak in.

Classic movies and new independent releases turn up at a number of theaters. Film buffs can check out the **Brattle Theater,** 40 Brattle St., Cambridge (T: Harvard [Red Line]; ☎ 617-876-6387; Internet: www.brattlefilm.org); the **Coolidge Corner Theater,** 290 Harvard St., Brookline (T: Coolidge Corner [Green Line C]; ☎ **617-734-2500;** Internet: www.coolidge.org); and the **Harvard Film Archive,** 24 Quincy St., Cambridge (T: Harvard [Red Line]; ☎ **617-495-4700;** Internet: www.harvardfilmarchive.org).

Chapter 23

Hitting the Clubs and Bars

●●

●●

*E*ven if you know nothing about Boston except what you saw on the TV show *Cheers,* you already know something important: The neighborhood bar is a big deal. A spell in a local watering hole is a great way to get to know any new city, and Boston is no exception. Many nightspots schedule live music; if you'd rather shake your bon-bon than bend your elbow, you'll find a number of places to do that, too. In this chapter, I guide you toward some congenial spots to indulge in your recreation of choice.

For locations of recommended nightspots, see the maps in Chapter 22.

The Basics

The state drinking age is 21; you must have a valid driver's license or passport. Have an ID ready if you look younger than 35 or so, especially near college campuses. Remember, the skeptical bouncer is all that stands between the management and a liquor-license suspension. Joking around or trying to talk your way in will only stall the line at the entrance.

When a club advertises a "21-plus" show, that means that only persons 21 or older may enter the club; "18-plus" means 18-, 19-, and 20-year-olds may enter but can't drink alcohol.

By law, bars close at 1 a.m. or earlier, clubs at 2 a.m. From Sunday to Thursday, the T shuts down by 1 a.m. systemwide, with the last car from some stations running shortly after 12:30 a.m. Be ready to spring for cab fare. On Friday and Saturday until 2:30 a.m., Night Owl bus service runs on some regular bus routes and on special routes that parallel the subway lines. The fare is one token or $1 in coins.

Unless otherwise noted, the establishments in this chapter don't impose a cover charge; of course, that's subject to change, depending on the entertainment on a particular night.

Making the Scene: Bars and Lounges

Cheers is the most famous tavern in town. The long-running sitcom remains so popular that the owners of the original bar, which looked nothing like the set of the TV show, opened a bar that looks exactly like the set. That bar is in Faneuil Hall Marketplace, on the south side of Quincy Market (T: Government Center [Green or Blue Line] or State [Orange Line]; ☎ **617-227-0150;** Internet: www.cheersboston.com). Cheers is open daily from 11 a.m. to 2 a.m. (food service until 11:45 p.m.).

The original **Cheers,** formerly the Bull & Finch Pub, is at 84 Beacon St. (T: Arlington [Green Line]; ☎ **617-227-9605**). Somewhat improbably, this location retains a loyal neighborhood clientele, but most patrons are out-of-towners looking for souvenirs and snapshots. The exterior sign is the one you remember from all those late-night reruns. This popular spot is open daily from 11 a.m. to 1 a.m.

The **Hard Rock Cafe,** 131 Clarendon St. (T: Back Bay [Orange Line] or Copley [Green Line]; ☎ **617-424-ROCK;** Internet: www.hardrock.com), is another fun tourist magnet. The Hard Rock is a huge, noisy space lavishly adorned with rock 'n' roll memorabilia. The food is better than average, and the downstairs room sometimes schedules live music. And guess what? You can buy a souvenir. The Hard Rock is open daily from 11 a.m. to 1 a.m.

Sky-high lounges

The romantic lounge at **The Bay Tower,** on the 33rd floor of 60 State St. (T: State [Orange or Blue Line]; ☎ **617-723-1666;** Internet: www.baytower.com), offers splendid city views, live music, and dancing. *Note:* You can't enter in denim or athletic shoes. The lounge is open Monday through Thursday 5 p.m. to midnight, Friday and Saturday 5 p.m. to 1 a.m.; it's closed Sunday.

Top of the Hub, 800 Boylston St. (T: Prudential [Green Line E]; ☎ **617-536-1775**), occupies the 52nd floor of the Prudential Tower. Sunset offers the best view, but any non-foggy time is good. The lounge schedules music and dancing nightly; dress is casual but neat. The lounge is open Sunday through Wednesday until 1 a.m., and Thursday through Saturday until 2 a.m.

Brew pubs

The microbrew fad, thankfully, seems to be on the wane. The surviving breweries specialize in deftly crafted creations and, as a bonus, tasty food.

John Harvard's Brew House, 33 Dunster St., Harvard Square (T: Harvard [Red Line]; ☎ 617-868-3585; Internet: www.johnharvards. com), attracts a boisterous student crowd with English-style brews made on the premises and reasonably priced pub grub. The pub is open daily from 11:30 a.m. to 1:30 a.m.

Right across from Fenway Park, and nearly as loud, **Boston Beer Works,** 61 Brookline Ave. (T: Fenway [Green Line D]; ☎ 617-536-2337), offers more than a dozen brews on tap and tasty food. The pub is open daily from 11:30 a.m. to 1:00 a.m. Boston Beer Works has another location at 112 Canal St. (T: North Station [Green or Orange Line]; ☎ 617-896-2337) — right across from the FleetCenter, and nearly as loud.

Classy cocktail spots

The top-shelf martini shakers reside in hotel bars, those elegant, expensive destinations where you can channel Nick and Nora Charles. (Don't think of these as more expensive than a regular bar; think of them as cheaper than booking a room.) Dress up a little. All stay open into the early morning.

The Bar at the Ritz, in the Ritz-Carlton, 15 Arlington St. (T: Arlington [Green Line]; ☎ 617-536-5700), was famous long before *Cheers* was even a pilot episode. The Ritz retains the crown with a combination of Brahmin atmosphere and killer martinis.

The Bristol Lounge, in the Four Seasons Hotel, 200 Boylston St. (T: Arlington [Green Line]; ☎ 617-351-2000), is a refined destination for cocktails, luscious American food, afternoon tea, and (on weekend nights) the decadent Viennese Dessert Buffet. The Bristol schedules live piano music every night.

The **Oak Bar** at the Fairmont Copley Plaza Hotel, 138 St. James Ave. (T: Copley [Green Line]; ☎ 617-267-5300), is the clubbiest place in town. Wood paneling, cigar smoke, a raw bar, and nightly live entertainment set the scene. Proper dress is required. The Oak Bar is open daily at 4:30 p.m.

The Atrium lounge in the lobby of the **Millennium Bostonian Hotel,** 40 North St. (at Faneuil Hall Marketplace; T: Government Center [Green or Blue Line] or Haymarket [Orange Line]; ☎ 617-523-3600), has less of a hideaway feel than many hotel bars. The wraparound windows afford a great view of the marketplace. Hear live piano music on weeknights.

Hibernian hangouts

That's a snappy way to say "Irish bars," which occupy an honored place in the Boston bar pecking order. Ponder which came first — the bartending job or the brogue — while you sip a Guinness.

My favorite is **Mr. Dooley's Boston Tavern,** 77 Broad St. (T: State [Orange or Blue Line]; ☎ 617-338-5656), a popular Financial District spot. World-class bartenders, hearty food, music, and imported draught beer in an authentic atmosphere — what more could you want? There's a $3 cover charge on weekend nights.

The Black Rose, 160 State St. (at Faneuil Hall Marketplace; T: State [Orange or Blue Line]; ☎ 617-742-2286; Internet: www.irish connection.com/blackrose), is considerably larger and rowdier. The Black Rose's live entertainment delights huge crowds who often sing along. The location makes this bar popular with tourists, but you'll find plenty of clued-in locals, too. You'll pay a cover of $3 to $5 at night.

Neighborhood bars

As promised, I point you toward some places where you can mingle with locals. This list was strenuously edited and comes with a suggestion: If your wanderings take you past an agreeable-looking establishment, pop in.

Start with Cambridge (T: Harvard [Red Line]), where the colorful mix of patrons makes for peerless eavesdropping. In Harvard Square, you'll see professors, students, and more colorful types at **Casablanca,** 40 Brattle St. (☎ 617-876-0999), and **Grendel's Den,** 89 Winthrop St. (☎ 617-491-1160).

In Central Square (T: Central [Red Line]), the **Green Street Grill,** 280 Green St. (☎ 617-876-1655; Internet: www.greenstreetgrill. com), has an amazing blues and jazz jukebox. Live music plays on weekends (with a cover charge, usually less than $10), and excellent food is served every night. A few blocks away, **River Gods,** 125 River St. (☎ 617-576-1881), is a fun, funky Irish bar that serves good food.

Beacon Hill (T: Charles/MGH [Red Line]) in Boston caters to the postcollegiate set. Check out the clean-cut types swilling beer at the **Sevens Ale House,** 77 Charles St. (☎ 617-523-9074), and the **Hill Tavern,** 228 Cambridge St. (☎ 617-742-6192).

The Good Life, 28 Kingston St. (off Summer Street; T: Downtown Crossing [Red or Orange Line]; ☎ 617-451-2622), is a madly popular after-work stop. The retro, lounge-y feel is a welcome holdover from the swing-dancing craze of the late '90s, without the zoot-suited poseurs at the bar.

A family-friendly pleasure dome

Imagine an establishment that incorporates a dance club, five full bars, and a restaurant. You can shoot pool on one of the 52 tables, take a virtual-reality movie "ride," or play slot machines (for fun, not money). You can tackle a classic or contemporary game in the 250-game video midway, play darts or table tennis, or just watch your kids have a ball. That's **Jillian's Boston,** 145 Ipswich St. (at Lansdowne Street; T: Kenmore [Green Line B, C, or D] or Fenway [Green Line D]; ☎ **617-437-0300;** Internet: www.jilliansboston.com), a 70,000-square-foot complex at the end of the Lansdowne Street nightclub strip. Jillian's is open Monday through Saturday 11 a.m. to 2 a.m., and Sunday noon to 2 a.m. The complex admits those under 18, who must be with an adult, before 7 p.m. Valet parking is available Wednesday through Sunday after 6 p.m., except during Red Sox games.

Nearby, **Radius,** 8 High St. (T: South Station [Red Line]; ☎ **617-426-1234**), attracts a chic Financial District crowd (no, that's not a contradiction). The restaurant is the headliner here, but the sleek bar is almost as much of a see-and-be-seen spot.

In the Back Bay (T: Arlington [Green Line]), the **Parish Café and Bar,** 361 Boylston St. (☎ **617-247-4777**), offers indoor and outdoor seating. Another after-work hot spot, this place is also a popular lunch stop because of a terrific sandwich menu.

In the South End (T: Back Bay/South End [Orange Line]), two friendly, cramped spots pack in the locals: **Anchovies,** 433 Columbus Ave. (☎ **617-266-5066**), and the **DeLux Cafe,** 100 Chandler St. (☎ **617-338-5258**).

Checking Out the Clubs

The information in this section is the most volatile in the book. I steer you toward some reliable places and neighborhoods, but I can't promise that what's hot tonight will even be there next month. Dance clubs that usually book DJs sometimes feature live music; live-music clubs rarely restrict themselves to one genre. Check the "Calendar" section of the Thursday *Globe,* the *Phoenix,* the *Improper Bostonian,* or the "Scene" section of the Friday *Herald* when you're making plans.

Throughout this section, I note hours for a few places. For the others, keep in mind most clubs open between 7 and 10 p.m. and must close at 2 a.m. Hours can change, however, depending on who's playing, who's booking, and whether a show is all-ages or 21-plus. If you need specifics, call ahead.

The original **House of Blues,** 96 Winthrop St., Cambridge (T: Harvard [Red Line]; ☎ **617-491-BLUE,** or 617-497-2229 for tickets; Internet: www.hob.com), rises above chain status by being so darn cool. This hot spot books everyone from promising locals to international super-stars for evening and weekend-matinee shows. The food is good, the crowds enthusiastic, and the music the real thing. Advance tickets ($7 to $30; matinees $5) are strongly recommended. The club is open Monday through Wednesday 11:30 a.m. to 1:00 a.m., Thursday through Saturday 11:30 a.m. to 2:00 a.m., and Sunday 4:30 p.m. to 1:00 a.m.

The House of Blues' **Sunday gospel brunch** is one of the liveliest events you'll ever experience. Call ahead for tickets (adults $26, children $13); seatings are at 10 a.m., noon, and 2 p.m.

Club-hop 'til you drop

Boston's most popular nightlife destination is Kenmore Square, specifi-cally **Lansdowne Street,** off Brookline Avenue outside the square, across the street from Fenway Park.

Head to Kenmore Square for the city's best dance club, **Avalon,** 15 Lansdowne St. (T: Kenmore [Green Line B, C, or D]; ☎ **617-262-2424**). This club is probably reinventing some aspect of itself as you read this. The multilevel space expanded in 1999 to accommodate more concerts, but the consistent reason to come here is "Avaland," the Friday night dance party. Management imports high-profile DJs and turns house dancers loose. The cover is usually $5 to $15, more for special events. Avalon is open Thursday through Sunday 10 p.m. to 2 a.m. The dress code forbids jeans and athletic wear, and requires jackets and shirts with collars for men.

Under the same management, **Axis,** 13 Lansdowne St. (T: Kenmore [Green Line B, C, or D]; ☎ **617-262-2437**), boasts a younger (collegiate and postcollegiate), looser crowd. Deafening rock, house, and techno music keep the leather-clad crowds moving. The cover charge is around $7 to $11. Axis is open Tuesday through Sunday 10 p.m. to 2 a.m.

You'll find a somewhat more sophisticated clientele at the **Paradise Rock Club,** 967 Commonwealth Ave. (T: Green Line B to Pleasant Street; ☎ **617-562-8804,** or 617-423-NEXT for tickets). This is one of the best-known live-music venues in the area — the medium size allows artists who aren't ready to tour solo to headline. This club is also famous for tangling with the Boston Licensing Board and losing its license for several months; you *must* have an ID. Tickets run $10 to $30.

Cambridge's **Central Square** (T: Central [Red Line]) draws enthusiastic crowds that go for music-making over scene-making. Many shows are 18-plus, with room for 30-pluses who can keep their fogeyish musings to themselves. (But *boy,* these places are loud.)

The **Middle East,** 472–480 Mass. Ave. (☎ **617-492-9181;** Internet: www.
mideastclub.com), books rock of all stripes in two rooms every night.
The cover ranges from $7 to $15.

The eclectic bookings at **T. T. the Bear's Place,** 10 Brookline St. (☎ **617-
492-0082,** or concert line 617-492-BEAR; Internet: www.ttthebears.
com), run the musical gamut. This place is a little crowded; expect to get
to know your neighbors. The cover runs from $3 to $15, but usually
under $10.

Three blocks away from T.T. the Bear's Place is the **Cantab Lounge,** 738
Mass. Ave. (☎ **617-354-2685**). The Cantab is a neighborhood bar that
happens to book great music — usually R&B or rock, sometimes jazz.
The cover seldom tops $7.

For jazz fans

The two biggest local clubs are two of the best in the country — an
enjoyable dilemma for devotees, a great opportunity for novices. You
simply can't go wrong at either place.

The **Regattabar** is in the Charles Hotel, 1 Bennett St., Harvard Square
(T: Harvard [Red Line]; ☎ **617-661-5000,** or 617-876-7777 for Concertix).
This is a large space where the crowd sometimes gets a little distracted
(and chatty). Tickets run $12 to $36. The Regattabar is open Tuesday
through Saturday, and some Sundays.

Scullers Jazz Club is in the Doubletree Guest Suites hotel, 400 Soldiers
Field Rd. (☎ **617-562-4111;** Internet: www.scullersjazz.com). The
room overlooks the Charles. The difficulty of getting to the hotel,
which is not near the T, means the crowd includes fewer casual fans —
a plus if your favorite artist is playing. Ask about dinner packages,
which include preferred seating. Show tickets cost $12 to $38.

Just for laughs

The **Comedy Connection at Faneuil Hall,** on the upper level of Quincy
Market (T: Government Center [Green or Blue Line] or Haymarket
[Orange Line]; ☎ **617-248-9700;** Internet: www.comedyconnection
boston.com), is the best comedy club around. Promising locals and big-
name visitors have packed the spacious room since 1978. Tickets run
from $8 (for unknowns) to more than $30 (for sitcom stars and the like).

You'll find fewer famous names but more potential in Cambridge at
the **Comedy Studio,** in the Hong Kong restaurant, 1236 Mass. Ave. (T:
Harvard [Red Line]; ☎ **617-661-6507;** Internet: www.TheComedyStudio.
com). This place is good for improv, inspired sparring with the audience,
and sketch comedy.

Two more names you need to know

Johnny D's Uptown Restaurant & Music Club, 17 Holland St., Somerville (T: Davis [Red Line]; ☎ **617-776-2004,** or concert line 617-776-9667; Internet: www.johnnyds.com), schedules a wild assortment of musical genres and styles. No matter what your taste, the schedule is worth checking out. If your taste runs to food, Johnny D's has that, too. Cover $2 to $16, usually $10 or less. Open daily 11:30 a.m. to 1:00 a.m. Somerville is just north of Cambridge.

Club Passim, 47 Palmer St. (T: Harvard [Red Line]; ☎ **617-492-7679**), is one of the few remaining legends in Harvard Square and actually lives up to the international reputation as a folk-music proving ground. The coffeehouse (which does not serve alcohol) has been around for more than 30 years; your favorite artist has almost certainly played here. The cover charge is usually $5 to $12 or so; for big names, the cover may top $20. Open daily 11 a.m. to 11 p.m.

Gay and Lesbian Clubs and Bars

Some dance clubs (see earlier in this chapter) schedule a weekly gay night; the largest and best known is Sunday at Avalon; at neighboring Axis, Monday is gay night. For entertainment listings, check *Bay Windows* (Internet: www.baywindows.com) and the *Phoenix* (Internet: www.bostonphoenix.com).

Club Café, 209 Columbus Ave., South End (T: Arlington [Green Line] or Back Bay [Orange Line]; ☎ **617-536-0966**), is a lively spot that serves drinks and food but is not so noisy to restrict conversation. Club Café attracts men and women with live music and video entertainment. Thursday is see-and-be-seen night. The club is open daily until 1 a.m.

Jacques, 79 Broadway, in the Theater District (T: Arlington [Green Line]; ☎ **617-426-8902**), is Boston's only drag venue. Jacques attracts a mixed (gay and straight) clientele with live music and performance art, too. The club is open daily until midnight.

Fritz, in the Chandler Inn Hotel, 26 Chandler St. (at Berkeley Street; T: Back Bay [Orange Line]; ☎ **617-482-4428**), will make you feel right at home: It's a regular old sports-mad neighborhood bar that's open daily until 1 a.m.

Part VII
The Part of Tens

"I want a lens that's heavy enough to counterbalance the weight on my back."

In this part . . .

People love top-ten lists — just ask Moses. The lists in this section aren't exactly biblical prophecy, but they do offer some inside information about blending in. You can do this in two ways: With your behavior and with a traditional thrifty Yankee attitude.

Chapter 24

The Top Ten Ways Not to Look Like a Tourist

● ●

In This Chapter

▶ Dressing like a local

▶ Keeping in step

▶ Talking the talk

● ●

*O*n a brief visit to Boston, you probably won't blend in. You probably won't want to. One of the best ways to acquaint yourself with a new city is to plead ignorance and seek directions and advice from the locals. This chapter offers suggestions for fitting in without becoming so assimilated that people are asking *you* for directions. Just remember that if you insist on leaving the conference without removing your nametag, the nametag may as well say, "Hi, I'm from out of town."

Always Dress in Layers

Even on the steamiest summer day, a midafternoon change in wind direction (or a stop at an enthusiastically air-conditioned store) can mean a sharp drop in temperature. You'll be glad to pull on a long-sleeved T-shirt or light sweater. And a spring or fall day that starts with a foggy morning can become toasty after the haze burns off — not a good time to have nothing on under your sweatshirt.

Keep Moving

Bostonians reputedly walk and talk faster than any other Americans — even New Yorkers. While sightseeing, step to the curb to check your map, count heads, or admire the architecture. Remember that the neighborhoods that attract hordes of tourists are also places where regular people live and work. When you block locals' paths while you get your bearings, you're forcing the home team off the sidewalks and into the paths of (scary sound effect) Boston traffic.

Stay in Touch with the Freedom Trail

Distinguished by red paint or red brick smack in the middle of the sidewalk, the Freedom Trail won't steer you wrong. If you lose track of where you are, follow the trail to an intersection or landmark. You don't need to keep to the trail religiously; in fact, I strongly suggest a bit of wandering. One observation to note: If you're standing right on the trail as you tangle with your map, you'll look like a big ol' tourist.

Don't Exclaim, "That Must Be the Old North Church"

As you follow the Freedom Trail away from the Paul Revere House, you'll come to a house of worship on Hanover Street. This is St. Stephen's, the last remaining Boston church designed by legendary architect Charles Bulfinch. The Old North Church is across the street, a block beyond the Paul Revere statue that faces St. Stephen's.

Be in Your Party Clothes Early

Bars close at 1 a.m. or earlier, clubs wrap things up at 2 a.m., and the line between "fashionably late" and "shut out" is all too thin. If the only admirers of your hot new outfit are the other people at the pancake house, don't say I failed to warn you.

Bring Cab Fare

Should you manage to scout out some late-night action, don't expect to jump on the T when you're through. On Sunday through Thursday nights, the T closes by 1 a.m. (every station posts the time of the last train in either direction). On Friday and Saturday, there's Night Owl bus service, but this doesn't go everywhere, and it shuts down at 2:30 a.m. After that, you'll be at the mercy of friends and cabbies.

Watch What You Say about Baseball

In cities that take sports less seriously, you can start a casual conversation with "How 'bout those (insert the name of the local nine)?" In Boston, just mentioning the Red Sox can land you on the business end of a lengthy lecture about Babe Ruth, Johnny Pesky, Carlton Fisk, Bucky Dent, Bill Buckner, and a bunch of other guys you couldn't pick out of a lineup. If you're up for that, great; if not, the weather is a reliable icebreaker.

Likewise, Chowder

This issue is less contentious than it once was, but still divisive. This disputed matter concerns a certain red ingredient found in the clam chowder in a big city some 200 miles south of the right-thinking people of Boston. You can sidestep the issue by ordering the version Legal Sea Foods attributes to Rhode Island (*never* Manhattan). In short, New England clam chowder does not contain tomatoes. Deal with that.

Pack the Right Shoes

Especially if you visit downtown, think twice before strapping on sandals. The Big Dig acts as a sort of gravel farm, and the closer you get to the site, the likelier you are to wind up with something uncomfortable in your shoe. Stick to closed footwear. And if you believe wearing socks with your sandals is an acceptable alternative, I'm sorry, but I'm going to have to pretend that we've never met.

Save the "I Pahked My Cah" Jokes

Everybody has an accent, even you — you just can't hear your own. The Boston accent isn't exactly poetic, but making fun of someone who speaks with one is both provincial and rude. That doesn't mean you can't enjoy the accent, though. Use your curious ear for discreet eavesdropping (the T is great for this), and you'll soon hear English being mangled in ways that will curl your hair.

Chapter 25

The Top Ten Free (or Almost Free) Activities

● ●

In This Chapter

▶ Finding free — or nearly free — cultural events

▶ Touring Boston on the cheap

▶ Locating the best people-watching spots

● ●

*W*hether your budget resembles an impoverished student's or a Microsoft millionaire's, a few extra bucks are always welcome. In this chapter, I point you toward activities that can help create financial wiggle room. For general information on all things budgetary, turn to Chapter 3.

Music Outdoors

In warm weather, musicians take to the streets and outdoor venues in droves. The free performances range from impromptu jam sessions to huge concerts that promote local radio stations. One congenial series brings jazz to Christopher Columbus Park, on the waterfront across the street from Faneuil Hall Marketplace, at 6:30 p.m. on summer Fridays. City Hall Plaza and the Hatch Shell on the Charles River Esplanade book larger events. Check around (in the papers or at the front desk) when you arrive — you'll definitely find something that appeals to you.

Music Indoors

Colleges and churches take up the slack when cold weather drives tunesmiths indoors. Students and instructors at local universities as well as prestigious conservatories perform throughout the school year.

The big academic names are **Berklee College** (Internet: www.berklee.edu), the **New England Conservatory** (Internet: www.newenglandconservatory.edu), and **Cambridge's Longy School** (Internet: www.longy.edu), but there's no telling what you may find while in Boston. Churches schedule secular performances as well as religious works; the best-known series runs year-round at historic Trinity Church, in Copley Square, Fridays at 12:15 p.m.

Check listings in the *Globe* "Calendar" section or the *Phoenix* before or when you arrive for more information about the Boston area's abundant free and cheap activities.

National Park Service Tours

Your tax dollars pay off like lottery tickets at the Park Service sites that dot eastern Massachusetts. Free or (at some locations) inexpensive tours complement and interpret the historic and cultural attractions. Check the Web site (www.nps.gov). Or drop into the **Boston National Historic Park Visitor Center,** 15 State St. (☎ 617-242-5642).

Movies

The **Free Friday Flicks** (Internet: www.wbz.com) film series brings family movies to the Esplanade every summer. The kid-friendly picture will probably be something that's available on video, but the experience — under the stars, ruffled by a breeze off the river — makes this feel like more than just another movie.

The **Boston Public Library** (Internet: www.bpl.org) schedules free movies year-round at the main branch, in Copley Square, and often at the neighborhood branches. Check ahead; you may stumble upon a gem.

Theater

This is another area with a substantial college component, and the usual potential and pitfalls of amateur stagecraft. Again, local listings can point you in the right direction. For the less adventurous (or more discriminating, if you prefer), professionals perform free on Boston Common in July and early August with the **Commonwealth Shakespeare Company** (Internet: www.commonwealthshakespeare.org). The top-notch troupe mounts one production per season with a cast that's about half Equity actors.

Museums

Your low-budget options are few but fun. Free: The USS *Constitution* Museum, the Institute of Contemporary Art on Thursday from 5 to 9 p.m., the Harvard University art museums all day Wednesday and until noon Saturday, and the Harvard natural history museums until noon on Sunday year-round and Wednesday from 3 to 5 p.m. during the school year. Cheap: The Children's Museum charges $1 per person on Friday from 5 to 9 p.m., and the Freedom Trail sites that do charge admission don't charge too much — the Bostonian Society's Museum in Old City Hall, $5 for adults; the Paul Revere House, $2.50. (The Museum of Fine Arts schedules pay-what-you-wish hours on Wednesday from 4:00 to 9:45 p.m. but "suggests" that adults "donate" $14.) If you're just in this for the shopping (and believe me, you're not alone), remember that every museum will let you into the gift shop without paying an admission fee.

People Watching

For the price of a cup of coffee or a drink, you can camp out and enjoy the passing parade just about anywhere. Three favorite destinations: the Hanover Street *caffès* in the North End; sidewalk tables and window seats on Newbury Street, in the Back Bay; and the outdoor tables at the Harvard Square Au Bon Pain.

Haymarket

Haymarket could fall under "People Watching," but this is such an unusual experience that it deserves special attention. This open-air market consists of stalls piled high with fruits, veggies, and sometimes fish. Located on Blackstone and North streets, near Faneuil Hall Marketplace, the market operates only on Friday and Saturday. If you're on the Freedom Trail, slow down and have your camera ready — the gregarious vendors, fanatical bargain-hunters, and colorful produce make a perfect photo op.

Street Fairs

You'll find alfresco diversions, from fashion shows to pony rides, all over town on weekends throughout the summer and fall. The North End, the Back Bay, and Harvard Square stage notable multiple-block parties; check the newspapers or ask at your hotel's front desk for details of festivities during your visit.

Hydrotherapy

Check out a map of Boston and Cambridge, both of which abound with waterfront property. Pack a lunch, a camera, or just a craving for a little downtime, and head toward the harbor or the river to kick back. Maritime traffic constantly crisscrosses the harbor, which lies within view of Logan Airport's flight patterns. Recreational craft on the Charles River include graceful sailboats and college crew shells.

You'll find excellent spots for a water break in downtown Boston on Long Wharf (follow State Street to the end) and off Commercial Street at Fleet Street and Hull Street; in Charlestown near the harbor ferry dock; and in the Back Bay on the Charles River Esplanade. The Cambridge side of the river is essentially one long park, with particularly enjoyable spots near Harvard and Kendall squares.

Another great experience involving water and not too much money is the ferry between Long Wharf, near the New England Aquarium, and the Charlestown Navy Yard. This costs $1.25 and affords a million-dollar view of the harbor.

Appendix

Quick Concierge

● ●

American Automobile Association (AAA)

Road service ☎ 800-222-4357; other services ☎ 800-222-8252. The Boston office is in the Financial District at 125 High St., off Pearl Street.

Ambulance

Call ☎ 911. This call is free from pay phones.

American Express

The main local office is at 1 State St. (☎ 617-723-8400); the office is open weekdays from 8:30 a.m. to 5:30 p.m. The Back Bay office, 222 Berkeley St. (☎ 617-236-1334), is open weekdays from 9:00 a.m. to 5:30 p.m. The Cambridge office, 39 John F. Kennedy St., Harvard Square (☎ 617-661-0005), is open weekdays from 8:30 a.m. to 7:30 p.m., Saturday 11:00 a.m. to 5:30 p.m., Sunday noon to 5 p.m.

Area Codes

Eastern Massachusetts has eight area codes, and every phone number is 10 digits (11 if you count dialing 1 first). Even if you're calling next door, you must dial the area code first. In Boston proper, the area codes are **617** and **857**; in the immediate suburbs, **781** and **339**; to the north and west, **978** and **351**; to the south and east, **508** and **774**.

ATMs

ATMs are widely available throughout Boston and Cambridge at banks, on the street, in convenience stores and supermarkets, and in some subway stations. (See Chapter 12.)

Baby-sitters

Ask your hotel's front desk or concierge for suggestions. See Chapter 4 for information about the agency Parents in a Pinch (☎ 800-688-4697 or 617-739-KIDS).

Camera Repair

Try Bromfield Camera & Video, 10 Bromfield St. (☎ 800-723-2628 or 617-426-5230), near Downtown Crossing, or the Camera Craftsman, 362 Commonwealth Ave. (☎ 617-267-5883), in the Back Bay.

Convention Centers

Hynes Convention Center, 900 Boylston St. (☎ 617-954-2000 or 617-424-8585 for show information; Internet: www.jbhynes.com). World Trade Center, 164 Northern Ave. (☎ 800-367-9822 or 617-385-5000, or 617-385-5044 for show information; Internet: www.wtcb.com). Bayside Expo Center, 200 Mount Vernon St., Dorchester (☎ 617-474-6000; Internet: www.baysideexpo.com).

Credit Cards

The toll-free emergency number for Visa is ☎ 800-847-2911. The number for MasterCard is ☎ 800-307-7309. American Express cardholders should call ☎ 800-221-7282 for emergencies.

Dentists

Check with the front desk or concierge at your hotel, or try the Massachusetts Dental Society (☎800-342-8747 or 508-651-7511; Internet: www.massdental.org).

Doctors

Check with the front desk or concierge at your hotel, or try a referral service. Every hospital in town has one, including Massachusetts General (☎ 800-711-4MGH) and Beth Israel Deaconess (☎ 617-667-5356). Before seeking medical treatment, be sure you understand your insurance carrier's policy on emergency care and preapproval.

Emergencies

Call ☎ 911 for the police, a fire, or an ambulance. This call is free from pay phones.

Hospitals

Closest to downtown are Massachusetts General Hospital, 55 Fruit St. (☎ 617-726-2000), and New England Medical Center, 750 Washington St. (☎ 617-636-5000). At the Harvard Medical Area on the Boston-Brookline border are Beth Israel Deaconess Medical Center, 330 Brookline Ave. (☎ 617-667-7000); Brigham and Women's Hospital, 75 Francis St. (☎ 617-732-5500); and Children's Hospital, 300 Longwood Ave. (☎ 617-355-6000), among others. In Cambridge: Mount Auburn Hospital, 330 Mount Auburn St. (☎ 617-492-3500), and Cambridge Hospital, 1493 Cambridge St. (☎ 617-498-1000).

Hotlines

AIDS Hotline (☎ 800-235-2331 or 617-536-7733); Poison Control Center (☎ 617-232-2120); Rape Crisis (☎ 617-492-7273); Samaritans Suicide Prevention (☎ 617-247-0220); Samariteens (☎ 800-252-8336 or 617-247-8050).

Information

Greater Boston Convention & Visitors Bureau, ☎ 800-SEE-BOSTON or 617-536-4100. Telephone directory assistance, ☎ 411. (Also see "Where to Get More Information" later in this Appendix.)

Internet Access

Kinko's is everywhere and offers Internet access. Locations include 2 Center Plaza, Government Center (☎ 617-973-9000); 10 Post Office Sq., Financial District (☎ 617-482-4400); 187 Dartmouth St., Back Bay (☎ 617-262-6188); and 1 Mifflin Place, off Mount Auburn Street near Eliot Street, Harvard Square (☎ 617-497-0125).

Liquor Laws

The legal drinking age is 21. Always be ready to show identification. At sporting events, everyone buying alcohol must show ID. Liquor stores and a few supermarkets and convenience stores sell alcohol. Liquor stores (and the liquor sections of other stores) close on Sundays, but restaurants and bars may serve alcohol. Some smaller restaurants don't have full liquor licenses; they serve wine, beer, and cordials, but no hard liquor. If you must have a mixed drink, ask when you make your reservations.

Maps

Pick up a map at any visitor information center (see Chapter 10 for more information), at most hotels, and from the clerks in most T token booths.

Newspapers/Magazines

The *Boston Globe* and *Boston Herald* are the city's daily papers. The free weeklies *Boston Phoenix* and *Stuff@Night* and the free biweekly *Improper Bostonian* carry arts coverage and entertainment and restaurant listings. Newspaper boxes around Boston and Cambridge distribute all. *Boston* magazine is a lifestyle-oriented monthly. (See "Information on the Web" later in this Appendix for *Boston Globe* and *Boston Phoenix* Web site information.)

Pharmacies

Nearly every neighborhood has a CVS; ask at your hotel's front desk. Downtown Boston has no 24-hour drugstore. The CVS in the Porter Square Shopping Center, off Mass. Ave. in Cambridge (☎ 617-876-5519), is open 24 hours, 7 days a week. The pharmacy at the CVS at 155–157 Charles St. in Boston (☎ 617-523-1028), next to the Charles/MGH Red Line T stop, is open until midnight. Some emergency rooms can fill your prescription at the hospital's pharmacy.

Police

Call ☎ **911** for emergencies. The non-emergency number is ☎ 617-343-4200.

Radio Stations

WBUR-FM, 90.9, is the local National Public Radio affiliate. WBZ-AM, 1030, carries news, sports, and weather, with traffic reports every ten minutes on weekdays.

Restrooms

The visitor center at 15 State St. has a public restroom, as do most tourist attractions, hotels, department stores, and public buildings. Most Starbucks locations and large chain bookstores have restrooms. Freestanding self-cleaning toilets (25¢) are in several high-traffic areas downtown. Inspect these carefully before using them — the generous time limit makes some of the toilets popular with IV-drug users. If you're walking the Freedom Trail, especially with children, be sure to use the restrooms at Faneuil Hall Marketplace before venturing into the North End, which has no public facilities. Restrooms are available at the CambridgeSide Galleria, Copley Place, and Prudential Center shopping areas.

Safety

Boston and Cambridge are generally safe for walking. As in any city, stay out of parks (including the Esplanade) at night, unless you're in a crowd. Use common sense: Walk confidently, try not to use ATMs at night, and avoid dark, deserted streets. Specific areas to avoid at night include Boylston Street between Tremont and Washington streets, and Tremont Street from Stuart to Boylston streets. Watch your step near the Big Dig (that is, most of downtown), where walking surfaces can be uneven. Public transportation in the areas you're likely to visit is busy and safe, but service stops between 12:30 and 1:00 a.m.

Smoking

All public buildings and many restaurants forbid smoking. Boston and Cambridge restaurants that do permit smoking must, by law, confine smoking to the bar. Brookline bans smoking in all restaurants and bars.

Taxes

The 5% state sales tax doesn't apply to food, prescription drugs, newspapers, or clothing worth less than $175. The state meal tax (which also applies to takeout food) is 5%. The lodging tax is 12.45% in Boston and Cambridge.

Taxis

To call ahead in Boston, try the Independent Taxi Operators Association (☎ 617-426-8700), Boston Cab (☎ 617-536-5010), Town Taxi (☎ 617-536-5000), or Metro Cab (☎ 617-242-8000). In Cambridge, call Ambassador Brattle (☎ 617-492-1100) or Yellow Cab (☎ 617-547-3000). For more information, see Chapter 11.

Time Zone

Boston is in the Eastern time zone. Daylight saving time begins on the first Sunday in April and ends on the last Sunday in October.

Tipping

The average tip for most service providers, including waiters and cab drivers, is 15%, rising to 20% for particularly good service. Tip bellhops $1 or $2 a bag, hotel housekeepers at least $1 per person per day, and valet parking and coat-check attendants $1 to $2.

Transit Information

For T subway, bus, commuter rail, and ferry information, call ☎ 617-222-3200. For airport transportation information, call ☎ 800-23-LOGAN.

Weather Updates

Call ☎ 617-936-1234 for forecasts.

Toll-Free Numbers and Web Sites

Major North American carriers

Air Canada
☎ 888-247-2262
www.aircanada.ca

Air Tran
☎ 800-247-8726
www.airtran.com

America West Airlines
☎ 800-235-9292
www.americawest.com

American Airlines
☎ 800-433-7300
www.aa.com

American Trans Air
☎ 800-225-2995
www.ata.com

Continental Airlines
☎ 800-525-0280
www.continental.com

Delta Air
☎ 800-221-1212
www.delta.com

Frontier Airlines
☎ 800-432-1359
www.frontierairlines.com

Midwest Express
☎ 800-452-2022
www.midwestexpress.com

Northwest Airlines
☎ 800-225-2525
www.nwa.com

Southwest Airlines
☎ 800-435-9792
www.iflyswa.com

United Airlines
☎ 800-241-6522
www.ual.com

US Airways
☎ 800-428-4322
www.usairways.com

Car-rental agencies

Alamo
☎ 800-327-9633
www.alamo.com

Avis
☎ 800-831-2847
☎ 800-TRY-AVIS in Canada
www.avis.com

Budget
☎ 800-527-0700
www.budget.com

Dollar
☎ 800-800-4000
www.dollar.com

Enterprise
☎ 800-325-8007
www.enterprise.com

Hertz
☎ 800-654-3131
www.hertz.com

National
☎ 800-CAR-RENT
www.nationalcar.com

Rent-A-Wreck
☎ 877-627-7736
www.rentawreck.com

Thrifty
☎ **800-847-4389**
www.thrifty.com

Major hotel and motel chains

Best Western International
☎ 800-528-1234
www.bestwestern.com

Clarion Hotel
☎ 800-CLARION
www.hotelchoice.com

Comfort Inn
☎ 800-228-5150
www.comfortinn.com

Courtyard by Marriott
☎ 800-321-2211
www.courtyard.com

Crowne Plaza Hotel
☎ 800-227-6963
www.CrownePlaza.com

Days Inn
☎ 800-329-7466
www.daysinn.com

Doubletree Hotel
☎ 800-222-TREE
www.doubletreehotels.com

Econo Lodge
☎ 800-55-ECONO
www.hotelchoice.com

Fairfield Inn by Marriott
☎ 800-228-2800
www.fairfieldinn.com

Hampton Inn
☎ 800-HAMPTON
www.hamptoninn.com

Hilton Hotel
☎ 800-HILTONS
www.hilton.com

Holiday Inn
☎ 800-HOLIDAY
www.holiday-inn.com

Howard Johnson
☎ 800-654-2000
www.hojo.com

Hyatt Hotels & Resorts
☎ 800-228-9000
www.hyatt.com

Marriott Hotels Resorts Suites
☎ 800-228-9290
www.marriott.com

Quality Inn
☎ 800-228-5151
www.hotelchoice.com

Radisson Hotels International
☎ 800-333-3333
www.radisson.com

Ramada Inn
☎ 800-2-RAMADA
www.ramada.com

Residence Inn by Marriott
☎ 800-331-3131
www.residenceinn.com

Travelodge
☎ 800-255-3050
www.travelodge.com

Ritz-Carlton
☎ 800-241-3333
www.ritzcarlton.com

Westin Hotels & Resorts
☎ 800-937-8461
www.westin.com

Sheraton Hotels & Resorts
☎ 800-325-3535
www.sheraton.com

Wyndham Hotels & Resorts
☎ 800-996-3426
www.wyndham.com

Super 8 Motel
☎ 800-800-8000
www.super8.com

Where to Get More Information

Cambridge Office for Tourism

Request a free guide to the place the tourist office insists on calling Boston's "Left Bank."

18 Brattle St., Cambridge, MA 02138. ☎ *800-862-5678 or 617-441-2884. Internet:* www.cambridge-usa.org.

Greater Boston Convention & Visitors Bureau

The bureau offers a comprehensive visitor information kit for $6; the kit includes a travel planner, guidebook, map, and coupon book with shopping, dining, attractions, and nightlife discounts. The "Kids Love Boston" guidebook costs $5. Call the main number to gain access to the "Boston by Phone" service, which provides information on lodging, attractions, dining, nightlife, shopping, and travel services.

2 Copley Place, Suite 105, Boston, MA 02116-6501. ☎ *888-SEE-BOSTON or 617-536-4100. Internet:* www.bostonusa.com.

Massachusetts Office of Travel and Tourism

Request the free *Getaway Guide* magazine, which includes information about attractions and lodgings, a map, and a seasonal calendar. Because this office covers travel and tourism for the whole state, the information has less Boston-specific material than the Convention & Visitors Bureau. But the material is still useful (and free!). The online "lobster tutorial" makes an excellent cheat sheet.

10 Park Plaza, Suite 4510, Boston, MA 02116. ☎ *800-227-6277 or 617-973-8500. Internet:* www.mass-vacation.com.

Information on the Web

www.boston.com

The *Boston Globe*'s city guide, the most complete and up-to-date resource around, includes everything from weather forecasts to movie reviews, plus enough links and listings to keep you busy for hours.

http://boston.citysearch.com

Ticketmaster's travel site contains copious lifestyle and entertainment listings, including restaurant reviews.

www.bostonphoenix.com

The alternative weekly offers abundant arts and entertainment coverage (listings and reviews), plus excellent listings for the gay, lesbian, and bisexual community.

www.massport.com

The Massachusetts Port Authority, which runs the airport, constantly updates this site with the latest weather and air-traffic information. The visitor-information area includes many useful links.

www.mayorsfoodcourt.com

Results of restaurant inspections (and reinspections), with numerical scores and pop-up windows that explain the regulations. Gross, but addictive.

www.bigdig.com

The Big Dig — see what all the fuss is about.

Information in print

Frommer's Boston

A comprehensive look at "the Hub," with more hotel, restaurant, and attraction listings than this book can accommodate. I have this on very good authority: The author wishes you well.

Frommer's New England

The perfect accessory on a multiple-state or -city visit to this appealing region.

Boston magazine

The slick monthly covers the arts, entertainment, and politics; gives the annual *Best of Boston* awards; and runs the city's best money-is-no-object ads. You can also check it out online at www.boston magazine.com.

Making Dollars and Sense of It

Expense	Daily cost	x	Number of days	=	Total
Airfare					
Local transportation					
Car rental					
Lodging (with tax)					
Parking					
Breakfast					
Lunch					
Dinner					
Snacks					
Entertainment					
Babysitting					
Attractions					
Gifts & souvenirs					
Tips					
Other					
Grand Total					

Fare Game: Choosing an Airline

When looking for the best airfare, you should cover all your bases — 1) consult a trusted travel agent; 2) contact the airline directly, via the airline's toll-free number and/or Web site; 3) check out one of the travel-planning Web sites, such as www.frommers.com.

Travel Agency_____ Phone_____

    Agent's Name_____ Quoted fare_____

Airline 1_____ Quoted fare_____

    Toll-free number/Internet_____

Airline 2_____ Quoted fare_____

    Toll-free number/Internet_____

Web site 1_____ Quoted fare_____

Web site 2_____ Quoted fare_____

Departure Schedule & Flight Information

Airline_____ Flight #_____ Confirmation #_____

Departs_____ Date_____ Time_____ a.m./p.m.

Arrives_____ Date_____ Time_____ a.m./p.m.

Connecting Flight (if any)

Amount of time between flights_____ hours/mins

Airline_____ Flight #_____ Confirmation #_____

Departs_____ Date_____ Time_____ a.m./p.m.

Arrives_____ Date_____ Time_____ a.m./p.m.

Return Trip Schedule & Flight Information

Airline_____ Flight #_____ Confirmation #_____

Departs_____ Date_____ Time_____ a.m./p.m.

Arrives_____ Date_____ Time_____ a.m./p.m.

Connecting Flight (if any)

Amount of time between flights_____ hours/mins

Airline_____ Flight #_____ Confirmation #_____

Departs_____ Date_____ Time_____ a.m./p.m.

Arrives_____ Date_____ Time_____ a.m./p.m.

All Aboard: Booking Your Train Travel

Travel Agency_____ Phone_____

Agent's Name_____

Web Site_____

Departure Schedule & Train Information

Train #_____ Confirmation #_____ Seat reservation #_____

Departs_____ Date_____ Time_____ a.m./p.m.

Arrives_____ Date_____ Time_____ a.m./p.m.

Quoted fare_____ First class _____ Second class

Departure Schedule & Train Information

Train #_____ Confirmation #_____ Seat reservation #_____

Departs_____ Date_____ Time_____ a.m./p.m.

Arrives_____ Date_____ Time_____ a.m./p.m.

Quoted fare_____ First class _____ Second class

Departure Schedule & Train Information

Train #_____ Confirmation #_____ Seat reservation #_____

Departs_____ Date_____ Time_____ a.m./p.m.

Arrives_____ Date_____ Time_____ a.m./p.m.

Quoted fare_____ First class _____ Second class

Departure Schedule & Train Information

Train #_____ Confirmation #_____ Seat reservation #_____

Departs_____ Date_____ Time_____ a.m./p.m.

Arrives_____ Date_____ Time_____ a.m./p.m.

Quoted fare_____ First class _____ Second class

Sweet Dreams: Choosing Your Hotel

Make a list of all the hotels where you'd like to stay and then check online and call the local and toll-free numbers to get the best price. You should also check with a travel agent, who may be able to get you a better rate.

Hotel & page	Location	Internet	Tel. (local)	Tel. (Toll-free)	Quoted rate

Hotel Checklist

Here's a checklist of things to inquire about when booking your room, depending on your needs and preferences.

- ❑ Smoking/smoke-free room
- ❑ Noise (if you prefer a quiet room, ask about proximity to elevator, bar/restaurant, pool, meeting facilities, renovations, and street)
- ❑ View
- ❑ Facilities for children (crib, roll-away cot, babysitting services)
- ❑ Facilities for travelers with disabilities
- ❑ Number and size of bed(s) (king, queen, double/full-size)
- ❑ Is breakfast included? (buffet, continental, or sit-down?)
- ❑ In-room amenities (hair dryer, iron/board, minibar, etc.)
- ❑ Other_____

Places to Go, People to See, Things to Do

Enter the attractions you would most like to see and decide how they'll fit into your schedule. Next, use the "Going My Way" worksheets that follow to sketch out your itinerary.

Attraction/activity	Page	Amount of time you expect to spend there	Best day and time to go

Places to Go, People to See, Things to Do

Enter the attractions you would most like to see and decide how they'll fit into your schedule. Next, use the "Going My Way" worksheets that follow to sketch out your itinerary.

Attraction/activity	Page	Amount of time you expect to spend there	Best day and time to go

Going "My" Way

Day 1

Hotel_____ Tel._____

Morning_____

_____

Lunch_____ Tel._____

Afternoon_____

_____

Dinner_____ Tel._____

Evening_____

_____

Day 2

Hotel_____ Tel._____

Morning_____

_____

Lunch_____ Tel._____

Afternoon_____

_____

Dinner_____ Tel._____

Evening_____

_____

Day 3

Hotel_____ Tel._____

Morning_____

_____

Lunch_____ Tel._____

Afternoon_____

_____

Dinner_____ Tel._____

Evening_____

_____

Going "My" Way

Day 4

Hotel _____ Tel. _____

Morning _____

_____

Lunch _____ Tel. _____

Afternoon _____

_____

Dinner _____ Tel. _____

Evening _____

_____

Day 5

Hotel _____ Tel. _____

Morning _____

_____

Lunch _____ Tel. _____

Afternoon _____

_____

Dinner _____ Tel. _____

Evening _____

_____

Day 6

Hotel _____ Tel. _____

Morning _____

_____

Lunch _____ Tel. _____

Afternoon _____

_____

Dinner _____ Tel. _____

Evening _____

_____

Going "My" Way

Day 7

Hotel_____ Tel._____

Morning_____

_____

Lunch_____ Tel._____

Afternoon_____

_____

Dinner_____ Tel._____

Evening_____

_____

Day 8

Hotel_____ Tel._____

Morning_____

_____

Lunch_____ Tel._____

Afternoon_____

_____

Dinner_____ Tel._____

Evening_____

_____

Day 9

Hotel_____ Tel._____

Morning_____

_____

Lunch_____ Tel._____

Afternoon_____

_____

Dinner_____ Tel._____

Evening_____

_____

Notes

Notes

Notes

Notes

Notes

Index

• *B* •

Notes

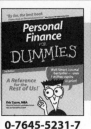  
 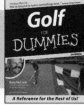 

FOR DUMMIES®

Helping you expand your horizons and realize your potential

INTERNET

0-7645-0894-6

0-7645-1659-0

0-7645-1642-6

Also available:

America Online 7.0 For Dummies
(0-7645-1624-8)

Genealogy Online For Dummies
(0-7645-0807-5)

The Internet All-in-One Desk Reference For Dummies
(0-7645-1659-0)

Internet Explorer 6 For Dummies
(0-7645-1344-3)

The Internet For Dummies Quick Reference
(0-7645-1645-0)

Internet Privacy For Dummies
(0-7645-0846-6)

Researching Online For Dummies
(0-7645-0546-7)

Starting an Online Business For Dummies
(0-7645-1655-8)

DIGITAL MEDIA

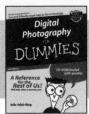

0-7645-1664-7

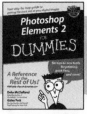

0-7645-1675-2

0-7645-0806-7

Also available:

CD and DVD Recording For Dummies
(0-7645-1627-2)

Digital Photography All-in-One Desk Reference For Dummies
(0-7645-1800-3)

Digital Photography For Dummies Quick Reference
(0-7645-0750-8)

Home Recording for Musicians For Dummies
(0-7645-1634-5)

MP3 For Dummies
(0-7645-0858-X)

Paint Shop Pro "X" For Dummies
(0-7645-2440-2)

Photo Retouching & Restoration For Dummies
(0-7645-1662-0)

Scanners For Dummies
(0-7645-0783-4)

GRAPHICS

0-7645-0817-2

0-7645-1651-5

0-7645-0895-4

Also available:

Adobe Acrobat 5 PDF For Dummies
(0-7645-1652-3)

Fireworks 4 For Dummies
(0-7645-0804-0)

Illustrator 10 For Dummies
(0-7645-3636-2)

QuarkXPress 5 For Dummies
(0-7645-0643-9)

Visio 2000 For Dummies
(0-7645-0635-8)

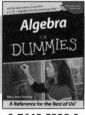
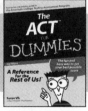